100 THINGS ROYALS FANS SHOULD KNOW & DO BEFORE THEY DIE

100 THINGS ROYALS FANS SHOULD KNOW & DO BEFORE THEY DIE

Matt Fulks

The Library of Congress has catalogued the previous edition as follows:

Fulks, Matt.
100 things Royals fans should know & do before they die / Matt Fulks.
pages cm
One hundred things Royals fans should know and do before they die ISBN 978-1-60078-909-0 (pbk.) 1. Kansas City Royals (Baseball team)—History. I. Title. II. Title: One hundred things Royals fans should know and do before they die.
GV875.K3F85 2014
796.357'6409778411—dc23
2013043424

This book is available in quantity at special discounts for your group or organization. For further information, contact:

Triumph Books LLC
814 North Franklin Street
Chicago, Illinois 60610
(312) 337-0747
www.triumphbooks.com

Printed in U.S.A.
ISBN: 978-1-62937-266-2
Design by Patricia Frey
Photos courtesy of Getty Images unless otherwise indicated

To Helen, Charlie, and Aaron, may you grow up with the same love of the Royals that your grandparents and great-grandparents instilled in me.

Contents

Foreword

Kansas City has a special baseball tradition, and it's a great honor to think that I've played some part in that tradition. Growing up in Ohio, with the Reds as *my* team and then getting the opportunity to start my professional career with Cincinnati, I didn't fully understand the history and tradition of baseball in Kansas City.

So when the Reds traded me to the Royals before the 1988 season, I just knew it was going to be a situation in which I could become an immediate member of the rotation. I knew of Dan Quisenberry, George Brett, Bo Jackson, and Bret Saberhagen, but that was about it. I hadn't heard of guys like Buddy Black and Mark Gubicza. Who's Jerry Don Gleaton? Who's Tom Gordon? I felt pretty confident that I'd make this club. I was a huge National League fan and didn't pay any attention to the American League. I quickly learned about the special baseball tradition—and talent—that exists in Kansas City.

Within 20 minutes of reporting to the Royals camp, I met a guy who looked like he was either a media type or a front-office type. Sure enough, it was general manager John Schuerholz. He said, "Welcome aboard; we're glad to have you here. We looked at your numbers as a starter and as a reliever. We really like you more as a reliever, so we're going to send you to Omaha to start the season and get some more experience as a reliever." My bubble burst immediately.

I became excited, though, once I found out that Gubicza, Black, and Charlie Leibrandt were established pitchers and, along with Saberhagen, made a great rotation. I ended up pitching really well in spring training and made it difficult for them to send me down, but they had Quisenberry and Gene Garber competing for the closer's job. I don't think either one gave up a run during the entire spring training, so they kept both of them. When the season started, they both struggled to get guys out. In early June I got my first call up to the Royals.

Once I arrived in Kansas City, Saberhagen and Gubicza became great influences on me, and right along with them was reliever Steve Farr. When I was first called up, my third game was a save situation against the Oakland A's. I had a 1-2-3 ninth, retiring Walt Weiss, Doug Jennings, and Carney Lansford. I only got one more save opportunity the rest of the year. Meanwhile, Steve was getting the save opportunities. He asked me one time, "Do you want to know why I was getting all those save chances? It's because I went into [manager] John Wathan's office and told him that I'd been setting up Quiz for so many years that I deserved the chance." He started the next season as the closer but injured his knee. I had been pitching well, so I was put into the closer's role during the second half. That probably ended up being my best season, start to finish. I ended the year with a 7–3 record, 18 saves, and a 1.37 ERA.

At the end of the season, Wathan called me into his office and said, "You've done a really nice job for us, and we're looking forward to bigger and better things from you next year." Guess what? That offseason I turned on ESPN, and there's National League Cy Young winner and closer Mark Davis with a Royals jersey and cap on, being introduced as the Royals' new closer. That didn't really match up with what Wathan had told me. So I went from a set-up guy to a closer back to a set-up guy.

After some injuries Mark suffered in 1990, I was closing again that season before becoming the full-time closer in 1991. Even though closing games is challenging, that's where I was most comfortable. In my major league career, 699 of my 700 games were in relief. I felt that coming out of the bullpen was best for my style of pitching. Even though I could throw four pitches for strikes like a starter, I enjoyed getting out and establishing all four pitches with the first batter I faced.

By the time I retired in 1999, I had 304 saves, which put me at the top of the career saves list for the Royals. Thinking about all of the great pitchers who have come through Kansas City, I'm extremely humbled. Being able to spend 13 years in the major leagues was the result of a lot of work, God-given ability, work ethic, proper mechanics, and opportunities to go out and perform. Of course, then there are more specifics like pitch selection and battery mates.

Mike Macfarlane was my favorite catcher. I think I threw more pitches to him than anyone other than possibly Kansas City's own Bill Sobbe, who was our bullpen catcher. I really enjoyed throwing to Mac, who was a great catcher and wonderful at calling games. With my style as a four-pitch closer, I had to be able to throw any of my pitches at any time in the count to any batter.

I was pitching in Fenway Park against power hitter Mo Vaughn. It was a full count, bases loaded, two outs, and we were up by one run. Mac called for a change-up. Of my four pitches, the change-up was the one I had the least command of, but Mac called for it, so I was going to trust him. I threw a 3–2 change-up with the bases loaded to Vaughn. He was so far out in front of the pitch that when he swung he threw his bat over the first-base dugout. The game was over. That would've been the fourth pitch in my mind that I would've thrown at that time, but when Mac put down the sign, I thought, *You know, that's the right pitch.* I threw it and executed it, and it was effective.

Throughout *100 Things Royals Fans Should Know & Do Before They Die*, you'll be able to read more about moments such as that one, along with stories about other great players who have given this organization such a wonderful and unique history. Because of teammates such as Mac, Brett, Kevin Seitzer, Frank White, Willie Wilson, and so many others, my name is mentioned as one of the

Royals' top closers of all time, along with Quisenberry, Joakim Soria, Greg Holland, and Wade Davis. I was lucky and blessed to be on good Royals teams and to become part of this organization's rich history. What an honor!

—Jeff Montgomery
Royals Hall of Fame, 2003

Introduction

It's hard to believe that I've been with the Kansas City Royals for nearly 50 years. Almost a half-century! There's no way when I joined the Royals as Bud Blattner's broadcasting partner in 1969 that I imagined being with the club 10 years, let alone more than 45. I was in my mid-20s and had visions of going to one of the Chicago teams or St. Louis. And I had opportunities in both cities, but by that time I didn't see a need or want to leave. I'd grown to love Kansas City...and I was a Kansas City Royal. It didn't hurt that when I sat down with Mr. Kauffman to talk with him about one of the opportunities, he said that he thought I'd be able to stay with the Royals for many years and develop something special in Kansas City. Boy, he was right.

As I think about more than 45 years with the club and how one or two moments from each season would account for nearly half of this book, compiling a list of the top 100 moments, people, and things to do seems daunting. Author and good friend Matt Fulks has pulled it off, though. Do I agree completely with the list? Not necessarily, but that's what makes a book like this fun to read and debate. Matt can make a compelling argument for his 100, the same way I could make a compelling argument for another 100, and the same way you could make a compelling argument for your 100.

Throughout *100 Things Royals Fans Should Know & Do Before They Die,* you'll read stories from 1985 and 2015, of course, as well as 1980 and 2014, and the other playoff years—1976, '77, '78. And you'll read stories about some of the great players and characters such as George Brett, Frank White, Dennis Leonard, Bo Jackson, Amos Otis, and Hal McRae. And as the title indicates, there are several things "to do," including visiting the Royals Hall of Fame and eating at Chappell's, one of the best sports museums you'll find in the Midwest. There's even a fun story on favorite barbecue restaurants of some former Royals.

The 100th story features a friend of mine for more than 40 years—and my broadcasting partner for 25—Fred White. (Matt isn't ranking Fred last; it's more of a rightful place of tribute.) As you'll read, we're reminded that Fred had a wonderful sense of humor and felt humbled by his association with the Royals.

Whether you're a fairly new Royals fan, captivated by the excitement of recent years, or you're a die-hard season-ticket holder since 1969, I'm sure you'll enjoy the stories you're about to read in *100 Things Royals Fans Should Know & Do Before They Die*. I know I did.

—Denny Matthews

National Baseball Hall of Fame's Ford C. Frick Award, 2007

1 Game 5 of the 2015 World Series

The comeback kids did it again for a second consecutive night. Only this time it was for the world championship, as the Kansas City Royals overcame a two-run deficit at Citi Field in the ninth inning and went on to beat the New York Mets 7–2 in 12 innings in Game 5, becoming the 2015 World Series champs.

It was the first world championship for the Royals since 1985. Unlike 1985's 11–0 win in Game 7, the decisive game in 2015 had a little more nail biting before the Royals took the crown.

One night after getting shell-shocked by another Royals late comeback, the Mets needed a big outing from ace Matt Harvey to extend the series. Harvey did not disappoint, delivering one of the top performances of the postseason, as he struck out nine through eight shutout innings.

Heading into the ninth, when Harvey learned that manager Terry Collins was going to bring in New York's closer, Jeurys Familia, to finish the game, Harvey pleaded with Collins to leave him in. "[Harvey] came over and said, 'I want this game. I want it bad. You've got to leave me in,'" Collins said after the game. "He said, 'I want this game in the worst way.' So obviously, I let my heart get in the way of my gut."

"It didn't work," Collins added. "It's my fault."

No one could blame Collins for sticking with Harvey. Although Harvey threw his 100th pitch in the eighth inning, the Royals weren't getting good swings. Harvey, who started Game 1 but didn't factor into the decision, allowed only four hits—all singles—and walked one batter through eight innings in Game 5. Even with the Mets down in the series, if Harvey delivered a complete-game win, especially a shutout, New York would have had incredible momentum heading back to Kansas City.

But the ninth was a different story, especially against this resilient, never-say-die bunch of Royals, who'd already staged late comebacks down by at least two runs in six out of 15 games during the 2015 postseason. With the Royals trailing 2–0 in this one, Lorenzo Cain worked a full-count walk, and then Harvey gave up an opposite-field double to Eric Hosmer, scoring Cain. That ended Harvey's night, as Collins went to Familia, who had blown a save opportunity about 24 hours earlier.

Familia got Mike Moustakas to ground out to first baseman Lucas Duda for the first out, but it advanced Hosmer to third base. Salvador Perez, who popped out for the final out of the World Series in Game 7 in 2014, rolled a soft grounder toward short. Third baseman David Wright fielded the ball, checked Hosmer, and threw to first for the second out. However, as soon as Wright threw it, Hosmer broke for home. He slid headfirst across home plate for the tying run as Duda's throw sailed past catcher Travis d'Arnaud. With Hosmer's gutsy base running, Familia had recorded his third blown save in a World Series, which hadn't happened since 1969.

With the blown save, Game 5 was headed to extra innings. "We never quit. We never put our heads down," said Perez, who was selected as the World Series MVP. "We always compete to the last out."

Perez helped the Royals get to that last out by leading off the 12th with a single against Addison Reed. Jarrod Dyson came in as a pinch-runner and stole second as the clock passed midnight in New York. After Alex Gordon's ground-out moved Dyson to third, manager Ned Yost called on Christian Colon to pinch hit for pitcher Luke Hochevar. Colon, who scored the winning run in the 2014 wild-card game against Oakland, had not played in the 2015

2015 World Series Roster

Pitchers	Catchers	Outfielders
Johnny Cueto	Drew Butera	Lorenzo Cain
Wade Davis	Salvador Perez	Jarrod Dyson
Danny Duffy		Alex Gordon
Kelvin Herrera	**Infielders**	Paulo Orlando
Luke Hochevar	Christian Colon	Alex Rios
Ryan Madson	Alcides Escobar	
Kris Medlen	Eric Hosmer	
Franklin Morales	Raul Mondesi Jr.	
Yordano Ventura	Kendrys Morales	
Edinson Volquez	Mike Moustakas	
Chris Young	Ben Zobrist	

postseason. But the long break didn't affect him as he singled to left and gave the Royals their first lead of the game at 3–2.

The Royals, though, kept the line going. Paulo Orlando reached on an error by Daniel Murphy, whose error in Game 4 started Kansas City's rally. Alcides Escobar doubled home Colon, making it 4–2. After Ben Zobrist was intentionally walked to load the bases with one out, Cain greeted relief pitcher Bartolo Colon with a bases-clearing double, giving Kansas City five runs in the inning, the most by a team in extra innings in World Series history.

Not taking any chances with a 7–2 lead, Yost brought in Wade Davis to close the game. Davis was the fourth Royals pitcher after Edinson Volquez, Kelvin Herrera, and Hochevar, who got the win, throwing five scoreless innings. After throwing two innings for the save the previous night in Game 4, Davis wasted little time in striking out Duda and d'Arnaud, putting the Royals one out from a championship.

Michael Conforto singled, but then Davis finished striking out the side by catching Wilmer Flores looking. Davis tossed his glove in the air and awaited backup catcher Drew Butera, commencing the celebration on the field. Fittingly, the clincher was the Royals' seventh comeback of the 2015 postseason after trailing by at least two runs. (They trailed by one run in Game 2 before eventually winning. That means that the Royals came from behind in eight of their 11 postseason wins in 2015.) "I couldn't have written a better script," Yost said.

The script of Game 5 began with the Mets jumping on Kansas City starter Volquez in the first inning via a leadoff home run by Curtis Granderson. It was the second time Volquez gave up a homer to Granderson, who hit one in the fifth inning of Game 1.

Granderson scored New York's second run of the game in an inning that could've been disastrous for the Royals. Volquez walked Granderson leading off the sixth inning before giving up a base hit to Wright. Murphy then reached on an error on a grounder to first that bounced off Hosmer's glove and loaded the bases with no outs. After Yoenis Cespedes popped out to Escobar for the first out, Duda lifted a deep sacrifice fly that scored Granderson and gave the Mets a 2–0 lead. Volquez avoided any more trouble by inducing a ground-out by d'Arnaud, ending the inning.

Volquez, who rejoined the team a day earlier following the death of his father Daniel in the Dominican Republic before Game 1, gave up two runs and two hits in six innings. He also walked five and struck out five. As solid as he was on the mound, Volquez went into the Royals history book for something he did at the plate. Volquez led off the top of the third with a single to right against Harvey. That's the first time a Royals pitcher has recorded a hit in a World Series game.

More importantly, though, for the first time in 30 years, the Royals were World Series champions. "To be able to win this is very, very special, with this group of guys," Yost said. "With their character, with their heart, with their passion, with the energy that they bring every single day, I mean, they leave everything on the field."

2 Game 7 of the 1985 World Series

Improbable teams have won the World Series, but none has come back from such improbable odds as the 1985 Royals.

After coming back from a 3-games-to-1 deficit against the St. Louis Cardinals—and following the same scenario against the Toronto Blue Jays in the American League Championship Series—the Royals seemed to hit Game 7 with an unbeatable attitude. "That's usually what happens when you tie [the series] up," said Royals Hall of Fame second baseman Frank White. "You have to hope that your ace is better than their ace for Game 7."

Indeed, as he'd been in most of his outings that year, Royals ace Bret Saberhagen was better than the other team's ace. In this case it was John Tudor. Saberhagen held the Cardinals to five hits and no runs. The Royals, on the other hand, turned in their most lopsided win of 1985 as they won 11–0.

In many ways right fielder Darryl Motley, who batted .364 in the 1985 World Series, symbolized the beginning and the end of the Royals' victory in Game 7. In the second inning after belting a foul ball down the left-field line and missing a two-run home run by a few feet, Motley got nearly the same pitch from Tudor. Motley didn't miss the second time. That dinger ignited the Royals' scoring binge. "I was trying to hit the ball out of the ballpark," Motley said. "My agent told me before the game that if I did something special, I'd remember it the rest of my life. That home run was a special moment for me."

Motley was expecting the pitch. After the Cardinals showed the Royals mainly off-speed pitches throughout the series, leadoff hitter Willie Wilson quickly picked up on a pattern by Tudor. Realizing that Tudor threw back-to-back fastballs and then a change-up,

The Bret(t)s—George Brett and Bret Saberhagen (No. 31)—embrace after the Royals defeat the St. Louis Cardinals 11–0 in Game 7 of the 1985 World Series. (AP Images)

Wilson gave Motley a heads up. "Tudor did that to every batter before Motley and, sure enough, he did it to Mot," Wilson said, laughing. "But Mot still doesn't give me credit for him hitting the home run."

Then there was the final out of the game and the series. As Wilson jogged toward his spot in center field for the ninth inning, he made a prediction to Motley. With the final outcome a foregone conclusion, Wilson proudly told Motley that he, Wilson, would be catching the final out, sealing the Royals' victory. Motley, though, told him this would be the one time he beat the fleet-footed Wilson to the ball.

With two outs St. Louis' Andy Van Slyke drove a ball toward right-center field. As Motley foretold Wilson, he charged over, camped under the ball, and clasped it tightly in his glove as the celebration began. "I got there first, but I could hear Willie coming," Motley said, laughing. "He was too late. I caught it and I still have the ball."

Between the two-run homer and final out, there were plenty of fireworks, and that's not even including the Royals' scoring barrage. After Tudor walked in a run in the third inning, Cardinals manager Whitey Herzog went to his bullpen. On the way to the clubhouse, Tudor, who hadn't been taken out of game that early all season, punched an electrical fan in the dugout. He cut his hand on the blade and had to go to a hospital for stitches.

Already leading 5–0 the Royals broke the game open in the bottom of the fifth with six runs. During the inning Joaquin Andujar, who won 21 games that season, was called on as the Cardinals' fifth pitcher of the game. He got into an argument with home-plate umpire Don Denkinger over balls and strikes.

Herzog, still fuming from Denkinger's controversial call in Game 6, went out to defend his pitcher. In the heat of the moment, Herzog reminded Denkinger of Game 6. "I told him, 'We wouldn't even be here tonight if you hadn't blown that call

1985 Roster

Pitchers
Joe Beckwith
Bud Black
Mark Gubicza
Larry Gura
Danny Jackson
Mike Jones
Mike LaCoss
Charlie Leibrandt
Dan Quisenberry
Bret Saberhagen

Catchers
Jim Sundberg
John Wathan

Infielders
Steve Balboni
Buddy Biancalana
George Brett
Onix Concepcion
Greg Pryor
Frank White

Outfielders
Dane Iorg
Lynn Jones
Hal McRae
Darryl Motley
Jorge Orta
Pat Sheridan
Lonnie Smith*
Willie Wilson

*Smith was on the World Series roster but not the Opening Day roster. He was acquired during the season from the St. Louis Cardinals.

last night,'" Herzog said. Denkinger, as Herzog walked away, fired a response: "You wouldn't be here either if your team was hitting." Denkinger had a point. Kansas City's pitching staff held St. Louis to 13 runs and a .185 batting average during the seven-game series. But Herzog heard enough and went back for more. Denkinger tossed Herzog a few moments later.

After Andujar's next pitch to Jim Sundberg—which was called a ball—the pitcher showed his disgust. Denkinger pointed him toward the clubhouse, kicking him out of the game. After going after Denkinger with a level of vehemence not far below George Brett in the Pine Tar Game, Andujar eventually left the game but not before taking a bat to a toilet and a sink. By the time the inning ended, the Royals were up 11–0.

Although the Cardinals were arguing, they had very little fight left. As the ninth inning began, broadcaster Denny Matthews began a countdown with each out, culminating with the most famous call in Royals history, that final Van Slyke at-bat.

High fly ball...
Motley going back...
To the track...
No outs to go!
The Royals have won the 1985 World Series!

Saberhagen, who won 20 games that season, cruised to a complete-game, five-hit shutout. He received World Series MVP honors after winning two games and sporting a staggering 0.50 ERA. "Looking back on my career, the Cy Young awards and the World Series MVP are nice, but to win the World Series is the thing I'll always cherish," Saberhagen said. "Every guy on the team has to go out and play good baseball in order to win the World Series. We had that in '85."

3 Putting the Wild in Wild-Card

Well, that was fast. Or so it initially seemed. Twenty-nine years of waiting, of frustration, of thinking every spring "maybe this is our year," to the mid-summer realization "there's always next year." After 29 years the Royals were finally here, in the postseason, in 2014. And in less than 29 minutes—or however long it took the Oakland A's to put together a five-run sixth inning—it was over. This time of the year teams don't come back from 7–3 deficits after seven innings, especially a team like Kansas City that had spent so much energy during the roller-coaster 2014 season just to reach the postseason.

But in front of a rocking, standing-room only crowd of 40,502 at Kauffman Stadium, the young and inexperienced Royals were brought back to life in the wildest of wild-card games. And all it took were two pinch-hitters, seven stolen bases, seven pitchers, a batter who had been 0-for-5, and 12 innings. "This will go down as the craziest game I've ever played," first baseman Eric Hosmer said. "This team showed a lot of character. No one believed in us before the game. No one believed in us before the season."

Pitcher Jon Lester, whom Oakland acquired at the trade deadline for an anticipated postseason run, held a comfortable 7–3 lead. That was bad news for the Royals, considering Lester has had Kansas City's number throughout his career regardless of the name on his uniform. In fact, Lester, who was 4–0 against the Royals in 2014, shut out Kansas City in Boston on July 20 and then two starts later on August 2—his first appearance for the A's—he beat the Royals again.

But things would change after the seventh inning of the wild-card game.

Down to six outs and nothing to lose against Lester, the Royals tightened the screws a little. Alcides Escobar led off the bottom of the eighth with a base hit and then promptly stole a base, one of seven on the night for the Royals. After Nori Aoki advanced Escobar with a ground-out to second, Lorenzo Cain singled to center. That made it 7–4 Oakland. With Hosmer at the plate, Cain stole second. Hosmer walked, which ended Lester's night. Relief pitcher Luke Gregerson gave up a single to Billy Butler, scoring Cain and moving Hosmer to third. *7–5 Oakland.* Terrance Gore, running for Butler, stole second. Perhaps focusing too much on Kansas City's speed on the base path, Gregerson threw a wild pitch to Alex Gordon that scored Hosmer on a dive at home. *7–6*

Oakland. Gordon ended up walking and then stole second. (In case you're not keeping track, that's four stolen bases for the Royals in the inning.) The inning came to a screeching halt, though, as Gregerson struck out both Salvador Perez and Omar Infante. It was the second time in the game that the hitless Perez struck out.

He'd get another chance.

The Royals tied the game in the bottom of the ninth, courtesy of pinch-hitter Josh Willingham, who was a late-season acquisition brought in to give Kansas City some veteran power at the plate. Hitting for Mike Moustakas against Oakland reliever Sean Doolittle, Willingham blooped a base hit. Jarrod Dyson, running for Willingham, was sacrificed to second and then stole third. He tied the game on a sacrifice fly by Aoki.

After Brandon Finnegan, who barely three months earlier was pitching for Texas Christian University in the College World Series, relieved Greg Holland and shut down the A's, the Royals seemed to be on their way to the American League Division Series. Hosmer led off the Kansas City 10th with an infield base hit and advanced to second on a sacrifice by pinch-hitter Christian Colon. Two batters later with Hosmer at third and two outs, Perez had a chance to redeem his eighth-inning strikeout. But the Royals All-Star catcher grounded out to second, making him hitless in five at-bats.

After neither team scored in the 11th, former Royal Alberto Callaspo delivered a pinch-hit RBI single off Finnegan that scored Josh Reddick and gave the A's an 8–7 lead. "First postseason in 29 years?" Finnegan said after the game. "I felt like I just ended it."

Yet, once again, just when it looked as if the Royals might be finished for the season, they gave everyone a foreshadowing to the next two weeks. With one out in the 12th, Hosmer tripled off the top of the wall in left-center. Colon, another rookie, knocked in Hosmer and reached safely on a high chopper to third base. That tied the ballgame. Colon then stole second—the seventh swipe of the night for Kansas City—giving the Royals a runner in scoring position with two outs and Perez at the plate once again. "I worry about it because I want to help the team," Perez said.

Perez, who looked silly at the plate throughout the game, reached out for a low and away pitch with two strikes and pulled the ball past diving third baseman Josh Donaldson. Colon, who has good speed, scored easily, giving the Royals a walk-off win—their first postseason victory since Game 7 of the 1985 World Series. "That's the most incredible game I've ever been a part of," Royals manager Ned Yost said. "Our guys never quit. We fell behind there in the fifth inning, sixth inning. They kept battling back. They weren't going to be denied. It was just a great game."

Of course, it was a controversial decision Yost made in the sixth inning that helped lead to Oakland's runs. Starter James Shields gave up a bloop single to Sam Fuld and then walked Donaldson. With two on and nobody out and Kansas City holding a 3–2 lead with Brandon Moss—who homered earlier—coming to the plate, Yost pulled Shields, who'd thrown 88 pitches, and brought in starter Yordano Ventura. *Yosted!* Instead of going to a reliever, Yost pulled "Big Game James" and brought in another starter, a questionable move by the much-maligned manager. Moss sent Ventura's third pitch 432 feet to dead center. "Just one of those things," Yost said.

But despite those things, this was just the beginning of something special for the Royals. Many point to the wild-card game as the moment the Royals really came together as a team and realized what they could do together. It was a game that showed them they could come back from nearly any deficit—a realization that served them well in 2015. "It was absolutely epic," Shields said. "You don't write a story like that."

Mr. K

There's never been a more unlikely owner in sports. And with all due respect to the team across the parking lot, there's never been one who has done so much for Kansas City. After Charlie Finley jilted Kansas City and headed for Oakland with the Athletics, a group of local businessmen, plus Joe McGuff and Ernie Mehl, longtime sportswriters and editors at *The Kansas City Star*, convinced Major League Baseball owners that Kansas City needed an expansion team. The only condition was that they had to secure an owner.

After much searching that owner came in the gift of longtime Kansas Citian and pharmaceutical billionaire Ewing Kauffman. He was everything Finley wasn't. Conservative in his thinking and loved by his employees and others around him, Kauffman loved Kansas City and felt the city needed a major league team. After further encouragement from close friends and his wife, Kauffman decided to step up to the plate for the city. "[Businessmen] like Earl Smith and Les Milgram really got the thing rolling, and then Ewing's wife, Muriel, put him over the edge," said Denny Matthews, who is one of a handful of people who has been with the club since its first season. "Muriel was the last one to kick him in the seat of the pants and say, 'Let's do it.'"

It's funny, but Kauffman didn't really understand the game of baseball. In fact he wasn't much of a sports fan at all. Sure, he played golf occasionally and gin (if you count cards as a sport) most days at the Kansas City Club. But he did care deeply about two things: guarding his investment and winning. Both served Kansas City well.

In the mid-1960s, Kauffman started the Ewing Marion Kauffman Foundation to help develop—in essence—entrepreneurs and to improve the education for youths. Among his ventures was Project Choice. In 1988 it gave students at Westport High School, Kauffman's alma mater, a chance to attend college on Kauffman's dime—if they graduated high school and stayed out of trouble. The program, which covered students from 1988–92, saw 767 students graduate from high school on time. (Almost 1,400 students signed up for the program.) Of those 767 students, 709 attended college.

As far as the Royals, Kauffman, being a wise and competitive businessman, hired baseball people to run the organization. Possibly the best in the bunch was Cedric Tallis, who had been the California Angels' vice president in charge of operations. Kauffman first met Tallis during a trip to California when Kauffman was considering purchasing the Royals. He then hired Tallis as the Royals executive vice president/general manager on January 16, 1968. Tallis quickly assembled a staff that included Lou Gorman, Joe Burke, Herk Robinson, and John Schuerholz. The latter thought twice about leaving the Baltimore Orioles organization, where he had spent two years with Gorman, and taking the Royals job because he pictured Kansas City as "cowboy hats and horses attached to hitching posts in front of the general store." Schuerholz said: "I'm not so sure anyone knew what an excellent franchise they were creating. The organization was consistently dedicated and focused on doing things as best as they could be done in the baseball industry…Mr. K gets most of the credit for [it] because he set such high standards."

Kauffman's competitive spirit and leadership helped the Royals become one of the most respected franchises in baseball as Kansas City won six division titles, two American League pennants, and a World Series championship. The club's success was part good baseball people—and a large part Kauffman's savvy and compassion. "In 1977, which was our best team, we went through a stretch when we lost five of six games," Royals Hall of Fame pitcher Dennis Leonard said. "After a doubleheader against Chicago, Mr. Kauffman came into the clubhouse, which he didn't do very often. I thought he was going to be chewing us out. Instead Mr. Kauffman gave us all about $250 and said, 'Take your wife out, relax, and have a good time.' We started to go on a streak during August and September where we won 10 in a row in mid-August, swapped a couple, and then won 16 in a row, lost one, and then won eight in a row. So we won 24 out of 25 games. It was phenomenal."

Kauffman's generosity could be seen in his financial dealings. "I went and talked to him one time about a contract, and he basically said to me, 'Fred, go down to spring training, and I'll take care of [the contract],'" Royals Hall of Fame shortstop Fred Patek said. "I went to Florida without a contract, but two or three days later, general manager Cedric Tallis showed me the contract. I couldn't believe it. It was about three times more than what Mr. Kauffman and I had discussed."

Although he was considered a hands-off owner, Kauffman, according to former general manager Herk Robinson, was involved with the club until the end of his life. Robinson recalls a dinner for the Royals Lancers on July 31, 1993. "We had been trying to get Stan Belinda from the Pirates," Robinson said. "Our scouts weren't terribly high on him, but [manager] Hal McRae was, and [pitching coach] Bruce Kison was. I thought if we could get Belinda, we could win the division. Some of our people didn't want to give up the players we gave up [Dan Miceli and Jon Leiber], which was a lot. I called [Kauffman] at home at 9:00, and he answered the phone. He seemed so happy and at peace. He asked how the ballgame was going, asked what Lancers were there, and told me to tell them hello. After I told him about the trade, he said, 'Sure, if you want to do that, let's do it.' That was the final deal that we made together. I got a call at 5:00 the next morning, telling me that he'd passed away."

On August 1, 1993, Mr. K lost a battle with cancer at the age of 76. His legacy, however, on the field and in the community lives on today through both the Royals and the Ewing Marion Kauffman Foundation. "Mr. K was a special man, not only to Kansas City but to me," said Frank White, who is the greatest success story from the Royals Baseball Academy, one of Kauffman's baseball innovations. "If it hadn't been for Mr. Kauffman, I wouldn't have been in baseball. He was very community-minded and he knew that Kansas City needed baseball, so he worked hard to purchase the new franchise. He stuck with the club during the lean times and he rewarded players with a chance to play championship baseball and the city of Kansas City to see championship baseball."

5 Brett Steps Up in Game 3

Among the general truths in baseball, there's this one: a position player can't dominate a game and lead his team to a win. A pitcher can throw a perfect game and overwhelm his opponent. A non-pitcher, though? No. There are too many factors. Defensively, he might have a chance to record only a few outs. Offensively, he'll likely get only three or four at-bats.

Someone forgot to tell George Brett all of that.

In the 1985 American League playoffs, the Royals looked as if they were going face another playoff disappointment, a similar fate as 1984. And 1978. And 1977. And 1976. Taking a 91–71 record into the postseason, the Royals headed north of the border to face the AL East champion Toronto Blue Jays, who had won a league-best 99 games. For the first time, the league championship series would be best of seven instead of best of five. In another first Toronto was hosting a postseason series.

The Blue Jays weren't hospitable hosts. They didn't have any problems with Charlie Leibrandt and the Royals in Game 1, winning 6–1. After taking a 2–0 lead in the third inning of Game 2, the Royals needed a run in the top of the ninth to tie the game at 4–4. Then after taking a 5–4 lead in the top of the 10th, the always reliable Dan Quisenberry couldn't hold the one-run lead in the bottom of the inning, and the Blue Jays took a two-games-to-none lead with a 6–5 victory.

Game 3 would be in Kansas City on Friday, October 11. Cue No. 5, George Brett.

In the third game, Brett went 4-for-4 with two homers and a double and he scored four of the club's six runs, including the go-ahead run in the bottom of the eighth. Defensively, he played a great game—highlighted by one of the best plays of his career. Brett backhanded a grounder by Lloyd Moseby and threw out Damaso Garcia at home plate. "You won't see a better play in baseball," manager Dick Howser said. "You can't do better than that. But he's done that all year both offensively and defensively." Joe McGuff wrote in *The Kansas City Star* on October 12: "If you were there, you saw a performance that will become a part of baseball's postseason lore along with Don Larsen's perfect World Series game, Babe Ruth's called-shot home run, and Reggie Jackson's three home runs in the sixth game of the 1977 Series."

Although the Royals lost the next game and still had to battle back from a three-games-to-one deficit against Toronto, things likely would've worked out differently had they not won Game 3 behind Brett. "George literally willed the Royals to win that game," said broadcaster Denny Matthews. "That was the biggest game of George's career and the most important in Royals history. If we don't win Game 3, we wouldn't have that World Series championship."

6 1977: The Best Royals Team Ever

It seems odd to say this about a team that didn't win a World Series or even make it that far, but here it goes: the 1977 club was the best team in Royals history. Of course, without reaching the World Series, it may also go down as the most disappointing season in Royals history. A year after winning its first American League West title, Kansas City didn't have a great start in 1977. Through the first three months, the Royals were lucky to be hovering around the .500 mark. After an 8–6 home loss to the Seattle Mariners on June 23, the Royals were 33–33.

But then something clicked.

The club started winning on a consistent basis, and the Royals weren't at or below .500 again the rest of the season. After sweeping the New York Yankees in mid-July, the Royals were 51–38 heading into the All-Star break. In case you don't have your calculator handy, that means the team went 18–5 after losing to Seattle on June 23. That was only the beginning of one of the best stretches in major league history. Ten days after the break, the Royals lost three out of four at Chicago and were tied for second place with the Minnesota Twins, five and a half games behind the division-leading White Sox. "A week after that series in Chicago, we had the White Sox in Kansas City," pitcher Dennis Leonard said. "Chicago was taking batting practice, and Mac [Hal McRae] was crawling on the ground on his belly [military style] toward the White Sox. Ralph Garr, who was with the White Sox, said, 'McRae, what the heck are you doing?' Mac said, 'We're coming after you.' The next thing you know, we went on that tear. I think that's the best team we ever assembled here in Kansas City."

The Royals indeed went on a tear. After losing to the Boston Red Sox on August 16, they won their next 10. And then after losing three of their next four, the Royals won 16 in a row, a team record that still stands. All told, beginning with the 10-game winning streak, Kansas City won 35 out of 39 games. "At the time with the White Sox, we were a game back [of the Royals] and playing pretty well," said Kansas City native and former Royals pitcher Steve Renko, who played for Chicago in 1977. "But with that tear that the Royals went on, we were just blown away. We were a good ballclub, winning 90 games, but we finished in second place, 12 games back!"

The Royals finished the regular season with a 102–60 record. It's the only 100-plus win season in club history. Kansas City then faced the 100-win Yankees for a trip to the World Series. In the five-game series, the two teams split the first two contests in New York and then the next two in Kansas City. Even after losing a chance to clinch the series in Game 4, the Royals came out slugging in Game 5...literally.

George Brett slid into third with the club's trademark aggressive style in the first inning, sparking a brawl at the base with Yankees third baseman Graig Nettles. After scoring two runs in that heated first, the Royals held a lead until the ninth inning. With Kansas City thin in the bullpen and ahead 3–2, manager Whitey Herzog brought in Leonard, who won Game 3 and also ended the regular season in a three-way tie for most wins in the AL with 20, to record the final three outs. "I was sitting on the bench, wearing my tennis shoes when Whitey asked me if I thought I could throw," Leonard said. "My arm usually bounced back quickly, so I told him I could, and I went down to the bullpen to warm up. My adrenaline was pumping, and my arm didn't hurt. Shoot, I felt like I was throwing 150 miles per hour...I threw a good pitch on the hands of the first batter, Paul Blair, and he blooped a broken-bat single. Then Roy White came up and fouled off several pitches before walking. So I left two guys on with no outs. Whitey had a decision to make and he took me out and brought in Larry Gura. The Yankees scored, Whitey brought in Mark Littell, and they scored two more runs by the end of the inning, and we lost the game and the series."

For a club that seemed destined for its first trip to the World Series, the season ended with a horrendous thud. "Even though we won three pennants and a World Series in St. Louis," Herzog said, "the 1977 Royals team was the best team I ever managed. We had the Yankees down two games to one. That was a playoff we should have won."

McRae, who also was a member of the 1980 and 1985 World Series teams, agrees with Herzog about the 1977 team's greatness. "That was the best team; the other clubs don't compare," McRae said. "But we were short in the [bullpen]. The Yankees had [Rich "Goose"] Gossage, and we had various guys closing for us. We went into the late innings with a lead but couldn't hold it. If we had Gossage or someone in the pen who could've shut the other team down, I think we would've played in more World Series than we did."

7 The 1980 World Series

It's one of the great mysteries in Royals history. How does a club that did so much, including reaching the World Series, and notching several individual accomplishments, become so forgotten? Somehow, that happened with the 1980 Royals. Even though they were the first major league team from Kansas City to reach the World Series, perhaps they're simply overshadowed by the team that won it all five years later.

In many ways, however, it's the 1980 team that links the perennial playoff teams of the 1970s to the 1985 World Series championship. "With the players who were here for an extended period of time like Amos Otis, John Mayberry, and Fred Patek and because of the success we had then on the field, I think we identify with a different group of fans than the players in '85 and certainly the players of today," said Dennis Leonard, who pitched for the Royals during 1974–86 but missed the 1985 World Series because of a knee injury suffered two years earlier.

In 1980 the Royals finished with an impressive 97–65 record before dispatching the New York Yankees in the American League playoffs for the first time in four attempts. However, as if they were dumbfounded over beating the Yankees and reaching the World Series, instead of coming back to Kansas City, the Royals, knowing they were going to be traveling to a National League city, stayed in New York, awaiting the winner of the Philadelphia Phillies-Houston Astros series. "There was some confusion about what to do, and maybe if we came home and rested, things might have been different," Leonard said. "Once you get on the field, though, you can't use it as an excuse."

But the time off can affect hitters. Finishing the playoffs on Friday and starting the World Series on Tuesday meant three full days of no games. "Once you get past a couple of days off, your timing is shot," said Willie Wilson, who had a club-record 230 hits in '80. "People don't realize how important it is to play every day. When you sit that long not going through competition, you're going to be slower than guys who have been playing. It hurts you. The Royals were better than the Phillies on paper, but it didn't work that way."

The layoff didn't hurt Amos Otis. In the second inning of Game 1 of the World Series, Otis put the Royals on top with a home run. In doing so, Otis became just the 16th player to homer in his first World Series at-bat. He went on to lead the Royals at the plate with two more home runs and a .478 batting average. "[Philadelphia] thought I was a fastball hitter, so they kept throwing me breaking balls," Otis said. "Pretty much every time up, I took the first pitch, which was usually a fastball, then they'd throw me a breaking ball, and I'd hit it." Willie Aikens, a 1980 newcomer, also blistered at the plate, hitting at a .400 clip with four home runs in two games. "I was fortunate to play with Amos until he retired, so I saw some of the things that he did in his career," Leonard said. "But [Otis and Aikens] both did an outstanding job. Everybody did. When you put the uniform on, especially on that stage, everybody's giving 100 percent. Sometimes it works out; sometimes it doesn't."

In the case of the 1980 Royals, it didn't. After tying the series at two games apiece, the Phillies took the next two, clinching the championship. Looking back now more than 30 years later, it's easier for the players to have some additional fondness for that trip to the World Series. "Playing in the World Series and producing the way I did was the highlight of my career," Otis said.

Leonard started both Games 1 and 4, one of the crowning achievements of his baseball life. "I think about the standout players who go through their whole careers without a chance to go to the World Series," he said. "Look at the Cubs with players like Ernie Banks and Billy Williams. To have the careers that they had and never play in the playoffs, let alone the World Series, then to think that I was in the right place at the right time—it's really special."

Even though the 1980 Royals aren't remembered as easily as the '85 club, that first World Series moment, which was triggered in part by George Brett's MVP season, was the impetus for what happened five years later. "That experience [in 1980] whet our appetites about the World Series," Brett said. "The World Series wasn't beating the New York Yankees; it was beating someone from the other league. Sure enough, we had that opportunity in 1985 and took advantage of it."

8 Ninety Feet Away

Ninety feet. That's all that separated the Royals from pulling off the improbable in the same place where their crazy 2014 postseason journey started 29 days earlier. For a brief moment in late September, it would've been more plausible to find Elvis eating a North Town Burger at Chappell's than it would be to even imagine the Royals getting past the wild-card game, let alone reaching the World Series.

And yet, here they were, 90 feet—just 30 yards—from tying Game 7 with two outs in the bottom of the ninth inning with one of the greatest pitchers in World Series history facing the Royals player who had came up big in a similar spot 29 days earlier.

After a strikeout by Eric Hosmer and a foul out to first by Billy Butler, Alex Gordon, who had an RBI double in the second inning, stood at the plate against San Francisco Giants ace Madison Bumgarner. Three days ago, Bumgarner mowed down the Royals for the second time in this World Series in a complete-game, four-hit shutout. Now he was one out from getting a five-inning save while allowing no runs and only one hit.

Gordon kept Kansas City's hopes alive, though, as he lined Bumgarner's 87 mph slider to left-center field. Center fielder Gregor Blanco misplayed the ball, and it rolled to the wall. Left fielder Juan Perez had trouble grabbing the ball, which allowed Gordon to motor to third base. In the aftermath some fans wished third-base coach Mike Jirschele would've sent Gordon home.

(Even an average throw from shortstop Brandon Crawford likely would've nailed Gordon by 27 feet for the final out of the series.) Others claim that had Gordon charged hard out of the box on contact, he might've been able to score easily. Either way, he stood at third with two outs and Salvador Perez at the plate.

Salvy was hitless in the game, though he'd been plunked above the knee by starting pitcher Tim Hudson in the second inning. Going by averages, Perez was one of the guys the Royals would want at the plate in this situation. He was tied with Butler for the highest batting average on the team in the World Series at .333. And let's not forget that 29 days earlier, Perez propelled the Royals past the Oakland A's in the wild-card game with a walk-off RBI single in the 12th inning.

But that hit was against Jason Hammel. To tie up Game 7, Perez would have to get a hit off Bumgarner. Whereas Hammel went low and away to Perez in the wild-card game, Bumgarner decided to throw high fastballs, which are the easiest to see and hardest to hit. Bumgarner threw six pitches—all fastballs—to Perez. Perez popped the last one up in foul territory near the Giants dugout at third base. Pablo Sandoval camped under it and made the catch. The Giants won the Game 7 contest 3–2, having recorded their third World Series title in five years.

The Royals ended the game with a man at third. "As magical as our run has been, to end up losing the ballgame by 90 feet is tough," Royals manager Ned Yost said. "But the hard part about this is that you work all year to climb to the top of the mountain and then—*boom*—you fall back and you've got to start right back at the bottom again next year. But we've gained a ton of experience. I don't think I've ever been as proud of anything in my life as I have been of this team and the way they performed this postseason. It was just fantastic."

The Royals were their typically resilient selves in Game 7. After the Giants scored two against starter Jeremy Guthrie in the top of the second, Butler led off the inning with a single before Gordon, who batted .185 in the series, knocked a double to center that scored Butler from first. After Hudson hit Perez with a pitch and Mike Moustakas advanced Gordon to third with a fly out to left, the Royals tied the game at 2–2 on a sacrifice fly to center by Omar Infante.

Making his second appearance in the 2014 World Series and second ever in the Fall Classic, Guthrie gave up four hits and three runs in three and one-third innings. With this being the last game of the season, each manager said his starting pitcher would be on a short leash. Giants manager Bruce Bochy went to his bullpen with two outs in the second and brought in former Royals pitcher Jeremy Affeldt. With one out in the fourth and runners at the corners in a 2–2 game, Yost brought in Kelvin Herrera. Designated hitter Michael Morse fought off a Herrera fastball and lined it to right, scoring Sandoval, who led off the inning with a hit. "We had the matchup we wanted with Morse and Herrera, and Morse did a great job of kind of just fighting off a high fastball and dumping it out into right field for the winning run," Yost said. "But Herrera was great… and Jeremy Guthrie was really throwing the ball well, too."

Morse's RBI hit made up Bochy's mind. Affeldt pitched another inning before Bochy plucked Bumgarner from the bullpen to start the fifth. Infante greeted him with a single, but that was the only base runner the Royals would have until Gordon reached in the ninth. For his five innings of work, Bumgarner got the save while Affeldt was the game's winning pitcher. Bumgarner, who was selected as the World Series MVP after winning two games and saving one, saw his ERA for the World Series drop to 0.43.

Wade Davis and Greg Holland closed out the game for the Royals. As they'd done throughout the World Series, neither pitcher allowed a run. Both ended the series with a 0.00 ERA. But just like that, the incredible month-long ride for the Royals was over. Through the improbable postseason run, which came 29 years after their last one in 1985, the Royals gained fans across the country and certainly brought the Kansas City community together unlike any other sports team, personality, or politician had ever done.

Just like they did after winning the American League Championship Series, Hosmer and several of his teammates went to the Power & Light District as a way to thank the fans. A rally honoring the team was held at Kauffman Stadium the morning after Game 7. "On a scale of one to 10 in terms of support through the postseason, it's got to be 14," Yost said. "It was phenomenal. What our fans did and the excitement in the city here for this last month, it's just been absolutely unbelievable."

9 "A.O., A.O., A.O."

"A.O., A.O., A.O." The chant kept ringing. Normally, that particular echo was reserved for Royals Stadium whenever Amos Otis came up to the plate in a big situation. This time, however, it was on the Royals' team bus.

The date was September 29, 1976. The Royals were in the final game of a three-game series with the rival Oakland A's, a team over which the Royals' lead in the standings had shrunk to two and a half games after dropping the first two contests in the series. Otis, who had been beaned in the head a week earlier by Oakland pitcher Stan Bahnsen, was benched for those first two games.

Manager Whitey Herzog made sure Otis was in the lineup for the series finale. Along with a four-hitter by pitcher Larry Gura, Otis performed as expected, helping lead the Royals to a 4–0 victory. He hit an RBI double and a home run. "I was fortunate, as always, that the pitcher hit my bat with the ball, and it went all the way out of the ballpark," Otis said, laughing.

When Otis reached the team bus after the game, his teammates started chanting: "A.O., A.O., A.O." "That's a very special feeling that's hard to describe," Otis said. "When you hear it from the fans, it's wonderful, but when you hear it from your teammates, it's special. They chanted quite a while. It put me on top of the world. I appreciated it very much."

But that was a game the Royals had to win. Ask nearly any member of that 1976 Royals team, and without hesitating they'll point to that game against Oakland as the turning point. "That game truly was a defining moment in Royals history," said broadcaster Denny Matthews. "It's probably second only to Game 3 of the 1985 playoffs in terms of importance in franchise history. If we don't beat Oakland in that game, we probably don't win the division." Added Royals Hall of Fame shortstop Fred Patek: "Oakland always beat us, and they knew they could beat us."

The A's showed that most recently in 1975 when the Royals finished with a then-club-record 91 wins but finished second to Oakland. However, 1976 seemed different. The Royals held first place in the American League West to themselves on May 19. By as late as August 6, they stretched it to 12 games behind great pitching from Dennis Leonard, Al Fitzmorris, Doug Bird, and Paul Splittorff, plus a tough lineup that included Otis, George Brett, John Mayberry, Hal McRae, and Al Cowens. But the Royals struggled mightily down the stretch. After a five-game winning streak in the middle of September, the club fell apart. Heading into the final road series at Oakland, the Royals had lost four out of five. Then they dropped the first two against the A's. Suddenly, that 12-game lead in the division was down to two and a half with four remaining.

So on Wednesday, September 29, Herzog pulled a couple rabbits out of his cap. He started Gura and backup catcher John Wathan and put A.O. was in center field.

Those moves and the win over Oakland helped the Royals clinch at least a tie with the A's for the division title. They went on to win their first AL West title outright a couple nights later.

Getting past rival Oakland helped start a new rivalry with the New York Yankees, which began during that postseason. In the best-of-five American League playoffs, the Yankees beat the Royals in a heartbreaking fifth game when Chris Chambliss hit a walk-off home run over the outstretched glove of Hal McRae. "There was a sense of relief getting to the playoffs, but as the series went on and we were tied two games to two, we felt we could win it," Leonard said. "Of course, that came to a crashing halt with Chambliss. But playing in that series and playing even with the Yankees—with the exception of that one pitch—fueled our fire going into '77."

In spite of the disappointing loss to the Yankees, the 1976 season set the Royals on a decade-long stretch of winning baseball. From 1976–85 the Royals won the AL West six times and made two trips to the World Series, including the championship against the St. Louis Cardinals in 1985. And in many ways, it all started with that one September game against Oakland in 1976. "Winning that game and the division," Patek said, "was the big thing that gave us confidence the next year and following. After that we felt that when we walked in the clubhouse [that] we couldn't be beat."

10 Frank White

From 1972 until 1990, eight men managed the Royals. But they had only two second basemen—a sleek fielder by the name of Cookie Rojas, who probably should've won at least one Gold Glove, and then a local kid named Frank White.

White grew up in the shadows of old Municipal Stadium. In fact, his Lincoln High School, which didn't have a baseball team, used to be so close that White and his buddies would climb to the top of the football stadium bleachers and peer over the fence to watch the Kansas City Athletics. There were even times when A's groundskeeper George Toma, whom White would get to know later with the Royals, would sneak the boys inside the stadium during the last couple innings of games.

Early in the Royals' existence, owner Ewing Kauffman hatched an idea for the Royals Baseball Academy with the belief that they could take a great athlete and turn him into a baseball player. The club held tryouts around the country to find the best athletes. The chosen players went to Florida, where they lived in dorms, attended junior college, and worked on the fundamentals of baseball. They weren't allowed to have cars there and they all were single—or at least supposed to be. The brightest prospect happened to be married. White was so talented, however, that Syd Thrift, the academy's director, convinced Kauffman to bend the rules for White, who was working as a clerk at Metal Protection Company in Kansas City.

The Academy folded before blossoming, but not before the club discovered its future second baseman, the married sheet metal worker, who played only summer baseball. Before White reached Kansas City in 1973, he had gone from outfielder to third baseman to shortstop. Early the next season, White platooned with George Brett for a few weeks at third before moving to second. With Rojas nearing the end of his career, it became apparent that White would take over for him. Once that happened in 1976, White went on to dominate second base in an era that featured some great players at the position—Willie Randolph, Lou Whitaker, Rod Carew, Paul Molitor, Julio Cruz, and Rich Dauer. That only pushed White more.

White made five All-Star teams during an 18-year career, during which he averaged .255, hit 160 home runs, and knocked in 886 RBIs. But it was on the defensive side where he really made his name. White won the Rawlings Gold Glove Award eight times. He won his first in 1977 and then the next five. He added two more in 1986 and '87. Gold Gloves are voted on by managers and coaches, which makes the award a little more special and maybe a little more difficult to win.

In 1988 at the age of 37, White enjoyed one of the finest defensive seasons of his career. In 148 games he had 293 putouts and 426 assists and committed just four errors, which were throwing errors to four different first basemen. He ended the season with a career best .994 fielding percentage, but he didn't win the Gold Glove. Instead it went to Seattle's Harold Reynolds, who committed 18 errors in 158 games and finished with a .977 fielding percentage. "That was the only year when I thought I was going to win a Gold Glove," White admitted. "I was truly disappointed and dejected when I didn't win it that year. That was the first and only time that I expected to win any type of award."

Though White impressively won eight Gold Gloves, the 1988 Gold Glove would have put in him even more rare territory among second basemen. (Ryne Sandberg won nine, and Roberto Alomar won 10.) "When you're depending on other people to vote," White said, "you never know what might happen."

That one non-Gold Glove, though, doesn't diminish White's dominance at second base. "Frank White was the best defensive second baseman I have ever seen—hands down," said Whitey Herzog, who managed White and the Royals from 1975–79. "There are four things you want a second baseman to do: go left, go right, come in, and go out. Frank could do those four things better than any second baseman I have ever seen. There's no doubt in my mind that if Frank had played in a market like New York or had we gone to the World Series in Kansas City in the 1970s, he would be in the Baseball Hall of Fame."

In 1995 White's No. 20 was retired by the Royals, and a bronze statue of him was erected outside Kauffman Stadium in 2004.

11 Getting Past the Yankees...Finally!

John Wathan isn't the most emotional guy in the world. There was one time, though, when he couldn't contain himself. Specifically, October 10, 1980.

The Royals had just capped off an incredible season by sweeping their most heated rival, the New York Yankees, in the American League Championship Series and were headed to the World Series for the first time in club history. "I ran off the field with tears in my eyes," said Wathan, who was playing right field when closer Dan Quisenberry struck out Willie Randolph for the final out. "It was such an unbelievable feeling. They had our wives down below to protect them from the fans, so we all hugged them on our way into the clubhouse for the celebration. It was the coolest thing ever."

That entire season was the "coolest" one in the Royals' 12-year existence. By 1980 after a fantastic stretch of three trips to the postseason in four years, the Royals expected to reach the playoffs. The '80 season, though, didn't start off so well. The club started off slowly before taking over first place in the division in late May. The Royals became a dominant team and stayed atop the standings for the rest of the season, enjoying a double-digit lead for most of the last two months.

Individually, it turned out to be a season of records. Rich Gale, who was one of five Royals starting pitchers with at least 10 wins, set a club record in decisions with 11 straight wins. Quisenberry had 33 saves, which was good for a tie as the league-best. At the plate the Royals led the American League with a .286 batting average. Willie Wilson's 230 hits, which remains a Royals record, led the AL.

The one player everyone watched that year, though, was George Brett, whose club-record 30-game hitting streak helped him get over the .400 mark in mid-August. He finished the season with a .390 average as the Royals took their 97 wins into the playoffs against the Yankees. After winning the first two games at home, the Royals trailed New York 2–1 in the third game heading into the top of the seventh. But then Brett came through with his biggest hit of the season. With two on and two out, Brett blasted a Rich "Goose" Gossage fastball into the upper deck. "I remember rounding the bases and how quiet Yankee Stadium got," Brett said. "Usually when we were there, it was the loudest place you'd ever been. To get a hit that silenced everybody was unbelievable…It was a great thrill not only to beat the Yankees, but to get the hit that beat them. Looking at my career, I'm most proud of that hit."

The Yankees started to rally in the bottom of the ninth before Quisenberry struck out Randolph, sealing the championship for the Royals. "It almost felt when George hit the home run that we had won a World Series, especially knowing we had Quiz," Wathan said. "It was so big because of all the heartbreaks we had had before then in 1976, '77, and '78. That was as emotional as I've ever been."

Four days later, the Royals faced the Philadelphia Phillies in Kansas City's first ever World Series. Each club won its first two games at home before the Phillies broke that streak in Kansas City in Game 5. Philadelphia went on to clinch the championship two days later. "Record-wise, 1980 was a great year, but it took me five years to get over [the loss to Philadelphia] mentally," Wilson said. "If we wouldn't have beaten St. Louis in 1985, I might never have gotten over losing. Getting back to the World Series after losing is what drove me."

That experience in 1980 definitely served the club well in '85. "When you reach the World Series," Wathan said, "it's relaxing in a sense because it's every boy's dream to reach the major leagues and then play in a World Series. Plus, it's very special because I think about all of the great players who never got a chance to play in a World Series, and I got a chance to play in two. Winning a World Series is icing on the cake. The main thing was getting there."

12 Bret Saberhagen

In 1984 the Royals, in light of the previous season's drug scandal and an aging pitching staff, made a bold move by going young—really young. The youngest of the bunch, Bret Saberhagen, made his debut on April 4, 1984, at the age of 19. The next season, en route to becoming the World Series MVP and the youngest pitcher in American League history to win a Cy Young Award (as well as the first Royals pitcher to win the award), Saberhagen led the club in wins (20), complete games (10), and strikeouts (158). While becoming the club's only two-time Cy Young winner, he won a franchise-record 23 games and posted a league-best 2.16 ERA in 1989.

As a young, inexperienced pitcher about to have a child, how in the world did you stay so focused in 1985?

Bret Saberhagen: The guys that were around us—we were more of a family than anything else. We did things together on the weekends during the offseason. We had barbecues and such. We were a close-knit group. We didn't have the best team on paper, but we went out and played baseball. It was easy to focus when you had guys who were pulling for one another and being friends away from the field and wanting to do well for each other.

How were you able to come back against the St. Louis Cardinals in the World Series?

BS: What helped us—being down three games to one to St. Louis—is that we'd faced something similar to Toronto in the playoffs. When we got into the same situation in the World Series, we felt we'd win it.

Bret Saberhagen, who won two Cy Young Awards and a World Series MVP during his eight years with the Royals, throws during a 1989 game.

Describe the experience of the '85 World Series.

BS: There were so many great moments in the I-70 Series. My mom told me about the governor's train that ran from Kansas City to St. Louis. She got a chance to ride on that. She said it was mainly blue at the start, and then a mix of blue and red in the middle, and by the time it got to St. Louis, it seemed like it was all red. That was just a very special time. Being that young and being in the playoffs the previous year—my first year when we lost to the Detroit Tigers—it seemed like it was going to happen year after year.

Did your and the team's success in 1985 raise expectations in 1986 and beyond?

BS: Yeah, it did. I came out in spring training in '86 and tried to do too much too soon to live up to the expectations. I ended up having a bum shoulder for part of that year. It didn't help out the team being on the disabled list. That was my toughest year, trying to live up to the expectations.

Among your accomplishments—the World Series MVP, the no-hitter, two Cy Young awards—is there one that stands out above the rest?

BS: The World Series. It's the toughest thing to achieve. You can have a good year, but to win the series, 25 guys have to go out and play good baseball. The Cy Youngs are great and talked about more than the World Series, but [a World Series championship] is something that takes a team to accomplish. Looking back on my career, that's something I'll always cherish.

Is it true that if someone made an error behind you, you'd turn around and laugh?

BS: Nobody wants to make an error. Gubie used to give the stare a lot. I'd tell him that he was going to make the guys nervous behind him, and then they'd be pissed at him. I'd just tell the guys that we'd get another ground ball and turn two.

Thinking about us, Gubie and I, coming up and making the team in 1984 and living with George—after about a month, Gubie finally asked if it was okay to use the telephone. Meanwhile, I was helping myself to whatever clothes he had in his closet, using his car whenever. After about a month and a half, [Brett] said, "I can't take you two youngsters anymore; I'm going to find you a place." Gubie and I ended up finding a place on the Plaza and rooming down there together. We ended up moving back in with George during the playoffs. He was a great mentor and cared about the younger guys, wanting to make sure they were going about things the right way.

I'm thinking neither you nor Mark Gubicza had to worry about Frank White making an error behind you.
BS: He was so smooth. He's one of the prettiest guys to watch field a ball and turn a double play. It was an honor to play on the same field with him.

You were known as a great prankster. Talk about how you used to give the hot foot, lighting someone's shoe on fire.
BS: We got [coach Bob] Schaefer one night. He was upset because [the match] was attached to his shoe when he was headed out to the field. Of course, it went off while he was out there. We timed it perfectly. He wasn't too happy about that because he was jumping around, and I guess he got embarrassed. I got reprimanded by the fire department because of it, saying how it wasn't a good example, and kids might see it and get burned. So I put the hot foot on the back burner, so to speak, after that.

13 69 Wins in '69

When he was working with young pitchers in the Baltimore Orioles organization, the late Moe Drabowsky would ask this question to new guys: who won the first game for the Kansas City Royals? Usually, the youngsters would think about it for a moment before guessing wrong. With some coaxing, they'd eventually get it right: their coach, Drabowsky.

And what a game it was.

On a cold April 8, 1969, at Municipal Stadium, the Royals and Minnesota Twins were tied at three going into the 12th inning. Drabowsky retired the Twins in order. The Royals promptly loaded the bases in the bottom of the inning after the Twins' rookie manager, Billy Martin, called for intentional walks to Chuck Harrison and Bob Oliver.

Royals manager Joe Gordon, who had managed the Kansas City A's in 1961, called on Joe Keough to pinch hit for catcher Ellie Rodriguez. Keough drove the first pitch over right fielder Tony Oliva's head, giving the Royals a 4–3 win. That first win was a point of pride for the well-known prankster Drabowsky, who was a 13-year major league veteran and had won a game in the 1966 World Series for Baltimore by the time he joined the Royals.

It seems being a part of that first team in Royals history is a bragging point for anyone involved. "People will ask about my favorite memory of broadcasting Royals games," said Denny Matthews, who was 26 at the time. "My answer is the very first game because it was the club's first game, and it was my first game as a major league announcer. As it turned out, I was doing the game in the 12th, so I was the first person to say on the air, 'Royals win!'"

That was redemption for Kansas City baseball fans. When the A's were in town, they weren't very good. Then there was owner Charlie Finley, who was somewhat of a renegade and a royal pain. So the second incarnation of Major League Baseball with a caring owner (Ewing Kauffman) this time and the club winning its first game was a welcome event.

Dave Wickersham, along with Drabowsky, pitched for both the Kansas City A's and the Royals. They also were the oldest Royals players in '69 at age 33. "I wanted to make that team so bad and be a contributor to the success because I'd lived here for four offseasons before 1969," Wickersham said. "Outside of my first year in the majors, my greatest thrill was making that Royals team. It was a fresh attitude because of Ewing Kauffman."

The roster was full of players who were either nearing the twilights of their careers or hungry to make it—some would say bottom-of-the-barrel guys—who'd been exposed by their previous clubs through the 1968 Expansion Draft. One major exception to that was a rookie outfielder named Lou Piniella, whom the Royals acquired a week before the opener in a trade with the other '69 expansion club, the Seattle Pilots (now the Milwaukee Brewers).

Piniella didn't disappoint. In the opener he led off the bottom of the first with a double and then scored the club's first run on a Jerry Adair single. Piniella went 4-for-5 that day, beginning a season in which he won the American League's Rookie of the Year award. As first seasons go, the Royals finished 1969 with a respectable 69–93 record. "As much as I liked Finley," said Keough, who played for the Royals from 1969–72, "when Ewing brought baseball back to Kansas City, he had a legacy to build and he wanted to start early. And I think we did."

The Royals were building something indeed. Just a few years later, Kansas City started battling for the division crown. "I enjoyed every minute of being in Kansas City with an expansion team,"

Keough said. "Every day that we had out there was a new experience and a great day."

14 The Big Red Influence of Hal McRae

Whether you love or hate Pete Rose, the Royals owe a lot to Charlie Hustle. During the championship years of the 1970s and '80s, the Royals were known as an aggressive club, especially on the base paths. Guys stretched singles into doubles and doubles into triples. They stole bases and never thought twice about sending a middle infielder flying toward left field if it meant breaking up a double play.

The player regarded as the impetus for that style of play is Hal McRae, who came to Kansas City from the Cincinnati Reds in December 1972 for Roger Nelson and Richie Scheinblum. He quickly points the finger at one of his old teammates, Rose. "We had good ballclubs in Cincinnati," McRae said. "Those guys all played hard, but I kind of took my lead from Pete. I enjoyed the way he played. We were teammates for about three years, and I tried to play that way because I thought that was the way to play the game. Plus I enjoyed playing that way."

McRae is regarded as one of the best and most aggressive players ever to wear Royals blue. "McRae is one of the real pros of the game," said former Royals general manager John Schuerholz. "He's as astute a student of hitting as I have ever seen and a clutch performer. When the game was on the line, you wanted to have [George] Brett or McRae at the plate."

When McRae arrived the Royals were young in every way as the club had been in existence for only three seasons. "When I got here, we had players from everywhere," McRae said. "Generally it takes time for that type of club to jell because you have players from all over the league. The club didn't possess a lot of players that came from winning situations. I think that made it difficult."

The Royals, though, would become a winning team, and McRae's Cincinnati roots deserve credit for giving Kansas City some attitude. He was known as someone who'd barrel roll into second base in an attempt to break up a double play. (He learned from Rose, who infamously plowed over catcher Ray Fosse at home plate in the 1970 All-Star Game—on a throw from Amos Otis.) McRae's most memorable barrel slide came during Game 2 of the 1977 American League playoffs in New York. With Freddie Patek on second and McRae on first, Brett grounded the ball toward third base. Graig Nettles threw the ball to second baseman Willie Randolph in an attempt to get the 5–4–3 double play. Instead of going straight to the base, McRae did a flying barrel roll beyond the second-base bag—actually, he *started* it beyond the bag—and Randolph couldn't get Brett at first. Patek scored on the play. "Before George hit that, Hal signaled to Freddie by pointing that if there was a play at second, he was going to take out the guy covering," said Royals Hall of Fame outfielder Willie Wilson.

The next season Major League Baseball brought in what was known as the "Hal McRae Rule," essentially outlawing rolling blocks and stating that the runner had to be able to touch second base, which McRae couldn't have done on the Randolph play. Shoot, Wilt Chamberlain couldn't have touched second base from where McRae started. "In the old days, we could slide into second or not slide," Wilson said. "If you were standing up and you went into a guy, it was okay. That's just the way we played. Then they brought in the Hal McRae Rule."

Because of the aggressive style that McRae brought to Kansas City, it could be rough on their own middle infielders. Opponents would have no problem taking out Patek, Frank White, or Cookie Rojas as a form of retaliation. "There were several guys around the league who had bad intentions when they came to second base, and we knew who they were," Patek said. "I remember one time in Texas, Toby Harrah came in and slid late and I threw the ball up in the seats. I told him, 'If you ever do that again, I'm going to hit you right between the eyeballs.' Well, it happened in the same game—him going from first to second. I dropped down a little and hit him right between the eyes, sent his helmet flying. As he was laying on the ground, I was standing over him and as he looked up half-dazed, he said, 'I know, Fred, I know. You told me.' We didn't want to hurt them, but it was a way of sending a message that we weren't going to be intimidated."

Of course, that retaliation went both ways, which benefited the Royals. "Any time a runner took me out at second base, I knew that Hal or George would go into second base hard and return the favor to our opponent's middle infielders," White said. "We had a luxury because there were about seven guys on our club who could go into a base as hard as anyone, but Hal and George were the best."

The aggressive base-running style worked well for the Royals because they played on artificial turf and lacked a true home run slugger. "We were a turf team with good speed and good athletes in Kansas City," McRae said. "We didn't possess a lot of power and we didn't try to hit for power, but we were able to use the turf, use the alleys and we were very aggressive, good base runners. We also had good pitchers and defense."

Although he was a solid defensive player, McRae became the American League's first premier designated hitter. He was a lifetime .290 hitter and led the AL in RBIs in 1982 with 133. In 1976 he batted a career-high .332 and lost the AL batting title to Brett on the last day of the season. With his all-out play in the outfield and on the base path as a designated hitter, McRae was one of the catalysts for the Royals' six AL West titles from 1976–85 and two World Series appearances, including, of course, the 1985 title against the St. Louis Cardinals. (Before joining the Royals, McRae had played in two World Series with the Reds in 1970 and '72.) "Going to the World Series in 1980 and to win it in '85 was exciting, but the most memorable aspect of my career here was the first year that we won the division, 1976," McRae said. "[It] was probably the proudest moment for me because we weren't a first-division ballclub up to that point. We broke through [in 1976] and we were able to continue the trend, so that was the most important year for me."

McRae, who was a three-time All-Star and was selected as the Royals Player of the Year in 1974 and 1982, became a member of the Royals Hall of Fame in 1989.

He went on to manage the Royals during 1991–94. During his tenure McRae had an infamous incident after a 5–3 loss to the Detroit Tigers game on April 26, 1993. He lost his temper while talking with reporters, yelled profanities, and trashed his entire office, throwing things off of his desk, including a phone. McRae, though, had a respectable 286–277 record before being fired during the 1994 strike. "Hal and I definitely had our moments, but there was a level of respect for Hal based on his understanding of the game and the way he managed," said Royals Hall of Fame closer Jeff Montgomery. "Of the five managers I played for, he became the best manager by the end of his tenure. He learned how to handle pitching staffs. He knew which buttons to push during the course of a ballgame. And all players enjoyed playing for Hal McRae."

Another of his players during that time was his son, Brian. "I found out how much respect my father had when we went around the league, especially my first go-around," Brian said. "Guys would come up to me and say how much they enjoyed watching him play the game the way it was supposed to be played. It was neat to hear that they liked how he played. They might not have liked playing against him, but they respected the way he played the game."

15 The Pine Tar Game

Steve Renko played in a lot of major league games for several teams—seven clubs in 15 years to be exact. The Kansas City native, who still lives in the area, spent his last season playing for the Royals. But one game during his one season with the team offered him a chance to play a crucial role in one of the weirdest and most memorable regular season games in baseball history.

On July 24, 1983, the Royals trailed their nemesis, the New York Yankees, 4–3 with two outs in the top of the ninth inning. U.L. Washington beat out an infield grounder for a base hit, which set up a confrontation between Rich "Goose" Gossage and George Brett. The Hall of Fame third baseman belted a Gossage fastball into the right-field seats, giving the Royals the lead…or so it seemed.

Since the Yankees were always up to no good, it shouldn't have come as a surprise to see Yankees manager Billy Martin approach home-plate umpire Tim McClelland. Unbeknownst to most everyone outside the New York dugout, the Yankees realized a week or two earlier that Brett had too much pine tar on his bat. Being the freakin' Yankees, they didn't say anything. No, they wanted to wait for the ideal situation to share their discovery with the umpires, and Brett's ninth-inning homer was the perfect moment to do so.

The umpires got the bat and started fooling around with it. They inspected it as if it held the secret code to solving the Rubik's cube. Finally, they measured it along home plate. Suddenly, with bat in hand, McClelland started toward the Royals dugout and signaled Brett was out. That started an outburst that hadn't been seen from the Royals before and hasn't been seen since. "I told George I thought they were going to call him out because he had too much pine tar on his bat," said Frank White, who was seated near Brett. "He said, 'If they call me out, I'm going to kill them.' I was laughing, but it looked like he wanted to kill them."

With the chaos around home plate, Royals pitcher Gaylord Perry, not exactly the bastion of rules following, somehow got the bat from McClelland and passed it on and on. That's where Renko comes in. "I was standing in front of our dugout, watching what was happening on the field, seeing Perry sneaking around behind all of the action," Renko said. "All of a sudden, a bat comes flinging toward me. I wasn't sure what to do with it, but I grabbed it and ran down the steps, up the tunnel, and toward the clubhouse. To do that you have to go through a narrow passage that winds around and eventually ends at the clubhouse. I was met in that passage by four or five guards, New York's finest."

McClelland, who was chasing Renko toward the clubhouse, asked for the bat. Renko said no, but he handed it to an official with the Yankees. That person promptly gave the bat to McClelland. The Royals played the game under protest. Three days later American League president Lee MacPhail overturned the call. So on August 18 the Royals stopped in New York to finish the game on their way to Baltimore. Brett, who had been ejected for his outburst, hung out at an airport restaurant as did many of the Royals.

In the typical fashion of the antagonistic Martin, he played ace pitcher Ron Guidry in center field, replacing Jerry Mumphrey, who had been traded to the Houston Astros between the second out of the ninth inning and the third out 25 days later. And Martin put left-handed first baseman Don Mattingly at second base. Of course, there was a different—albeit prepared—umpiring crew. When the game resumed, the Yankees threw to first to say Brett didn't touch first when he homered. "When the umpire signaled that Brett was safe," Renko said, "Billy yelled out of the dugout, 'How do you know? You weren't even there!'"

Davey Phillips, one of the new umpires, pulled out a notarized letter signed by the previous crew, saying Brett touched first. So Martin had pitcher George Frazier throw to second base in protest. Martin didn't try any more shenanigans. About 10 minutes later, the Royals finished off the Yankees 5–4 in one of the most bizarre games in the rivalry's history.

After nullifying his home run because his bat had too much pine tar, umpires try to restrain George Brett during the July 24, 1983, game against the New York Yankees.

And Renko's decision of what to do with the bat proved to be the right one. "If I had thought about it, I would've taken the bat and thrown it in the bat rack instead of running with it," he said. "But if I had done that or if I made it to the clubhouse, then the ruling might've held up, George wouldn't have gotten the home run, and we wouldn't have gotten the win."

That bat is currently on display in the National Baseball Hall of Fame.

Brett Hogs Club's Top Hitting Spots

Besides boasting the highest single-season batting average in team history at .390, George Brett holds the top spot in several offensive categories for the Royals.

Total Bases (Single Season): 363 in 1979
Slugging Percentage (Single Season): .664 in 1980
On-Base Percentage (Single Season): .454 in 1980
On-Base Plus Slugging Percentage (Single Season): 1.118 in 1980
Longest Hitting Streak: 30 games (July 18-August 18, 1980)
Career Games Played: 2,707
Career At-Bats: 10,349
Career Runs Scored: 1,583
Career Hits: 3,154
Career Doubles: 665
Career Triples: 137
Career Home Runs: 317
Career RBIs: 1,596
Career Batting Average: .305
Career Walks: 1,096
Career Total Bases: 5,044
Career Extra-Base Hits: 1,119
Career Intentional Walks: 229

16 Willie Wilson

There's no denying Willie Wilson's ability on the field, his blurring speed, and his ability to hit effectively from both sides of the plate. He's one of the best in the history of the Royals. During 1976–1990 he was a catalyst for the artificial-turf fast Kansas City clubs, stealing 612 bases, including a club single-season record 83 in 1979. In 1980 he collected more than 100 hits from each side of the plate, helping lead the Royals to their first World Series appearance. And then he won the American League batting title in 1982 with a .332 average. On the flip side, there's no avoiding the issues Wilson had off the field, including his involvement in a drug scandal in 1983 and his bankruptcy in 2000, the year he joined the Royals Hall of Fame. In recent years, though, Wilson has moved back to the Kansas City area, where he remains active in the community with the Royals and with the Negro Leagues Baseball Museum.

You came up in 1976, when the Royals were about to win their first American League West crown. Did it take you time to learn how to win?

Willie Wilson: They were already winning. I didn't want to get there and disrupt what they were doing. I think what happened—they were good enough to win the pennant. With the addition of Dan Quisenberry, Rich Gale, U.L. Washington, and me, it made them good enough to get to the World Series in 1980. I learned how to win in the regular season, but then we had to learn how to win in the playoffs and then how to win in the World Series. There's a learning process all the way through.

Even when you guys won the American League pennant in 1980, it seemed like there was this thought of, "Well, we're headed to the World Series. Now what do we do?"
WW: That's what I mean. I had 12 strikeouts and four hits in the 1980 World Series, but then I had 11 hits and four strikeouts in the 1985 World Series. It took me five years to get there, but you learn. The young Royals now are trying to learn all of this.

You mentioned 1980, which was an awesome year for George Brett and the team obviously, but you had a monster year, too.
WW: That was my first full active year. I remember how exciting it was. In 1979 we didn't get there, so '80 was my first chance in postseason. The playoff atmosphere was incredible, especially against the Yankees. I was around in 1976, '77, and '78, but I didn't really participate. But I knew the feeling the guys had after losing and I didn't want to experience that. And there was a sense—once we beat the Yankees—of what do we do now? Well, we sat around New York for three days, which was probably a mistake.

Describe the World Series-winning season of 1985.
WW: It was a great season, but it wasn't one when we had the best record or the best team. I think we had the best confidence. We felt like we were going to win. When we were down three to one to the Toronto Blue Jays and then three to one to the Cardinals, we never gave up. We never said we were going to lose. That was most exciting for us. Who wins three straight like that in the playoffs and then three straight like that in the World Series? It was a magical year for us. When the pressure was on against St. Louis, we felt we'd done it once, we could do it again. It goes to show that you never give up.

How do you hope Royals fans remember you?
WW: I hope they think of me as gritty, feisty, and someone who showed his emotions on the field. The game was fun for me, but I went at it hard and tough.

How would you describe your story and where you are now?
WW: To me, life is a lot like golf. You can have a good nine holes in the beginning but a great nine holes on the back. I don't consider [the negative things that happened] a bad beginning but rather a learning beginning. You learn from things you do and you put that to use. That's what I'm trying to do now—put all of this to good use.

17 Salvy

If someone needed to find Salvador Perez but had never seen him, perhaps the best way to direct that person would be to instruct him or her to look for the Royals player who appeared to be having the most fun of anyone on the diamond.

As the Kansas City Royals chugged through the 2015 regular season toward what had been the stated goal all along—the World Series—their 25-year-old catcher Perez made the journey a conspicuously joyous one. After each game he would dump a bucket of Gatorade on whichever one of his teammates was standing for an on-field postgame interview. When players started trying to avoid the beverage showers, Perez switched it up, idling without a bucket and attracting attention, so that a teammate to whom he had delegated the dumping could accomplish the mission and keep the surprise intact. Perez was rarely spotted without a wide grin. After many wins he responded with unrestrained enthusiasm, hollering in triumph and bounding out to meet his teammates with emphatic hugs and elaborate handshakes.

Behind home plate, however, Perez meant business and he did his job well in 2015, as he had in his two previous full seasons as catcher for the Royals. In July, Perez, who had turned 25 in May, was selected to his third All-Star Game and after the season he won his third Gold Glove. That's after catching 150 games in 2014 and 142 in 2015. "When it's all said and done, his reputation is going to be every bit as good as Pudge Rodriguez's is," manager Ned Yost told *The Kansas City Star* in 2014. "Salvy's going to end up being one of the best catchers to come out of Latin America of all time."

Rodriguez, the 14-time All-Star and 13-time Gold Glove winner who was named the American League MVP in 1999, is not the only masterful catcher to whom Perez's performance has drawn comparisons. Senior team advisor Bill Fischer gave general manager Dayton Moore a similarly dramatic report on Perez's ceiling after he watched Perez play in the Arizona Rookie League in 2007. "I've just seen the Latin Johnny Bench," Fischer said to Moore. And Fischer would know. He was the pitching coach for Cincinnati Reds' "Big Red Machine" of the 1970s.

Although Bench was an offensive force for the Reds, Perez had not put up overly impressive batting statistics, finishing both the 2014 and 2015 seasons with a .260 average. He did have 21 home runs in 2015, improving upon the 17 the previous year. Like many of the Royals, however, Perez had a knack for the clutch hit. He most notably knocked in the run that gave Kansas City its win in the wacky wild-card game in 2014 and he continued to deliver the following season. With runners in scoring position in 2015, Perez had a .311 batting average. He had 138 hits in the regular season, and 42 of them came in such situations.

He wasn't too shabby with a bat during the '15 World Series either. En route to being selected as the World Series MVP, Perez batted .364 (8-for-22) with two doubles, two RBIs, and three runs scored during the World Series. He had three hits in Game 4, including an RBI single as part of Kansas City's three-run eighth inning. In the clinching Game 5, Perez had only one hit, but it was a big one: the leadoff single in the 12th inning that pinch runner Jarrod Dyson turned into the game-winning run. And it was on Perez's ground-out in the ninth inning that Eric Hosmer scored the tying run that sent the game into extra innings.

Of course, Perez performed so well behind the plate that whatever he did in the batter's box was merely a bonus. As the Royals closed in on their second World Series in as many years, the 6'3", 230-pound Perez did it all while getting knocked around. Foul tips found him often, thanks mostly to his size, but he rarely left games. Yost found a couple of occasions where he felt the need to take Perez out of games early, but Yost, a former catcher, knows the beating is part of the gig. "But Sal is suited perfectly for it," Yost said. "He's a big guy, extremely tough, and he can take a beating."

Part of that determination stems from a love for the game. Another part of it comes from an unmistakable affection for the other members of the organization. "Everybody just feeds off his enthusiasm and energy that he brings to the ballpark every day," Yost said. "That's why I think all the players can unite behind Salvador, knowing that he helps bring the energy every single day."

In fact, Perez was asked after Game 5 of the '15 World Series if the disappointment of popping out for the final out of the '14 Series outweighed the excitement he was feeling as a World Series champion. In typical Perez fashion, he sported a wide grin as he answered: "Kansas City is No. 1. Who cares about what happened last year?"

18 Greinke Wins the Cy Young

Thank you, Zack Greinke!

By receiving the 2009 American League Cy Young Award in a landslide of 25 of 28 first-place votes, you brought incredible joy to every Royals fan at a time when every Royals fan needed it. "It certainly was a day of celebration for our organization, our fans, and everyone in Kansas City," Royals general manager Dayton Moore said on the now-defunct SportsRadioKC.com a day after the Cy Young announcement. "We haven't had a lot to celebrate over the last 15 years, but [that] was certainly a special day. I am happy for Zack and what he's accomplished."

Greinke accomplished a lot during the 2009 season. For starters he rang up 242 strikeouts in 33 games and registered an incredible major league-leading 2.16 ERA. He also had six complete games. It was the first time in Greinke's career when he spent most of the year not focusing on strikeouts, which seems a bit ironic since his 242 were good for second in the American League. By not focusing on getting a swing and miss with every pitch, Greinke was able to conserve pitches and have more left in the tank later in games. "It'd be nice to get my control better, so I can hit my spots a little more instead of just throwing strikes and letting them put it in play," Greinke said during the press conference after the Cy Young announcement. "It'd be nice to throw a quality strike. I think I can do it; it's just a matter of more focus so you don't fall behind in the count."

The award was well-deserved in '09. Yes, Felix Hernandez, Justin Verlander, and CC Sabathia all had great seasons. But let's face it, Greinke played for a club that struggled defensively and offensively. Yet he remained relatively consistent. His ERA and total number of strikeouts help show that.

Greinke gave Royals fans a reason for hope in 2009 and beyond. People couldn't wait to flock to Kauffman Stadium to see what hitter he might fool next. Even on a rain-drenched night, fans waited hours for the game to start just because it was Zack Greinke Night. Greinke pitching against the Boston Red Sox on television on the same night as the National Hockey League exhibition game at the Sprint Center was said to have affected that game's attendance.

Three years before the Cy Young, Greinke walked away from the Royals during spring training of 2006 for personal reasons. Some wondered if he'd come back at all. As everyone eventually found out, Greinke was diagnosed with social anxiety disorder and depression. He missed the '06 season except for three outings in late September.

Besides coming back to Cy Young form three seasons after his breakdown, the great thing about Greinke that year was that in spite of his eight losses compared to 16 wins—which would've been much better with run support—he rarely disappointed. His average run support on the season was just 3.73 runs, which tied for 70th worst in the majors. Nonetheless, Greinke went out, game after game, batter to batter, and competed unlike any Royals pitcher in recent memory. "That's the fun part," he said. "You do whatever you can to get ready and see if your game plan works. It's fun facing the hitters that aren't as good because you challenge them and say, 'Hey, I dare you to beat me.' You just go right at them. When you face the amazing hitters, you do a completely different gameplan. Some hitters make the adjustment real fast. For instance, at the end of the year, it was awesome watching [Minnesota Twins catcher Joe] Mauer. I got him out in Kansas City a certain way and then I thought I had him set up for something again [the next week in Minnesota], but then he makes an adjustment and beats me.

"When you're in the game, you notice every little detail and you can see when some players are good at making adjustments with you and other guys make stupid mistakes all the time. That's neat, too, because you'll look at the guy and think, *What's wrong with him?* There are so many things that are fun about the game."

In December of 2010, the Royals traded away their ace, but they received fair value in return. The Milwaukee Brewers sent Alcides Escobar, Lorenzo Cain, Jake Odorizzi, and Jeremy Jeffress to the Royals for Greinke and Yuniesky Betancourt. Odorizzi was used to help acquire pitcher James Shields from the Tampa Bay Rays before the 2013 season, while Cain (2014) and Escobar (2015) went on to be selected as American League Championship Series MVPs.

19 .400, By George!

Being George Brett would've been a tall order at any time during his career, but not nearly as much as it would've been in 1980. As longtime broadcaster Fred White pointed out often, Brett seemed to be involved in every pressure moment for the Royals during the 1970s and 1980s and he always seemed to produce. "I was able to get all my butterflies to fly in the right formation in pressure situations," Brett said, laughing. "I used to tell myself in pressure situations: *Don't try harder, try easier*. I was able to alleviate a lot of tension and try easier. So it slowed everything down instead of speeding everything up."

To Brett everything must've been in super slow motion—or at least it seemed that way—throughout his whole career. Possibly no other moment defines George Brett's pressure-peaking performances better than Game 3 of the 1980 American League Championship Series against the Yankees and fireball closer Rich "Goose" Gossage. After Royals shortstop U.L. Washington beat out an infield single with two outs in the seventh, Brett blasted Gossage's first pitch into the upper deck at Yankee Stadium for a three-run homer. A few outs later, the Royals were headed to their first World Series. "That, by far, was the biggest hit of my career. *Ever*," Brett said matter of factly. "That was the best swing I ever took in my life." Really, that swing was a climax of more than 175 solid ones that Brett took during the 1980 season, including a particularly memorable hit seven weeks earlier.

* * *

The image is embedded in Royals history: George Brett standing at second base on a sweltering afternoon in mid-August with his arms raised and his right hand grasping his helmet. In the background the numbers on the scoreboard explain the hoopla: .401.

Although Brett's average had been climbing the previous 28 games, during what turned out to be a 30-game hitting streak, this was the crescendo. Eclipsing .400 this late in the season was unheard of. Rod Carew passed .400 in 1977, but that was in early July. It looked nearly impossible that Brett would surpass .400 on this Sunday against Toronto, considering he went into the Blue Jays game batting .394, needing a 4-for-4 performance. Even after three hits, there was no way he would hit in the eighth—not with two outs and three batters ahead of him. But sure enough, Washington singled, and Amos Otis walked. John Wathan was at the plate next. "I was batting second a lot that year and I remember we were about to go on the road," Wathan said. "When my name got announced, the crowd started to roar. Ball one, it got a little louder. Ball two, a little louder. Then a strike, and there were some boos. Eventually, I got walked and got a tremendous ovation. I didn't know what was going on, but then George got a double, went over .400, and the place went nuts."

Blue Jays pitcher Mike Barlow, who had struck out Brett the previous night, entered the game. In typical Brett dramatics, he belted Barlow's fourth pitch over left fielder Garth Iorg's head for a bases-clearing double. "The ovation was unbelievable," Brett said. "I looked around and saw what the average was and saw the standing ovation, so I just took my hat off and raised my arms up. It was special going over .400 at home. Little did I know what was going to happen over the next six weeks of the season."

The chase for Ted Williams' .406 mark of 1941 was on.

* * *

Everything about Kansas City was hot in 1980. It was a record-setting summer with 17 straight days in July over 100 degrees. The Royals were just as steaming. They took lone possession of first place in the American League West on May 23 and never looked back. They went up by 10½ games on July 14 and held a double-digit lead for the rest of the season except for one day, July 22, when it was nine and a half games. Less than two weeks after Brett eclipsed .400, on September 1 the Royals were up by 20 games.

Long before then Brett had shaken off his typical early-season slump, when he was batting around .250 in mid-May. He hit an unbelievable .494 for the month of July. "The hotter it was, the better I seemed to play, which is why I always got off to slow starts in April," Brett said. He started a club-record 30-game hitting streak on July 18 with a .366 average. It was at .404 on August 18, the final day of the streak.

Little did anyone know that Brett's march toward immortality would continue, despite the growing media demands, for the rest of the season. Even Brett didn't put much stock into the possibility that he might finish the year at .400—at least not for the first two or three weeks. "Then I told myself that this opportunity might not come up again and I didn't want to shortchange myself at all," he said. "I became a hermit. I never went out. I stayed in my room all day and went back there after games. In giving myself every opportunity to reach this milestone, I probably should've just continued doing what I was doing to ease the pressure a little bit. I started thinking about [.400] an awful lot."

September 19, 1980, marked Brett's final game at .400. During the season's last two weeks, his average dropped to .384 before he finished the year at .390. That was the highest average for a season since Ted Williams in 1941. (Since then, only San Diego's Tony Gwynn has been higher. Gwynn finished the 1994 strike-shortened season at .394.) "I always think how my life would be different if I had ended at .400," said Brett, who was 27 years old in 1980. "Obviously it wouldn't be any different. But to be the last guy to reach that milestone is a great moniker to have by your name. To come so close and fail, yeah, I'm disappointed by it, but it was a great experience."

20 Bo Knows

On the day he signed with the Royals, Bo Jackson crushed a batting practice pitch to the base of the Royals scoreboard—about 450 feet away, even though he had not swung a bat in weeks. The next pitch landed in nearly the same spot.

And with that—the legend of Bo's days in Kansas City was born. The hapless Tampa Bay Buccaneers had drafted Jackson, the Heisman Trophy winner, with the first overall pick in 1986. Rather than play for such an awful organization, Jackson announced on June 21 that he was picking baseball over football. The Royals were the big winners. Jackson became the first Heisman winner since Pete Dawkins in 1958 to bypass a football career—at least at first.

Just as he did at Auburn, Jackson would play both baseball *and* football. The latter would come to fruition after the Raiders, the main rival of the Kansas City Chiefs, took a flier on him, drafting him in the seventh round of the 1987 NFL Draft. "Because of what happened with Tampa, I think many teams passed on him," said Tom Flores, the Raiders coach from 1979–87. "We figured that if he were interested in playing football, we would be interested in him.

"The first time I saw Bo run in practice was incredible. He'd run inside, but he loved to bounce to the outside and run in the open field. He loved to run, and we all loved to watch him. In fact when we first watched him, several of the players and coaches could only exclaim, 'Oh!' as if they were watching a fireworks display. In many ways we were watching one. It was hard to imagine that a guy as big as Bo could have that kind of speed and explosion."

The same explosiveness could be seen on the baseball field. Even though he holds three of the Royals' top four single-season records for strikeouts—including the top spot with 172—neither fans nor teammates knew what they were going to see. Perhaps no other play or moment better displayed Jackson's baseball ability and superhuman athleticism than his throw on June 5, 1989, in Seattle's Kingdome—the same stadium where Bo ran over Seahawks linebacker Brian Bosworth on *Monday Night Football* less than two years earlier. The unsuspecting Seattle athlete this time was Mariners second baseman Harold Reynolds.

The Royals and Mariners were tied 3–3 in the bottom of the 10th inning with Reynolds at first base. Scott Bradley lined a Steve Farr offering into the left-field corner. The speedy Reynolds, who

Two Other NFL Stars (and QBs) Drafted by the Royals

The Royals have another tie to NFL greats. The club drafted *both* Hall of Fame quarterbacks Dan Marino and John Elway in the 1979 MLB Amateur Draft. Marino was selected in the fourth round, and Elway was taken in the 18th round.

Both players opted for college instead and would eventually be taken in the 1983 NFL Draft, which was famous for the number of quality quarterbacks selected. That year Elway went first overall, Marino went 27th, and the Chiefs drafted Todd Blackledge with the seventh overall pick. Too bad the Chiefs couldn't draft quarterbacks as well as the Royals.

was running on the pitch, rounded third when Jackson grabbed the ball as it bounced off the wall. In a split instant, Jackson spun and, flat-footed with one foot on the warning track, fired a throw toward home plate. The laser reached catcher Bob Boone an instant before Reynolds touched the plate. "I'm about to throw a courtesy slide and I see the ball in Bob Boone's mitt," Reynolds said. "I say, 'You've got to be kidding me.'" As Frank White said in 2006: "That is the greatest throw I've ever seen in my baseball career." Appropriately, the Royals scored two runs in the top of the 13th and won the game 5–3.

Jackson had other signature moments for the Royals, showcasing his athletic gifts.

Major League Debut—September 2, 1986

He faced Hall of Fame pitcher Steve Carlton during his first major league game. In the bottom of the second inning, Jackson launched a ball over the left-field foul pole. Umpire John Hirschbeck called it foul. On the next pitch, Jackson singled on an infield hit to second base. "He just beat out a ball to second base," marveled Royals pitcher Mark Gubicza. "Everyone else would've been out by half the base line."

Before injuring his hip while playing football, multi-sport athlete Bo Jackson could mesmerize on the base path, in the outfield, and at the plate for the Royals.

The First Home Run—September 14, 1986

Just a few days after going 4-for-5, Jackson launched a 475-foot home run to left-center at Kauffman Stadium against Mike Moore of Seattle. His '86 season was an abbreviated one because of the late-season call-up, but Jackson would end up having four 20-plus home run seasons for the Royals.

The All-Star Game—July 11, 1989

With Ronald Reagan on the television broadcast with Vin Scully during the first inning of the 1989 All-Star Game from Anaheim, California, Jackson greeted Rick Reuschel's second pitch with a blast to center field estimated at 448 feet. Scully interrupted the president to declare: "Look at that one—Bo Jackson says hello!"

During that same game, Nike featured a television commercial with the "Bo Knows" tagline, a funny short playing up his multi-sport abilities. (Musician Bo Diddley would end it by saying, "Bo, you don't know diddley!") Given such attention on the national stage, one could argue that Jackson was as major a superstar athlete as Kansas City ever had. With his Pro Bowl selection following the 1990 NFL season, Bo became the first professional athlete to be selected for All-Star Games in two major sports.

Spider-Man Lands in Baltimore—July 11, 1990

Playing center field Jackson robbed the Baltimore Orioles' Joe Orsulak of an extra-base hit to the gap in left-center. Jackson was running so hard on the play, though, that as he hit the warning track he ran up the wall instead of crashing into it. He was a few inches from the top, nearly horizontal to the track below. He darted across the wall, seemingly defying gravity like something out of a *Matrix* movie. "Bo was a walking highlight film," Jeff Montgomery said. "You never knew what you were going to get from him. He would do remarkable things with his foot speed, his bat, or his arm. I was very fortunate to play with him."

Bo vs. Prime Time at Yankee Stadium—July 17, 1990

Although others have tried to play two professional sports, two of the greatest athletes of the past 50 years played baseball and football at the highest levels: Jackson and Deion "Prime Time" Sanders. The Royals actually drafted Sanders a year before they selected Jackson. They picked Sanders in the sixth round of the June 1985 draft out of high school, but he didn't sign. They then selected Jackson in the fourth round of the June 1986 draft. (The New York Yankees picked him in the second round in 1982, and the California Angels selected him in the 20th round in 1985.)

One of the only times the two multi-sport stars faced each other on the diamond was during a mid-week series in mid-July 1990. Jackson put on a show in the series' second game. In three at-bats he had three home runs and seven RBIs against Andy Hawkins. The second dinger was estimated at 464 feet. "The second home run was an eye-opener," said George Brett, who hit three homers at Yankee Stadium in 1978. Unfortunately, we'll never know if Jackson would've had four in the game. With two outs in the bottom of the sixth, Sanders lined a ball to center that Jackson dived for but couldn't get. Sanders ended up with an inside-the-park home run; Jackson ended up with a partially dislocated shoulder and a trip to the disabled list.

Bo's Return vs. The Big Unit—August 26, 1990

In Jackson's first game since going on the DL, the Royals were playing host to Seattle with Randy Johnson on the mound for the Mariners. In his first at-bat—despite saying he had not taken batting practice—Jackson launched Johnson's first pitch to the fountains in left-center. That gave him four consecutive home runs, which remains a Royals record. "He's the best athlete I've ever seen," Bret Saberhagen said. "You never wanted to miss an at-bat because you never knew what special thing was going to happen."

Unfortunately, his spectacular athletic career ended way too early. On January 13, 1991, on a seemingly harmless play in an NFL game against the Cincinnati Bengals, Jackson suffered a hip injury, which ended his NFL days. The Royals released him during spring training 1991. Bo played briefly for the Chicago White Sox and Angels, but he wasn't the same player. His baseball career ended with the 1994 strike. "God has his way of opening up our eyes to see reality," Bo said when announcing his retirement. "The way he opened my eyes is to allow me to have this hip injury. That is a rough way to go, but I had to accept the fact."

21 Golden Alex Gordon

One of the greatest success stories in Royals history is Alex Gordon. This is the same Alex Gordon who grew up as a Royals fan in Nebraska but was the second overall pick in the 2005 draft because he was college baseball's best player. He was selected as *Baseball America*'s Minor League Player of the Year in 2006 and then skipped Triple A in 2007 on his quick ascension to the majors. He won the Platinum Glove Award after the 2014 season as the best defensive player in the American League. And then he gave Royals fans a late New Year's gift in January 2016, when he signed a four-year contract to stay in Kansas City.

Despite all these accomplishments, it wasn't the skyrocket path everyone expected. See, when he came up to the major leagues, Gordon was seen as the Royals' savior—the next George Brett, even manning Brett's former spot at third base. But he struggled early. Gordon battled injuries and then seemed destined to mediocrity

Golden Royals

In 2012 Alex Gordon became only the third Royals player to win the Gold Glove award more than once, along with Amos Otis and, of course, Frank White. Salvador Perez and Eric Hosmer joined that select group after each won his second in 2014. (Each added a third following the 2015 season.) When Gordon, Hosmer, and Perez won the Gold Glove in 2013, it gave the Royals their most Gold Glove recipients in a single season in franchise history.

Otis, the Royals' first Gold Glove recipient, won the award in 1971, '73, and '74. White, meanwhile, dominated second base for so long that he won eight Gold Glove awards: 1977–82 and 1986–87. Catcher Salvador Perez and first baseman Eric Hosmer each won their first Gold Glove in 2013, giving the Royals three recipients that year, the most ever in franchise history.

Other Kansas City Gold Glove winners include Al Cowens (1977), Willie Wilson (1980), George Brett (1985), Bob Boone (1989), Bret Saberhagen (1989), Jermaine Dye (2000), and Mark Grudzielanek (2006), and Alcides Escobar (2015), who is the first Royals shortstop to win the award.

at best. It didn't help that the organization seemed to have its next third baseman, Mike Moustakas, tearing up the minor leagues.

Early in the 2010 season, when Gordon was batting .194 with one home run, Royals coach Rusty Kuntz didn't think Gordon looked comfortable at third, so he suggested to general manager Dayton Moore that they move Gordon to another position. "Maybe we can put him in a different spot and free up his mind," Kuntz told Moore. "If he moved 150 feet farther from home plate, his hands and feet would be great. That will allow his natural athleticism to come out."

So, the Royals sent Gordon and Kuntz to Triple A Omaha for the conversion. "That was a tough, challenging time in my life," Gordon said. "Rusty was in Omaha for the first two or three weeks and spent as much time as possible with me every day during batting practice. He was the perfect person to have out there."

Evidently. In 2011, Gordon's first full season in Kansas City as an outfielder, he hit .303, eclipsing .300 for the first time in his career. And he happened to win the American League Gold Glove as a left fielder. On his way to winning it, he led all outfielders in assists with 20, which eclipsed Kansas City's previous record of 16 by Jermaine Dye and Mark Teahen. As if that's not enough, half of Gordon's assists threw out a runner at home plate.

Besides winning the 20th Gold Glove in Royals history, Gordon won the award again in 2012, becoming the first Royals player since Frank White in 1986 and 1987 to win it in back-to-back seasons. He won it again in 2013. And 2014. Although his streak ended in 2015, Gordon is the only Royals player besides White to win the Gold Glove in at least four consecutive seasons.

22 Game 4 of the 2015 ALDS

Besides being in the Royals' favor, there's nothing seemingly spectacular about the final score of 9–6 in Game 4 of the 2015 American League Division Series. But when great Royals postseason games are debated decades from now, this is one that's sure to be near the top of the list, along with the phrase, "Keep the line moving."

The Royals were down to their final six outs of the season with the Houston Astros leading by four runs 6–2, heading into the top of the eighth at Houston. To make matters worse, Kansas City's Ryan Madson gave up back-to-back home runs to Carlos Correa (his second of the game) and Colby Rasmus in the bottom of the seventh that pushed Houston's lead from 3–2 to 6–2.

But then it happened.

Mike Moustakas, who was batting .143 at the time in the postseason, came in the dugout before the eighth inning and reminded his teammates that it wasn't over. The G-rated version: "It was just that we're not losing this game. We've worked too hard and we've come too far," Moustakas said.

It wasn't exactly John Belushi's "Germans bombing Pearl Harbor speech" from *Animal House*, but it worked. The first five batters in the inning—Alex Rios, Alcides Escobar, Ben Zobrist, Lorenzo Cain, and Eric Hosmer—singled, cutting Houston's lead to 6–4, while the players kept saying to each other in the dugout, "Keep the line moving."

With the bases loaded, the next batter, Kendrys Morales, chopped a ball up the middle against reliever Tony Sipp, but it went off the glove of rookie shortstop Correa for an error. Zobrist and Cain scored, tying the game at 6–6. After Moustakas struck out on a 3–2 pitch for the first out of the inning, catcher Drew Butera, who had replaced Salvador Perez defensively earlier, welcomed pitcher Luke Gregerson into the game by turning a 10-pitch at-bat into a walk. "Hitting's contagious and, when you see six guys in front of you put together good at-bats and keep the line moving, you don't want to be that guy that just goes up there and swings at it—one, two, three—and heads back to the dugout," Butera said. "That was my plan—to keep the line moving and get on base."

With the bases loaded once again, Alex Gordon grounded out to second baseman Jose Altuve, scoring Hosmer and giving the Royals an improbable 7–6 lead. "The thing about this club is that they don't quit," said Royals manager Ned Yost. "After giving up three runs in the bottom of the seventh, they came in on fire. Our bats were really silent until the eighth inning, but having watched them as much as I've watched them, you know that sooner or later they're going to break out."

After Wade Davis retired the Astros in order in the bottom of the eighth, Kansas City's bats remained hot. With Zobrist on first after a walk from reliever Josh Fields, Hosmer launched a two-run homer to right-center that gave the Royals a couple of insurance runs. Davis gave up a lead-off single to Correa in the bottom of the ninth before finishing off the Astros by striking out Rasmus, who earlier hit his third home run of the series, and pinch-hitter Preston Tucker and then getting Carlos Gomez to fly out. "Having Wade come out in the eighth inning and get a six-out save gave us the best opportunity to win that game," Yost said.

This Game 4 comeback was reminiscent of 2014's epic comeback against the Oakland A's in the wild-card game, when the Royals trailed 7–3 after seven innings before winning in the 12th inning. Once again, the never-say-die Royals, who would have seven comebacks of at least two runs during the 2015 playoffs and World Series, showed their mettle in the postseason.

23 Buzz Kills

Steve Busby was in the first Royals Hall of Fame class, joining Amos Otis in 1986. Some will say that had it not been for a rotator-cuff injury that first emerged in 1976, Busby was on his way to *the* Hall of Fame. It's easy to see why. "Buzz" was a workhorse for the young Royals of the 1970s. During his best season, 1974, Busby won 22 games, threw 20 complete games, pitched 292⅓ innings, and struck out 198. From 1973 to 1975, his first three years in the major leagues, he averaged close to 19 wins and 177 strikeouts a season. Then there's this: he became the first pitcher in major league history to throw no-hitters in each of his first two seasons.

April 27, 1973 at Detroit

Buzz threw the first no-hitter in Royals history during his rookie year, and it took awhile for it to hit him. "I didn't really realize the gravity of it," he said years later. "I was caught up in the moment and in awe of all the attention that it drew. The second one was different because I had been through it before. I enjoyed the second one more at the time than I did the first one."

As he's quick to point out, Busby was anything but spectacular during that first one. His six walks in the game help tell that story. In fact, Busby, 23 years old at the time, struggled throughout the early part of his rookie season. He was 1–2 with an 8.04 ERA. If things didn't turn around in a hurry, "Buzz" probably was headed north on I-29 to Triple A Omaha.

Though Busby was far from perfect that April night in Detroit, he was unhittable against a solid Tigers offense that boasted the likes of Norm Cash, Bill Freehan, and Mickey Stanley. "I know it sounds ludicrous to say that I wasn't pitching well, considering I threw a no-hitter," Busby says, "but every time I threw a strike, I think it was a surprise to the Detroit hitters. I was all over the place. The weather was miserable, though, and the Tigers weren't really interested in trying to hit."

The Royals didn't do much better offensively, though they scratched across a run in the fifth inning. Then Kansas City added another in the eighth. Around the eighth inning or so is usually when teammates avoid the no-hitter-throwing pitcher in the dugout. In Busby's case the other Royals avoided him in the early innings, too—and pretty much whenever he pitched. "I'm not the most sociable person anyhow, but when I was pitching, I was always kind of in a grumpy mood," Busby said. "That was just me competing. That night was no exception. Nobody said [one word] to me. Looking back, I don't know if it was because of the old baseball thing about not mentioning the no-hitter or because the guys just knew that's how I was when I pitched."

The Royals added another run in the top of the ninth inning, giving Busby a three-run cushion. In the bottom of the inning, Busby walked the first hitter, Duke Sims, before Rich Reese laced a screaming line drive down the first-base line. Since John Mayberry was holding Sims on the base, Reese's shot went right at "Big John," who then stepped on first for the double play. "In most situations with either John not holding the runner on or nobody on base, that's a double for Reese, and everything is up in smoke," Busby said. "It just worked out that way."

One pitch later, Bill Freehan popped out, ending the game and cementing Busby in Royals lore. It also gave baseball its first no-hitter with the designated hitter in the lineup. Buzz impressively took a no-hitter into the sixth inning of his next outing. And crazy as it sounds, he went hitless into the sixth again in 1974—immediately after his second no-hitter.

June 19, 1974 at Milwaukee

Ah, yes, that second no-hitter, which came about 14 months after his first. After being admittedly wild in his first no-no, Busby had a little more control against the Brewers during Kansas City's 2–0 win. His only blemish in the game was a second-inning walk to George Scott on a 3–2 count. Busby was ahead in the count 0–2 before throwing four balls. "I never considered myself as a pitcher with the kind of stuff to translate into a no-hitter and I still don't think of myself that way," Busby said. "In the [Milwaukee game], though, I thought I pitched much better than I did against Detroit. I was around the plate and had only the walk to George Scott. Because I was throwing strikes, I threw fewer pitches. And because I was throwing strikes, there were more great defensive plays."

Al Cowens, George Brett, and Cookie Rojas each accounted for defensive gems. In the second inning, Cowens ran down a deep drive in right field by future Royals teammate Darrell Porter. Two innings later Cowens went to nearly the same spot and caught a ball launched by Scott. Those were two of the only five balls that left the infield. In the sixth inning, Busby said Brett saved a no-hitter when he went behind the bag at third and threw out Don Money by a half-step. "I still consider that the best play I ever saw a third baseman make," Busby said.

Then with two outs in the eighth inning, Rojas, the 35-year-old second baseman, dove to his left for a ball that was headed to right field and threw out Bob Hansen at first. "Cookie was getting a little long in the tooth, but he dove headlong about 20 feet on the outfield grass, snared it, scrambled to his feet, and threw out Hansen," Busby said. "Those two plays—the one by George and then Cookie's—I remember like I'm watching them now on replay. They were incredible."

Around the time of those two plays is when Busby said he started thinking about the possibility of a no-hitter. "As a pitcher you always know there is a no-hitter going on," he said. "When you get to about the seventh or eighth inning, it becomes a possibility at least in my mind. Against both Detroit and Milwaukee, it helped that they were tight ballgames, so I could concentrate on something other than the no-hitter. If it was a blowout, it'd be tougher to focus."

Busby worked a relatively smooth ninth as he struck out Bob Coluccio, got Tim Johnson to fly out to Amos Otis in center, and then saw Money pop out to Rojas.

Besides the two no-hitters, Buzz threw three complete-game shutouts in 1974 and '75. Unfortunately, he tore his rotator cuff in 1976 and was never the same, though he pitched into 1980. "Busby was one of the best pitchers I ever saw," Rojas said. "It's a shame that he hurt his arm. He had great stuff, great command. He's the one who started the third-to-first pickoff move. He was very successful at doing that. I think he would have been a tremendous pitcher for many, many years to come."

24 Dan Quisenberry

There's a funny story about how Dan Quisenberry ended up signing with the Royals. Legendary scout Rosey Gilhousen had scouted Dan's older brother, Marty, who ended up hurting his arm in college. Gilhousen didn't have an interest in the younger Dan. Neither did many scouts, even though Dan was an NAIA All-American at what's now the University of La Verne in California.

Ben Hines, Quisenberry's coach at La Verne, called Gilhousen to see if he'd take a look at Dan for the upcoming 1975 draft. The Royals liked Quisenberry and needed a reliever, but they weren't going to select him in the draft. But Gilhousen made a promise: "If you don't get drafted," he told Quisenberry, "I'll sign you."

The draft came and went without any teams selecting Quisenberry. So late one night a day or two after the draft, Quiz called Gilhousen to make good on their deal "Look," Gilhousen said, "it's too late to do it tonight, and I'm going out of town tomorrow, but I'll stop by next week, and we'll sign the contract."

Anxious and perhaps not wanting Gilhousen to renege on the deal, Quisenberry offered to go to Gilhousen's house to sign the contract at that moment. "I'm about to go to bed," Gilhousen said. "You have 10 minutes." Quisenberry hopped in his Gremlin and sped off to sign his first professional contract. "I got $500 a month," he said in 1983. "My bonus was a Royals bat that Rosey had in the house, a Royals pen, and a Royals lapel button. I was really pretty excited, especially about the lapel button."

Four years later on July 8, 1979, Quisenberry and his submarine delivery emerged in Kansas City when the Royals desperately needed a closer. Sure, guys such as Al Hrabosky and Doug Bird had done the job previously but not well enough to get past the

New York Yankees in the postseason. "When he first came up in '79, the first time I caught him in the bullpen, I thought, *Why is this guy here?*" said former catcher John Wathan. "He was a side armer who maybe threw 83 miles per hour. Who was he going to get out? We quickly learned that it would be most everybody. His routine in the bullpen was to do the crossword puzzle early in the game. All the guys in the bullpen would try to guess the attendance at home games. So around the fifth inning, Quiz and I would sneak into George Toma's office and call to find out the attendance. We would then guess close enough that we won all the time. Nobody could figure out how we did it. Then he would start to get serious around the sixth inning."

In Quiz's first full season as the club's closer in 1980, he led the Royals with a then-franchise-record 33 saves, which tied for the lead in the American League that year. He went on to lead the league in saves four more times and was selected as the Royals Pitcher of the Year four times. His record of 45 saves in 1983 stood as the club record until Jeff Montgomery tied it in 1993. (Greg Holland surpassed Quiz and Monty with 47 in 2013.) Quisenberry was a five-time winner of the AL Fireman of the Year award.

He finished his Royals career in 1988 with 238 saves and a 2.55 earned run average. As great as he was on the mound, he was as quirky and funny and friendly away from the field—not to mention intelligent. (He majored in business, religion, sociology, psychology, and history at La Verne.) "Charlie [Leibrandt], Sabes [Bret Saberhagen], Quiz, and I were hanging out at a bar in Boston called Daisy Buchanan's, and people would come up to talk to us," Mark Gubicza said. "Quiz was always so funny. He started telling people that night that he was going to invent an underwater Nautilus machine that would make everyone bigger and stronger. A huge audience gathered around him, thinking he was telling the truth. He was talking about how he put a Nautilus machine underwater to add to the resistance. I was on the ground laughing, and people thought I was stupid because I was laughing at Quiz's 'invention.' He kept it going and going. By the end I think if he would've had it, he would've sold out. The thing about him was that he could keep a straight face the whole time. Most of us can't tell jokes because we start laughing, but he did it with a straight face the whole time. You never could tell if he was being honest or just pulling your leg."

While on a family vacation in Colorado in January 1998, Quiz was having headaches and getting dizzy. When he got back to Kansas City, doctors discovered a brain tumor. After they removed it on January 8, they announced it was a Grade IV malignant astrocytoma. The prognosis was bleak. Quiz was inducted into the Royals Hall of Fame that summer, but he lost his battle with cancer on September 30, 1998.

"Quiz was a character," Saberhagen said. "He was a genuine human being. I'll never forget. He was going through his cancer stuff, and it was a month or two before he passed away. I came to Kansas City as a member of the Red Sox. He called the clubhouse just to talk to me. He was a great guy. I miss him."

"The loss of Quiz was huge," Wathan said. "Dan was a close friend to all of us. He was a good family man and very Christian man. Not to mention, he was a big part of our success. He's one of the best guys I've ever known."

"When you saw Quiz out of uniform, you would've bet everything you had that he wasn't an athlete," said Gubicza. "Not that he didn't have an athletic body, but his vocabulary, the clothes he wore, and the way he projected himself—you never would've thought he was hanging out in a clubhouse a couple hours before. He was an awesome human being who left a huge impact on everyone who knew him."

25 Tour Kauffman Stadium

For a unique Royals fan experience, a tour of Kauffman Stadium is a must. Unlike some stadium tours, the Royals offer multiple tour package options with varying stops (and varying prices, of course). "We have our basic tours but want to make the experience memorable and worthwhile for each visitor," said Morrie Carlson, the Royals manager of tours and educational programs.

Carlson and his staff of tour guides have designed tours that run year-round. Even though the tours vary, stops generally allow fans to see the press box, interview room, Royals dugout, visitor's clubhouse, the outfield experience, and the Royals Hall of Fame. Other tour options include the dugout suite, the diamond club, triple crown suite, and view level overlook. One tour even includes golf cart transportation.

Along the way there are plenty of photo opportunities. "It's great to see grown men get so excited about getting their picture taken in the dugout," said Carlson, who's as entertaining as the stops along the tour.

Of course, for fans who want the ultimate experience (and are willing to pay a premium), there are two game day all-access tour options. Both of these tours visit the diamond club, the crown club, the Fox Sports television booth, the Royals Radio Network booth, the CrownVision control room, a guided tour of the Royals Hall of Fame, and an on-field viewing of batting practice.

The differences in the two come in the two seating options. One includes a ticket to the Frank White signature lounge, a player autographed baseball, a player autographed bat, a Kauffman Stadium cap, and a Royals yearbook. The other includes a crown club ticket, a personalized Royals jersey, a player autographed

Touring Kauffman Stadium, the beautiful ballpark known for its crown scoreboard and outfield fountains, is a must for any Royals fan.

baseball, a player autographed bat, a Kauffman Stadium cap, and a Royals yearbook. "Kauffman Stadium is a great place to show off," Carlson said. "Any tour option is a great way for people to see Kauffman in a way they might not be able to see it otherwise."

Except for the all-access tour, Kauffman Stadium tours are available year-round. For the 2016 season, the prices are $350 for the all-access tour, $17 (adults) for the legends tour, $30 (adults) for the All-Star tour, $55 (adults) for the grand slam tour, and $120 for the group tour, which includes 20 tickets. Visit Royals.com or call (816) 504-4222 for more information.

26 Hoz and Moose

There are countless reasons why the Royals went to back-to-back World Series in 2014 and 2015. After all, those two clubs embodied the word "team" perhaps as well as any other current major sports team. But much of the success can be pointed back to a simple question in 2011: "When are we going to flip the switch?"

That was a question that Gene Watson, the Royals director of professional scouting, kept asking general manager Dayton Moore. In not so many words, many Royals fans wondered the same thing. The Royals were coming off a 95-loss season in 2010, but they had a world of talent in the minor leagues, including the 2007 and 2008 first-round draft picks Mike Moustakas (second overall) and Eric Hosmer (third overall), respectively. And there were names such as Salvador Perez, Danny Duffy, and Kelvin Herrera.

No offense to those last three names, but there was more anticipation for the two first-round picks. Hosmer and Moustakas seemed to be the future of the organization, the younger players who would help build the club around the likes of Alex Gordon and Billy Butler. "They fit right in with what we're doing," manager Ned Yost said of Hosmer and Moustakas during spring training in 2011. "They're both quality kids in the clubhouse and outside the clubhouse. We know they're extremely talented, but their make-up is off the charts for kids their age. They're special kids."

Early in 2011 Hosmer was the first one who looked to be ready for a ticket to Kansas City. During the first month of the 2011 season, he was leading all of the minors in batting average (.439) and on-base percentage (.525). Moore received a call from Chino Cadahia, who joined the Royals as a special assistant in 2011, and Jack Maloof, who was one of the organization's hitting coaches. They started talking to him about Hosmer: "This guy is ready for the major leagues. What are you waiting for?"

A few weeks later on May 6, 2011, Hosmer made his major league debut against the Oakland A's. Although he went hitless in that game, he made a huge impact on that season. He went on to hit .293 with 19 home runs and 78 RBIs in 128 games.

Hosmer's fellow corner infielder, Moustakas, made his debut about a month later, on June 10 in Anaheim and singled off Angels (and future Royals pitcher) Ervin Santana for his first major league hit. Moustakas didn't get off to the same meteoric start as Hosmer, batting .182 in his first 53 games through August 16. After that, though, things began to click. Moustakas had a 15-game hitting streak and batted .379 for the rest of the season.

In a perfect world, each player and their baseball-appropriate nicknames of "Hoz" and "Moose" would have kept rising from the 2011 season and put the Royals on their backs to reach the post-season in back-to-back seasons for the first time in three decades. That's not exactly how it worked. Both players have had their share of struggles. After hitting 34 doubles, 20 home runs, and 73 RBIs in his first full season in Kansas City in 2012, Moustakas spent time at Triple A Omaha in 2014 as his batting average dipped to .212.

Hosmer's average dropped to .232 with only 124 hits in 2012 and then nine home runs in 2014.

Appropriately, perhaps, each player had a coming out party, if you will, during the 2014 postseason. In fact, in back-to-back American League Division Series games against the Los Angeles Angels of Anaheim, "Hoz" and "Moose" propelled the Royals with a game-winning home run. In Game 1 at Anaheim, Moustakas, a California native, hit a solo homer in the 11th inning that gave the Royals a 3–2 lead. In Game 2 Hosmer hit a two-run homer in the 11th that put the Royals ahead 3–1. "We came up and had similar paths, and it just made us better," Moustakas said after Game 2 of the 2014 ALDS. "Everything we went through in those minor leagues and even earlier in the season just made us better and got us ready for this situation."

Throughout the 2015 postseason, Hoz and Moose each came up with key hits and defensive plays as well. Look no further than Game 4 of the ALDS against the Houston Astros, when the Royals mounted a five-run rally in the eighth inning and avoided elimination. Moustakas started everything, according to his teammates, with a rallying cry before the Royals came up to the plate in the eighth. During that inning Hosmer had an RBI single and then scored the tying run on a ground-out by Gordon. (Hosmer then iced the 9–6 win with a two-run homer in the ninth.)

Incidentally, besides Hosmer and Moustakas, the other three players made it to Kansas City in 2011. About 10 days after Hosmer's debut on May 18, Duffy pitched for the Royals. Two months after Moose came up, Perez saw action for the first time for the Royals on August 10. Herrera made his debut as a September call-up on the 21st of that month.

27 White Cleans Up Nicely in '85

There's no way to describe just how much Frank White meant to the Royals as a player (and beyond). That's part of the reason he's in the club's Hall of Fame, had his No. 20 retired, and has a statue at Kauffman Stadium. Although he was known around baseball as one of the best defensive second basemen ever to play the game, he gained one more distinction in 1985: he became just the second second baseman in major league history to bat cleanup in a World Series. He did just fine with seven hits, including three doubles and a home run, along with six RBIs, four runs, and three walks.

You played on incredible teams throughout the 1970s, but what was it about the '85 club that put the team over the hump?
Frank White: We knew we had a pretty good club going in with good, young pitching. We were coming off a playoff year, so we figured we had a chance to win. We didn't really play on fire in '85, but we held our own. Really, I felt we were a little stuck early in the year and then we made the trade for Lonnie Smith from St. Louis. When Lonnie came in, he was an aggressive player. He started stealing bases. Then Willie Wilson picked it up from there. The whole team became more aggressive. We started breaking up more double plays. Lonnie was the leadoff guy, a hard-nosed guy. I really think he was the missing piece for that '85 season.

How important was manager Dick Howser?
FW: Dick was good because he didn't panic. He didn't throw things around or have a lot of meetings. He believed in his players. With whatever we were facing, he'd say, "Piss on it; we'll get it done." He knew when to fight for his team and when to lay back and let his

team do its thing. He had control of the reins, but he didn't pull back on them too often. He led by a quiet, calm professionalism.

How did the Royals bounce back from such big postseason deficits?

FW: When you're down like that, you have nowhere to go. Suddenly, it's not a series; it's one game at a time. Our feeling was that we were down three to one, but we had to take this game and the next game and the next game. We felt that if we could tie it up, the momentum would switch to us. With that one-game-at-a-time mentality when they were setting up the TV lights for the losers—us—in the clubhouse in St. Louis, Willie told them, "You guys might as well take those down." Then I came in and said, "We can't lose this game." When someone asked why, I said, "We're two blocks from the hotel. If we lose this game, we'll never get home." Things like that helped us focus. We felt we weren't going to lose. When your back's against the wall, you're either going to give up or you're going to fight. We decided to fight one game at a time and go from there.

When you guys went to St. Louis, were there signs and banners welcoming the "World Champion Cardinals" home?

FW: They even had one on the tower at the airport. That's the confidence they had. But up three to one I'd be pretty confident, too. As an athlete you're at that point of the year when you have the winter to rest, so you put everything you have into that one game. If you win that game, you start again the next game.

In Game 3, the first game in St. Louis, you hit a two-run home run and an RBI double in a 6–1 win. You hit cleanup, becoming just the second second baseman in World Series history to do so. What did that mean to you?

FW: That was probably, in my opinion, the greatest thing that I ever had to do for my ballclub. When you go from a guy hitting

Hitting for the Cycle

Many people consider Frank White a light-hitting second baseman in spite of him batting cleanup in the 1985 World Series. But besides compiling 2,006 hits in his career, White is one of four different Royals players who have hit for the cycle—a single, double, triple, and home run in one game. White and George Brett are the only two Royals who did it more than once; each did it twice.

1. Fred Patek	July 9, 1971	at Twins	2B, 1B, 3B, HR
2. John Mayberry	August 5, 1977	vs. White Sox	1B, HR, 3B, 2B
3. George Brett	May 28, 1979	vs. Orioles	3B, HR, 1B, 2B
4. Frank White	September 26, 1979	at Angels	1B, HR, 2B, 3B
5. Frank White	August 3, 1982	vs. Tigers	HR, 2B, 1B, 3B
6. George Brett	July 25, 1990	at Blue Jays	1B, 3B, 2B, HR

An interesting footnote: Royals minor league outfielder Brian Anderson hit for the cycle in a spring training game against Arizona on March 19, 2010. That alone might not seem spectacular until considering that Anderson hit for the cycle, knocked in seven runs, and scored three runs—in the first four innings. The Royals beat the Diamondbacks that day 24–9. Despite Anderson's impressive performance, the Royals converted him to a pitcher that season.

eighth or ninth for most of his career to cleanup in the biggest game of your club's history, that's a huge deal. They could've gone to George Brett, but he wanted to stay at third in the lineup. Hal McRae couldn't bat because of the DH not being used, so he was relegated to being a pinch-hitter. Still shocked, I told Dick I'd do it, but I told him, "If I do well, they'll write about it being a great decision. If I don't do well, they'll say how I shouldn't have been there in the first place." One thing I did tell myself, though, was that I was going to just be me. I wasn't going to try to be George or Hal or Steve Balboni. I was going to do what I'd always done, which helped me relax. To find out later that Jackie Robinson was the only other second baseman to bat cleanup in the World Series made it even more special.

Was 1985 the pinnacle of your career?
FW: It has to be. You play the game to be a champion. That's why you put the uniform on in the first place. When you get that achieved, when you become a world champion—regardless of what the other years are like or however many more games you might've won in another year—that takes the top spot over anything you've done as a team. When you look at the thousands of guys who have played and will play this game and will never get to experience a division championship or a playoff game and especially a World Series, that has to be No. 1.

28 The Gubie Stare

Throughout the Royals' history, there have been intense players. There have been guys like Hal McRae and George Brett, who'd take out a second baseman with a barrel roll if it meant breaking up a double play. Or starter Dennis Leonard, who once beaned a much bigger Don Baylor and then stood in front of the mound ready for a confrontation (and got one). Or closer Al Hrabosky, who'd stand behind the mound and—after a few moments of calmness—would slam the ball into his glove and march to the top of the mound with smoke seemingly coming out of his Fu Manchu moustache. But perhaps the most intense Royal of all time was pitcher Mark Gubicza, who was instrumental in the club's 1985 World Series championship.

During 1984–96, Gubicza, a hard-throwing right-hander with a wicked slider, won 132 games (third all time for the Royals) and recorded 1,366 strikeouts (second all time). In 1988, a year after an uncharacteristic 18 losses, Gubicza won a career-best 20 games, the seventh pitcher in club history with at least 20 wins. That season he also had a 2.70 ERA, which was the third lowest in club history at the time. (By 2013 it ranked seventh.) And he threw more innings (2,218⅔) than anyone except Paul Splittorff.

In addition to his impressive stats, Gubicza was remembered for something else: a glare that became known as the "Gubie Stare." "I'll always remember how intense he was on the mound," Frank White said. "He threw sinkers and thought every ball should be caught. You didn't want to make a mistake behind him, but he was a fun guy on the team and fun to play behind." Brett echoed White's sentiment. "[Bret Saberhagen] and Buddy [Black] would turn around and laugh at you if you made an error behind them… but you'd get the old Mark Gubicza stare if you made one when he was pitching," Brett, said laughing. "But Gubie was a guy that you wanted in your foxhole with you because he wasn't going to quit until he was dead."

How did Gubicza's intensity come about? Perhaps it was his Philadelphia roots. Or his hockey roots. "[The stare] wasn't directed toward the player who made the error," he said. "It's just that you want to get everyone out, and you feel you have to try harder on the next batter when an error is made. As a starting pitcher, you get to play once every five days, so you have built up energy, and if it looks like someone behind you isn't giving their all, it is difficult to hide your emotions. In hockey they talk about Mark Messier's stare. He expected not only a tremendous amount out of himself, but he expected his teammates to have that same kind of intensity."

In many ways, Gubicza resembled his mentor, Leonard. Both righties challenged hitters, were highly competitive, and they'd throw a fastball through a batter if needed. "I'd always ask him how he was able to channel his emotions," Gubicza said. "He finally came up to me one time and said, 'You know what? You have a half hour after a game to either—one, celebrate your win, or two, throw something if you have to. But after that half hour's up, it's over because you have to start moving toward your next game.' He was so driven that after that half hour was up, he was preparing for his next start."

As much success as Gubicza had on the field in his career that culminated with induction into the Royals Hall of Fame in 2006, he thought he was getting away with something when he made the club in 1984 after a season in Double A. Gubicza, then 21, and Saberhagen, 19, actually did everything possible to ensure a spot on the Opening Day roster. "Sabes and I hid our luggage among all the other luggage, hoping they'd forget about us," Gubicza said. "We snuck onto the bus and were hiding because we thought that if they didn't notice us, maybe we'd make the team. We got on the plane, and still nobody said anything to us. As we were driving in from the airport, I figured it was too late for them to send us down and that we were safe. Of course, I learned that they could send you down at any given time, but at that point I didn't think it was possible."

Away from the field—besides sometimes being naïve—Gubicza was the most shy and reserved pitcher from that young staff of 1984 and '85. "No one expected Gubie and Sabes to make the club out of spring training in 1984. When they did make it, obviously they needed a place to stay," Brett said. "Instead of putting them in a hotel near the ballpark, I had two extra bedrooms in my house, so I told them that they could stay with me until they found a place. After about three weeks, Gubie asked me if he could use the phone and get something to eat from the refrigerator. I said, 'Mark, you can use the phone anytime you want to and you can eat anything out of the refrigerator that you want.' Meanwhile, Saberhagen would come down first thing in the morning, go raid my closet, put on my clothes, and take off for the day. They stayed with me for the first month and they weren't in a hurry to find a place to live. Finally, I called people I knew to get them out of the house."

"I definitely remember that," Gubicza said, laughing at Brett's story. "We were all lucky to have great teammates that liked each other and were great competitors...For me it was luck with great timing and seizing the opportunity."

29 Don Denkinger's Call

This might irritate St. Louis Cardinals fans—as if they'd be reading this book—but here it goes: Don Denkinger can't be blamed for the Royals winning the 1985 World Series. Oh, sure, he has been, but he shouldn't be.

In case you've been living in a van down by the river since 1985, here's how things played out in the final inning of Game 6. In the bottom of the ninth with the Royals trailing the game 1–0 and the World Series three games to two, pinch-hitter Jorge Orta led off the inning by grounding a ball toward first base. Cardinals first baseman Jack Clark fielded it cleanly and flipped to pitcher Todd Worrell, who was covering first. Although Worrell seemed to touch first before Orta on the bang-bang play, umpire Don Denkinger called Orta safe. "As a pinch-hitter, in my mind, I just was going to try to get a good at-bat and see if I could get on base," Orta said 25 years later. "I wanted to help start a rally. When I hit that soft ground ball, my instincts said to run as hard as I could.

I hustled down the line and was called safe on the play. And I thought I was safe, yes."

Immediately after the game, Worrell disputed that account. "Orta's foot hit my heel," he said, "and I had the ball by then. The umpire said something about how my foot came up off the base. But I'm told the TV replays show that Orta was out by a half-step. Games come down to umpires' judgments sometimes. I can't be real mad about it because they're human. He tried his best to get the call right. Sometimes they make the wrong call."

Right or wrong call, the Cardinals self-destructed after that. First, Clark missed a pop-up in foul territory off the bat of Steve Balboni, who went on to single. "The play that really made a difference in that inning was the pop fly that landed in front of our dugout that Jack Clark didn't catch," Orta said. "I don't think enough people talk about that play. That was an out they should've had."

Instead with no outs and two on, catcher Jim Sundberg tried to sacrifice bunt, but the Cardinals threw out Orta at third. With runners at first and second and one out, a ball got past Cardinals catcher Darnell Porter, which moved pinch-runner Onix Concepcion and Sundberg up 90 feet. Pinch-hitter Dane Iorg, who had been hitless in the series, delivered a base hit that scored Concepcion and Sundberg—with the latter crossing home plate on a headfirst dive—and sent the series to a seventh game. The hit should've turned Iorg into a hero. But because of the controversy from earlier that inning, Iorg's hit often remains forgotten in World Series lore.

Any time there's mention of 1985 or blown calls in baseball, Denkinger's name comes up—and usually with a cuss word immediately before or after. There's one thing to remember, though. "We scored the winning run with one out," Royals pitcher Mark Gubicza said. "We still had an out [left in the inning] if the play went differently at first. The way things had been going for us that season, who's to say that whoever was coming up next doesn't hit a home run, and we win anyhow? It was a magical season for us. [The Cardinals] had every opportunity in the world to come back in Game 7, but we blew them away...Hey, they had us down three games to one. If you can't close it out at three games to one, don't blame it on the umpire. Yeah, [the call] went our way...[But] you have to be able to close out a team when you have them down like that."

Either way that rally and Royals win gave the club extra confidence that began immediately and carried on for more than 24 hours. "After we came back and won Game 6, the attitude was if we'd won the World Series," Frank White said. "All of our families were in the clubhouse, which was so exciting. We knew we had John Tudor for Game 7, so everyone started chanting, 'We want Tudor. We want Tudor.' Then it changed to 'Let's play now. Let's play now.' That's just how the momentum switched."

Indeed. With all of the whining and complaining from the eastern side of Missouri about Denkinger's call in Game 6, there was one more game to be played in the series. And we all know how that turned out. "After that game with the way the Cardinals fell apart and were complaining and arguing, we were confident," Orta said. "In Game 6 they took their guard down and gave us a chance to come back the next day and beat them."

30 1978: The Forgotten Season

Here are some facts to know about the 1978 Royals:

- They won the American League West with a record of 92–70.
- They won the club's third straight division title.
- Their 92–70 record was the third best in Major League Baseball behind the New York Yankees (100–63) and the Los Angeles Dodgers (95–67).
- Nearly 40 years later, the 92–70 mark remains tied for the fourth best record for any Royals team.
- The Royals spent 99 days in first place.

And somehow it seems to be the forgotten team from the glory years. The Royals battled injuries throughout the 1978 season but still saw great individual play. Pitching in nearly 300 innings, Dennis Leonard won 21 games. He was second in the American League with 20 complete games and third in strikeouts (183). Paul Splittorff won 19 games. Then there was Larry Gura, who had perhaps the greatest major league season of his 16-year career. He finished with a 16–4 record and 2.72 ERA. Offensively, Amos Otis led the team in average (.298), home runs (22), and RBIs (96, a career high). He finished fourth in the MVP voting, which Jim Rice won. Otis didn't hit above .298 again in his career.

The American League West was tight throughout the season—so tight that the Royals went from fourth to first in a three-day span in mid-June. That was the start of a stretch when the Royals won seven out of nine games. The Royals took command of the division on August 27. Kansas City met the Yankees for a third straight year in the playoffs, and the two teams split the first two 1978 games in Kansas City. Each won decisively with New York taking the opener, 7–1, and the Royals taking Game 2, 10–4.

The highlight of the playoffs, however, might've been Game 3, even though the Royals lost in the Bronx. With the series tied 1–1, George Brett delivered a classic October performance. Facing New York's Jim "Catfish" Hunter, Brett, batting leadoff, knocked Hunter's third offering over the right-field wall. But he was far from finished. In the third inning, Brett gave the Royals a 2–1 lead when he hit another solo homer to right. Then with the Royals trailing 3–2, Brett led off the fifth inning with his third homer.

In the top of the eighth, the Royals took a 5–4 lead against Yankees closer Rich "Goose" Gossage, who was in his first season with the Yankees since signing as a free agent. Otis, who led off the inning with a double, scored on a hit by Darrell Porter. Then with one out, Porter scored when Al Cowens grounded into a fielder's choice. That wasn't enough to salvage Brett's performance. Yankee catcher Thurman Munson hit a two-run home run in the bottom of the eighth inning that gave New York the decisive 6–5 lead. So instead of Brett's three-homer game being relived each October, it went down as just another incredible chapter in Brett's Hall of Fame career. "It's too bad we didn't win it for George," said pitcher Paul Splittorff, who started Game 3. "He had one hell of a game."

After the Yankees won the series, Royals manager Whitey Herzog lamented his roster more than anything else. "They go out and sign Reggie Jackson, Sparky Lyle, and Gossage," he said. "And who do we sign? [Utility infielder] Jerry Terrell…All we needed was Gossage, and if we'd paid him $600,000, we could have had him but [the Royals' front office] wouldn't do it."

The Royals, though, would find an alternative to Gossage. In the middle of the next season—on July 8, 1979 to be exact—a 26-year-old closer named Dan Quisenberry made his major league debut for the Royals.

31 Moore and Yost Return Royals to Postseason

What a difference a year makes. Or seven or eight. Royals general manager Dayton Moore, a longtime baseball man, desired to cultivate the Royals into winners more than you can imagine. That's been the case since he became the club's sixth general manager on June 8, 2006. Developing a winner, though, takes time—especially with how depleted the Royals farm system was when Moore took over.

And it certainly took time. In Moore's seventh full season, 2013, the Royals finished 86–76. It was the club's first winning season since 2003 and the most number of victories since winning 92 in 1989. Even though the Royals were in the chase for a wild-card berth until the last week of the season, they fell short and finished third in the AL Central—seven games behind Detroit. Key players on the 2013 roster were homegrown, including Billy Butler and Alex Gordon—both of whom were selected by GM Allard Baird—Greg Holland (10th round, 2007), Eric Hosmer (first round, 2008), Mike Moustakas (first round, 2007), and Salvador Perez (non-drafted free agent signing, 2006). After the winning record and wild-card push in 2013, many fans remained unhappy and sought more progress. Still, Moore felt there was reason to look ahead optimistically to 2014. "I believe that all our players that are signed long-term or under team control are going to get better," he said during his 2013 postseason press conference. "Is it just going to happen? No. They are going to have to continue to work hard, apply instructions, and make adjustments. They are going to have to continue to commit to becoming great players."

Winning never comes easy. But decades of losing can do funny things to a fan base, whether that fan base is old enough to remember the glory days of the 1970s and '80s or young enough to be part of today's society of instant gratification. So, after enduring losing season after losing season and bad trade after bad acquisition under previous general managers, seven seasons of waiting for "the process" to work was an eternity.

Sending Zack Greinke to Milwaukee for (mainly) a light-hitting shortstop named Alcides Escobar and an outfielder named Lorenzo Cain, who had played a whopping 43 games in the big leagues in six professional seasons? And then you're going to trade the future greatest Royal ever, Wil Myers, along with two stud minor league pitchers for a short-term starter in James Shields and a barely average pitcher named Wade Davis?

Are you serious?

Those moves, though, turned out to be quite deft and have more than vindicated Moore.

Critics also questioned Moore for backing manager Ned Yost, whom he'd hired in May 2010 to lead this club. Yost was Moore's guy, who he knew well from their days in the Atlanta Braves organization, when Moore was in the front office and Yost was coaching.

Throughout 2013 and '14, in particular, Royals fans came up with all sorts of words to describe Yost, and most of them aren't very pleasant. He's unapologetic. He could come off as condescending. And he'd made moves that fans and former players alike thought were boneheaded, which fostered the term "Yosted" to describe anything and everything negative in life.

It was a controversial decision Yost made in the sixth inning of the wild-card game that almost kept the Royals from advancing in the 2014 playoffs. After starter Shields gave up a bloop single and then issued a walk with two on and nobody out and Kansas City holding a 3–2 lead with Brandon Moss—who homered earlier—coming to the plate, Yost pulled Shields, who'd thrown 88 pitches, and brought in starter Yordano Ventura. Moss launched Ventura's third pitch 432 feet to dead center. It seemed as though social media might combust at once with thousands of fans and other detractors saying how the Royals had been "Yosted." Funny, though, the Royals overcame any questionable judgment decisions in that first postseason game and went on to make 2014 the "Yostseason."

That Yostseason should've caused the doubters to eat crow, but the negative perceptions mean little to the Royals manager. "I don't need vindication," Yost said after the Royals swept the Baltimore Orioles in the 2014 American League Championship Series. "I'm comfortable with who I am. And everything that I look at, I don't look at much. But I'm the dumbest guy on the face of the earth. But I know that's not true…I am smart enough to hire really, really good coaches and use them. But I'm real comfortable in my own skin. I don't feel like I need vindication. I'm not looking for it, don't care for it. My whole goal—none of this was ever about me. Winning a championship was all about this city, our fans, and these players. I've been there six times before; I know how special it is. And I wanted my players to experience it. I wanted the city of Kansas City to experience it and our fans."

And, thanks to Dayton Moore, who built a deep farm system and assembled a club with pitching and speed that could win at spacious Kauffman Stadium, Yost was able to take that group of players, push the right buttons, use each player to his strength, foster a cohesive clubhouse, and lead them to back-to-back World Series for the first time in club history. "These kids, from the minute you saw them, you knew they were going to be special," Yost said after winning the 2014 ALCS. "Then they won championships in A ball together, and they won championships in Double A together, and they won championships in Triple A together. And then their goal was to get up here and win a championship, and today they accomplished that."

Along the way Yost became the first manager ever to win his first eight postseason games as a skipper. And then, on June 18, 2015, when the Royals beat the Milwaukee Brewers, Yost became the winningest manager in Royals' history.

Then there's Moore, who, in spite of the detractors, became just the second Royals general manager to oversee a World Series championship in Kansas City (his mentor, John Schuerholz, was the other) and first to lead the Royals to back-to-back World Series appearances. During that stretch the Royals saw their win-loss record improve every year from 2009 to 2015, the longest stretch of annual improvement since Connie Mack's Philadelphia A's did so from 1919 to 1925. As Luke Hochevar said of Moore after the 2015 World Series: "He proved that one man's dreams are bigger than other people's opinions."

32 John Schuerholz

When many baseball fans think of John Schuerholz, they think of the Atlanta Braves. That's understandable, considering Schuerholz guided the Braves to 14 straight division titles and the 1995 World Series Championship as general manager. Royals fans know, of course, that Schuerholz spent 23 years in the Kansas City organization, including his last nine as the general manager, beginning in October 1981.

What comes to mind when you think about your time with the Royals?

John Schuerholz: An excellent organization with great people. Absolute, strong, good construction plan at the beginning of the expansion franchise. Dynamic, consistent ownership, leadership, and support. Great fan support. Mutual admiration between organization and community and community to organization. Sensationally talented players. It would take me all day to name them. I'm not sure Major League Baseball knew how wise it was to put a franchise back in Kansas City when Charlie Finley left for Oakland under the cover of darkness. I'm not sure anyone knew what an excellent franchise they were creating. Mr. Kauffman gets most of the credit for that because he set high standards. He was going to run the Royals like he did Marion Labs. It was a wonderful experience.

Did Lou Gorman, the Baltimore Orioles director of player development, have to convince you to leave Baltimore with him?
JS: Lou basically told me I was going. [Laughs.] I'm embarrassed to say this, but my thought of Kansas City when Lou told me that was cowboy hats and horses attached to hitching posts in front of the general store. Obviously, it was not that at all. It was the most enjoyable 23 years a person could spend in a community. I absolutely loved it.

What was the philosophy in the early days of building the organization?
JS: We made a commitment from the beginning that it was going to be a building process. Mr. K wanted to win the next day because that's who he was. He was a winner in everything he did. He had that passion and energy and focus to winning, but he was bright enough to build companies with good foundations. When you build the strength, it can sustain itself. Scouting and player development were our No. 1 premise. Two [was] pitching development and then scouting and player development. Because of Kauffman Stadium's expanse in the outfield and the artificial turf, we had to have exceptional athletes at every defensive position.

You mentioned Charlie Finley, who was a hands-on owner without question. Was Ewing Kauffman hands on?

JS: He was hands off, but his aura was always around us. We knew we couldn't disappoint Mr. K. We knew what he expected and the confidence he had in us, which never swayed. Sure, he was aggravated when we lost but never dismayed. He'd say, "Win with dignity and lose with grace." When I made the deal that blew up in our face that brought a player [Vida Blue] to our organization that introduced drugs into our clubhouse and then the drug scandal that followed in 1983, I thought that was it for me. We had to manage our organization through that chaos and through that thunderstorm of negative circumstances. Every day I had a meeting in the clubhouse with the media, answering questions about how the Royals would deal with this and how we were embarrassed and how it was a kick in the organizational stomach. We worked through that because we had the unwavering support of Mr. K. As we were working through it, one day he called me to his office. He sat me down across from his desk and—with his steely blue eyes—said to me, "Look, we made you general manager of this team because of our confidence in your ability, your intellect, your knowledge, and your aggressiveness. I do not want you to pull in your horns and lose your aggressiveness because of this trade. That's what makes you who you are." How many owners would say that? Now you know why I have such admiration for Mr. K.

At the time, leaving a successful organization like the Royals to go to the struggling Atlanta Braves was a very surprising move.

JS: My friends in Kansas City thought I'd completely gone daft when I left the Royals. I remember it like it was yesterday when I called Dean Taylor, who had left me in Kansas City to work in the commissioner's office, and told him that I'd accepted the job as a general manager with another organization. When I told him it was the Atlanta Braves, he said, "You're kidding me!" I told him the more shocking news that I wanted him to come join me. He said, "I'll be there." [Taylor would later re-join the Royals under Dayton Moore as vice president of baseball operations and assistant general manager in 2006.] I left the IBM of the American League, the Kansas City Royals, and joined the Atlanta Braves, who at that time were not highly regarded. That's an understatement. I never thought I'd leave Kansas City. I'm surprised to this day that I did.

You obviously have good feelings about your time with the Royals.
JS: A large part of my heart and soul are still there. I love that organization, that community, that stadium, and the legacy of excellent baseball from the mid-1970s to the mid-90s. I'm going to say that there's reason to have good hope that that can be regenerated. I want that to happen. That'd be wonderful to me. It was a sensational time in my life that I remember fondly.

33 Leo vs. the Bird

In a career that included 144 wins, a franchise-best 103 complete games and 23 shutouts (both likely will remain at the top forever), and 1,323 strikeouts, it might be unfair to say that a couple of games defined Dennis Leonard's career. However, right or wrong, a game midway through Leonard's third season has remained a hallmark performance in his career and one of the top memories for longtime Royals fans. "Including postseason games, that midsummer game in 1976 remains one of the most electric contests I've ever broadcast," said Royals announcer Denny Matthews.

Right before the 1976 All-Star break, the Royals hit the road for a series in New York and Detroit. Leonard, a Brooklyn, New

York, native, was initially scheduled to pitch against the Yankees. With a chance to pitch against a team he liked as a kid and in front of friends and family in Yankee Stadium, Leo couldn't wait.

Royals manager Whitey Herzog, however, nixed Leonard's start. He told Leo, who was 9–3 at the time, that he wasn't going to be pitching in New York because of his upcoming appearance in the Mid-Summer Classic. "I remember telling my dad that I wasn't going to be pitching because I made the All-Star team. He told everybody, so I'm thinking how cool it was," Leonard said. "Well, P.S., Whitey apologized to me after the series, saying that he didn't know what happened, but I wasn't going to be on the All-Star team. So, I went from being a big, tall stud, to a little, itty-bitty nothing."

Instead of having him face the Yankees, Herzog slated Leonard to start in Detroit against Mark "the Bird" Fidrych. The Tigers pitcher burst onto the major league scene in 1976 at a time when the game still had plenty of characters. But Fidrych's persona stood above the other goofballs in baseball. He'd get down and dust off the pitching rubber with his hands. He talked to the ball. Oh yeah, and he had dazzling stuff, especially a wicked sinker. "He made such an impact on that Detroit ball club," said Royals Hall of Fame shortstop Fred Patek with a believe-you-me chuckle, "Sure, he'd pound on the mound and talk to the ball, but he was an exceptional young man on the mound. People talk about his antics, but he had great stuff. There's no doubt about it."

Everywhere Fidrych pitched, fans flocked to see both his incredible talent and his undeniable quirkiness. Although he never faced the Royals in Kansas City, his rookie season brought an unforgettable contest against Leonard and the Royals on this warm night in Detroit. "My father-in-law, God bless him, flew to Detroit to meet us," Leonard said. "The night before I was to pitch, we were in a little piano bar—I was drinking water—and I told him, 'Fidrych, my ass. I'm going to beat him tomorrow.'"

"You had the feeling from the outset that this game could be something special," Matthews said. "And it was. Fans hung on to every pitch because each one meant something. Not many baseball games give you something compelling like that."

On July 9, a capacity crowd of more than 51,000 at Tiger Stadium, mainly wanting to see "the Bird," instead saw a masterful outing by Leonard. He held the Tigers to four hits and struck out eight in a complete-game performance. With George Brett and John Mayberry on base in the top of the fourth inning, Hal McRae singled to left, scoring Brett. That was the only run of the contest.

Fidrych and Leonard both went the distance, but it was Leonard who held true to his prediction from the night before. "That was just one of those games," Leonard said, "when we were really determined."

34 Splitt's Legacy

It's one of those great but seldom told stories in Royals lore. In September 1972 during the first inning of a game at Anaheim, pitcher Steve Busby, who was from nearby Fullerton, California, was making his third big league start. In the top of the first inning with the Angels leading 4–0, Busby launched a grand slam off Angels relief pitcher Lloyd Allen.

Well, almost.

As Busby reached first base in his home run trot, umpire John Rice stood with his arms raised. Rice had called time, he said, right before the pitch, so that he could throw a few Royals out of the game for arguing an earlier call. Busby, who was an excellent hitter, disappointedly went back to the batter's box for a two-run single to center field. The following season, the American League introduced the designated hitter.

Years later, after shoulder surgery wiped out his 1977 season, Busby's roommate, Paul Splittorff, came to the hospital for a visit. Busby said: "As I'm lying there, he says, 'Hey, remember that deal in Anaheim a few years ago? Well, that was me.' Evidently he suggested something that John Rice didn't like, and that did it. But Splitt was the only one on that end of the bench who didn't get thrown out, so I had no idea. I think that's part of the reason he felt bad all those years. We laughed about that often for the next 35 years or so."

That story helps describe Splittorff, the Royals Hall of Fame pitcher who lost a battle with cancer on May 25, 2011, at the age of 64. Teammates, broadcast partners, and friends will tell you that Splittorff was loyal and honest. He never wavered.

He has one of the most unique legacies in Royals history. For Royals fans 40 and older, Splittorff was the big left-hander with the glasses and high leg kick who won some of the club's biggest games. He was good enough to be inducted into the team's Hall of Fame in 1987. For fans who don't remember life before cable television, compact discs, and personal computers, they'll best remember Splittorff as the television and radio analyst. To anyone who *knew* Splitt, he was much more. "He was a rock solid guy who was very fair and objective," said longtime broadcaster and close friend Fred White. "He always told you how he felt about things. There wasn't much gray in his life; it was black and white. He was also a very giving person." Added Busby: "I'm not sure I've ever been around a guy who was more fiercely loyal and private as Splitt. If you were friends with him, he would do anything for you and not expect anything in return."

On the field and in the clubhouse, Splittorff was a silent leader. He knew how to get involved with the clubhouse barbs, but he was willing to take young players under his wing and show them

The Yankee Killer Who Ruled Fenway

Paul Splittorff owns the Royals career records for wins (166), starts (392), and innings pitched (2,554). You could also say that he owned the New York Yankees and Boston Red Sox.

Splittorff was known as the "Yankee Killer" because of how well he threw against New York, whether at home or in the Bronx, and for beating the Yankees twice in the playoffs. (Not to mention, he struck out Reggie Jackson 23 times.)

Oddly, though, Splittorff did well against the Red Sox at Fenway Park, which is not traditionally good for left-handed pitchers because of the Green Monster in left. Splittorff's career numbers at Fenway look more like a righty's: 3–1 record, 2.91 ERA in 34 innings, and no home runs. "It doesn't surprise me that a left-hander did well there if you're talking about Splitt," said teammate and friend Steve Busby. "In his mind he decided that he would prove a left-handed pitcher could do well there. Really, whatever he did, if he felt it was worthy of his doing it, he worked to be as good as he possibly could be. That included every part of his life."

Former Royals manager Whitey Herzog felt comfortable starting Splittorff in Yankee Stadium or Fenway Park. "I never had any concern about pitching him anywhere, against anyone," Herzog said. "He took the ball every fifth day or whenever I needed him out there and he always gave 100 percent. He never got mad at anybody or blamed anybody or complained about a teammate or the manager. I'm sure he got terrifically mad at people sometimes, but he never let it be known. Having him on your baseball team, as a manager, was a privilege. And I was very, very privileged to manage Paul Splittorff for four-and-a-half years."

As good as he was, as many Royals records as he holds, and as tough as he was against the likes of New York and Boston, Splittorff never threw a no-hitter. But he came very close. Splittorff threw three one-hitters, including a particularly memorable one for catcher John Wathan during a home game on September 2, 1977, against the Milwaukee Brewers. "He shook me off only one time during the game," Wathan said with a chuckle. "That's something catchers take pride in. This one time, though, was against Charlie Moore, who ended up getting a base hit. I kidded Splitt through the years that if he'd just listened to me, he probably would've gotten the no-hitter. He'd always say, 'No, it wasn't the pitch; it was the location.' I liked to tease him about that."

how to be big leaguers. Part of that was through his example. Day after day, game after game, they saw how hard he worked. There's no other way to explain how a two-sport (baseball and basketball) athlete at tiny Morningside (Iowa) College, who was given such a small shot at being a big league pitcher that it took an expansion team selecting him in the 25th round of the 1968 draft, ended up as the club's first drafted player to reach the major leagues, its first 20-game winner, and the winningest pitcher in the organization's history. "If I had to describe Paul, I'd do it in two words: very professional," said Hall of Fame manager Whitey Herzog, the Royals' skipper during 1975–79. "I have to say that he's one of the greatest persons I ever managed."

After Splittorff's playing career ended, White encouraged Splitt to try broadcasting. The two ended up working together on both Royals and college basketball broadcasts. "He got into broadcasting by paying his dues just like the rest of us," White said. "I never sat down next to him for a game when he wasn't totally prepared. And he always came up with at least one thing in a broadcast that you didn't know. Whatever the opposite of a diva is, that's Paul Splittorff."

Longtime TV partner Bob Davis further emphasized Splittorff's humility. "When we first started doing the games together, he introduced me to everyone at the different parks, which helped tremendously," Davis said. "He could've been aloof or acted like a star, but he never did that...He was just one of the guys—but a pretty special one."

For more than 40 years, Splittorff gave everything he had to the Royals organization. He got the first win in the organization's history in 1968. He started and won the first game at Kauffman Stadium in 1973 and finished with 166 career wins. And he was on the air for more Royals broadcasts than anyone except White and Denny Matthews. "He really cared about people, the Royals, and this community," White said. "He was our go-to guy for pitching, for broadcasting, and for friendship."

35 Dick Howser

In 1980 the New York Yankees gave Dick Howser, who'd been a coach with the club for a decade, a chance to manage, replacing Billy Martin. Howser led New York to a major league-best 103 wins. The only problem was that they were facing baseball's hottest hitter in 1980 on a team that ran away with the American League West—George Brett and the Royals. Leading two games to none in the best-of-five series, Brett launched his first famous home run off Rich "Goose" Gossage in Game 3 that not only gave the Royals their first trip to the World Series, but it also gave them the manager who would take them to their first World Championship.

Overlooking the 103 wins, Yankees owner George Steinbrenner fired Howser. It's funny how karma works. About eight months later and just after the 1981 strike, the Royals fired Jim Frey, and Howser was available. The Yankees reached the postseason in the goofy playoffs of '81, but they wouldn't get back again until 1995. The Royals under Howser marched toward 1985.

Before Frey was fired, Howser was broadcasting minor league games on ESPN with longtime Royals announcer Fred White. "I don't know that it made a difference to the Royals, but it made him visible to baseball people about three or four nights a week," White said. "The timing was perfect to get Howser. Even though outsiders saw Jim Frey as the manager who took the Royals to the World Series in 1980, many around the club saw things begin to unravel late that season. In 1981 they were 30–40 in late August.

So with the strong candidate in Dick available, the Royals made the change."

It was obvious to the players that Howser was the opposite of Frey. Though a nice guy, players will say that Frey could be wound tightly during games. Howser was more laid back. "We followed Dick because he was our leader," Willie Wilson said. "If he panicked, we panicked. But he never panicked. He did the same things and talked the same way regardless of the situation. For us it was about going out there and doing what we had to do to be successful."

Although he's best known for leading the Royals to their World Series victory in 1985, Howser's best managing job may have come in 1984. Coming off the drug scandal of 1983 and facing injuries throughout the season, the Royals sat in sixth place in the AL West on July 18 with a 40–51 record. During the final 10 weeks of the season, they went 44–27 and won the division. ESPN selected Howser as its Manager of the Year.

Then there was '85. The resilient team never gave up and came back from three-games-to-one deficits against both the Toronto Blue Jays and St. Louis Cardinals en route to the World Series championship. There were many keys to winning that season, but one of the top reasons was Howser. "He was a great manager because from spring training in '85, he addressed each player and told each guy his role," said Jorge Orta. "He was able to communicate with his players. He emphasized that everyone needed to be ready to play every day."

Howser had previous roots in Kansas City, winning Rookie of the Year in 1961 with the Kansas City A's. An All-Star selection that season, he batted .280 with 171 hits. After that auspicious start, he produced seven average seasons with two other clubs—the Cleveland Indians and Yankees. He made his true mark, though, as a manager, a tenure that was highlighted by the Royals' championship season in 1985.

"We weren't as talented as Toronto or St. Louis in 1985, but something about our team was magical," Mark Gubicza said. "We were treading water late in the season, but with guys like Frank White, George Brett, and Hal McRae leading us, we didn't panic. I think that also was a direct reflection of Dick Howser. His famous line was, 'Don't worry about it; piss on it. We'll get this thing done.' There was never panic on his face, which is why he was so good. We knew he was backing us. And we knew that he put people in places to give them a chance to be successful."

Howser managed the Royals into the 1986 season, but three days after managing the American League club in the All-Star Game on July 18, doctors diagnosed him with a malignant brain tumor. Less than a year later on June 17, 1987, Howser lost the battle with cancer. He was 51. That same year his No. 10 became the first jersey the Royals retired. "It was very sad to see him go way too soon," Bret Saberhagen said. "He gave me an opportunity at 19 years old in my first week in the big leagues and entrusted the game to me. Out of the all the guys I played for, he was my favorite manager."

36 The Corked Bat and Other Amos Otis Stories

Amos Otis could be considered the Royals' first five-tool player—a player who can hit for power, hit for average, can run, can field, and can throw. The five tools don't always translate into a star player, but it did in Otis' case. He came to Kansas City from the New York Mets after the 1969 season in exchange for Joe Foy. Otis, a three-time Royals Player of the Year, won three Gold Glove awards, received five All-Star nods, and was in the first Royals Hall of Fame class in 1986.

Will Steal for Steak Dinner

Even though he was a five-tool player, the aspect of Amos Otis' game that he took the most pride in was stealing bases. He holds the club record for steals in a game with five, which he did in a September 1971 game against the Milwaukee Brewers.

With two outs in the Royals' half of the seventh inning and the score tied at 3, Otis singled, promptly stole second, and then third. He scored what turned out to be the winning run when a future teammate, catcher Darrell Porter, threw to third, trying to get Otis, and the ball went to the outfield. "That's certainly one particular game that stands out," Otis said. "I also had two infield hits and went 4-for-4, so I figure I had nine hits when you count the five stolen bases."

Not only did he steal 340 bases during his Royals career, but he also was so good at reading pitchers that he made wagers based on that ability. "I made bets with my teammates—such as U.L. Washington—that I could steal second base standing up against a certain pitcher," Otis said. "We'd bet a steak dinner with all the trimmings in the next town we visited. Then I'd steal a base and wipe the dust off the tops of my shoes. I stole about 25 bases standing up like that."

You were a much better hitter than you give yourself credit for.

Amos Otis: No, I was just very fortunate because pitchers did seem to hit my bat more often than I hit them. That's the way it was. I just had a lot of good friends who were pitchers and they hit my bat.

Since you hit one of the most famous home runs in Royals history, which almost went out of then-Royals Stadium, off Rollie Fingers, the mustachioed reliever must have been a very good friend.

AO: Rollie was one of my best friends because he wanted to see how far I could hit one. He hit that bat with the cork in it that I was using that night. And that's right: it would've left the stadium, but it hit the flag pole going up…It was still rising when it hit the flag pole. There should be an asterisk next to the person who hit the longest home run at Royals Stadium. People claim Bo Jackson got it, but I got it. But I think the cork had a lot to do with that.

You didn't really use a corked bat, did you?
AO: A few times. I only weighed 150 pounds when I played, so I needed all the help I could get. The bat started out at 35 ounces, but when they got through putting the cork in it, it weighed 28 ounces, so I could get some pretty good bat speed.

Speaking of weight, there's a story from one of your old Royals teammates, Jerry Terrell…
AO: Oh, that son of a gun.

So you know which story he likes to tell about how you guys got into some type of body weight contest because he was always lighter than you. When you guys weighed off for trainer Mickey Cobb, did they rig it so that Terrell weighed more than you, and you consequently ate everything in sight?
AO: Yeah, they were pulling a fast one because they kept putting five and 10-pound weights in [Terrell's] back pocket. Then he'd step on the scale. I guess I had to let him beat me at something because he couldn't beat me at anything else. [Laughs.]

Obviously fans in Kansas City loved you, but New York fans loved to boo you in Yankee Stadium. Did you enjoy playing in New York?
AO: You love to have the fans get on you because that means they recognize who you are and that you're a complete ballplayer. They only boo the guys who are good ballplayers.

Wasn't it in New York where your "special" glove came in handy?
AO: [Laughs.] That's right. That was a special glove. My older brother, Edward, gave me that glove during my first year of high school. That's the only glove I used in high school, a few years in the minor leagues, and my whole big league career except when it was stolen three times. [I got it back all three times.] The hole got

in the glove because I used to put so much pine tar and stickum inside the glove. The middle of it started cracking and peeling, so I cut a little bit off. The next thing I knew, I cut a hole big enough to put a softball through. And, yes, it came in handy in places like New York when the fans got rowdy. Instead of making an obscene gesture and getting fined, I could stick my fist through that hole and let them know what I thought.

37 Former Royals Offer Their BBQ Recommendations

As any Kansas Citian will tell you, we have the best barbecue in the country. For us natives, that's not really up for discussion. What is debatable, however, is which KC restaurant has the best barbecue in the city.

The following are various barbecue joints to hit up on the way to Kauffman Stadium. They're perfect for tailgating, taking back to the house, or eating in. To help you further decide which tasty meal to eat while rooting on your team, we have included the recommendations of several former Royals.

(Note: Restaurants are listed in alphabetical order.)

Arthur Bryant's Barbecue
Locations: 17th and Brooklyn Avenue, the Legends, Ameristar Casino
Specialties: beef sandwich, ribs, baked beans
Favorite of: Joe Keough, Brian McRae. "George Toma would shoot me if I said anything else," Keough said.

Fiorella's Jack Stack
Locations: Martin City, Country Club Plaza, Freight House District, Overland Park
Specialties: Poor Russ sandwich, Martin City Mayor sandwich, hickory pit beans, cheesy corn
Favorite of: Ed Hearn, Jeff Montgomery, Steve Renko, Mike Sweeney. "I still have it shipped occasionally out here to California," Sweeney said.

Rally Sauce and the Luck of the Z-Man

Did barbecue help the Royals in 2013?

It might sound odd to people outside of Kansas City—or vegetarians—who don't understand the significance of barbecue in this city. However, facts are facts from two significant barbecue events during the Royals' 2013 season.

After a disastrous stretch of games that left the Royals with a 23–32 record on June 4, which included Kansas City losing eight straight and 13-of-15 games, Billy Butler had some of his new Billy's Hit it a TON Barbecue Sauce, which was produced by Zarda Bar-B-Q, delivered to the stadium.

Wouldn't you know it, the Royals won that night, June 5, against the Minnesota Twins. And the next game. And the next.

Suddenly, with a bottle of the sauce in the dugout being used in postgame celebrations, the Royals won six in a row and nine of their next 10, and the "Rally Sauce" was born.

Fast forward two months. On August 6 the Royals were shut out at home against Minnesota 7–0. Turns out that before their victory, the Twins ordered 50 Z-Man sandwiches from Oklahoma Joe's. (The Z-Man is a sandwich with smoked brisket, melted provolone, and two onion rings on a toasted Kaiser roll, a meal we highly recommend).

Sensing the power in their sandwiches and not wanting to hurt their hometown Royals, who were above .500, Oklahoma Joe's sent 51 Z-Man sandwiches to the Royals' clubhouse on August 7. The result of that game? The Royals defeated the Twins 5–2. They then went on to win the first two games of their next series against the Boston Red Sox.

After hitting a home run against the Atlanta Braves on June 25, Eric Hosmer points to Billy Butler's rally sauce, which helped fuel the Royals during the 2013 season.

Gates Bar-B-Q (home of the famous "Hi, may I help you?")
Locations: six around Kansas City
Specialties: ribs, Gates fries, sandwiches, Yammer pie
Favorite of: John Mayberry, Frank White, Willie Wilson

Hayward's Pit Bar B Que
Location: College and Antioch Road in Overland Park
Specialties: smoked sausage platter, burnt ends, Ol' Fashioned BBQ Sammich, french fries, onion rings
Favorite of: Buddy Biancalana

LC's Barbecue
Location: 5800 Blue Parkway in Kansas City, Missouri
Closed Sundays except for Royals and Chiefs home games
Specialties: ribs, huge beef sandwich, french fries, cobbler
Favorite of: John Wathan. "Hole-in-the-wall joints like LC's are great," Sweeney said.

Oklahoma Joe's Bar-B-Que
Locations: Kansas City, Kansas; Olathe; Leawood
Specialties: pulled pork sandwich, Z-Man sandwich, red beans and rice
Favorite of: Mike Boddicker, George Brett, Tom Burgmeier, Al Fitzmorris, David Howard, Joe Randa. "I say Oklahoma Joe's, although a friend of mine we call 'Meat Mitch' does the best barbecue in town," Brett said.

Zarda Bar-B-Q
Locations: Blue Springs, Lenexa
Specialties: burnt end or pulled pork sandwich
Favorite of: Jim Eisenreich

38 A True Shortstop

While sitting at a table near the front of Chappell's Sports Museum and Restaurant in North Kansas City, we received a lot of double-takes. Actually, it's the graying man in the red golf shirt—the shortest of the group—who gets the most looks. He certainly receives more attention than most 5'4" guys. But Fred Patek is used to it.

For many of the onlookers, it's the realization that Patek, who made up half of one of baseball's best double-play combinations during the 1970s—first with Cookie Rojas and then with Frank White—is back in the public more and more after several years of isolation. For others it's the realization that Patek looks so good despite all that he's been through during the last two decades. For most, though, it's just the realization that *this* is Freddie Patek. "I've always tried to do a lot in the community and keep a good reputation," Patek said. "That's part of it. I still have people that I did something for years ago come up to me and say something, which is nice because it was meaningful to them. When I played, though, because I was small people related to me. They'd see this little short guy playing pretty good, which is also part of it."

The very humble Patek was very good for a 5'4" player. Heck, he was good for a 6'4" player. During his career with the Royals from 1971–79, he was a three-time All-Star and led the American League in triples (11) in 1971 and stolen bases (53) in '77. He was the first player to steal a base at Kauffman Stadium and the first to score a run there. He was the first Royal to hit for the cycle, which he did on July 9, 1971. During his 14-year, big league career, Patek compiled a .962 fielding percentage.

As if all of that weren't enough, while playing for the then-California Angels in a game at Boston in 1980, Patek became just the second shortstop in major league history to hit three home runs in a game. (He also doubled off the top of the Green Monster.) "The thing I remember most from that game," Patek said, "is that the fans in Boston gave me a standing ovation after the third home run. They did it so long that I went back out and tipped my hat.

Beating the Heat

The term "hotter than Hades" might've been the best way to describe the field at then-Royals Stadium before grass was installed. Throughout the 1970s and most of the 1980s, the Astroturf was basically a thin piece of carpet installed directly on top of asphalt. And it felt that way during most afternoon games. "When it was hot out, [groundskeeper] George Toma would put a thermometer on the Astroturf, and if it was 100 degrees air temperature, it was about 140 degrees on the turf. It was 30 to 40 degrees hotter on the turf than the actual temperature," George Brett said. "We used to have buckets of ice in the dugout. You'd come in between innings and—with your cleats on—stick your feet in the ice. Back then our spikes had a thin layer of fiberglass, and the heat would go right through it. Between pitches I could go stand on the dirt, but the poor outfielders were stuck."

"Yeah, when it was 130 degrees, we'd come off that turf and put our feet—spikes and all—in buckets of ice to keep our feet from getting blisters," Fred Patek said. "Sometimes you might go through seven pairs of shoes during the game. There wasn't anything you could do, and we tried everything, including freezing the insoles before the game, but even that lasted only an inning or so."

"I used the buckets of ice, too, but I had another trick," Frank White said. "Our clubhouse was right behind the dugout, so I'd have a change of shoes just inside the door of the air-conditioned clubhouse, and I'd change about midway through the game. It'd feel pretty good at first, but they'd get hot again quickly. You just had to accept the fact that you were going to get particularly hot during those afternoon games."

That's really unique for a visitor, but Fenway and the Boston fans were special."

Like many Royals who played throughout the 1970s, however, Patek is remembered as a member of the great Kansas City clubs that couldn't get past the New York Yankees in three American League Championship playoff series—1976, '77, and '78. For many years that was tough for Patek to handle. "At that time it was important," Patek said. "It would've been great to go to the World Series, but it's okay that I didn't. Today those losses look so small compared to what life is all about. Those losses gave me a lot of knowledge later in life about how to deal with disappointment. Losses like those are hard, but when you look back in the reality of life, they weren't quite as big in the real world. When you go through difficult times, you find out about life is all about."

Patek knows that better than most. On July 21, 1992, two days after the Royals inducted Patek into their Hall of Fame, his youngest daughter, Kim, was in a car accident on I-29. The accident left her paralyzed from the neck down. For the next three years, Fred and his wife, Jerri, cared for Kim around the clock. There were times she nearly didn't make it through the night. In June of 1995, Kim died at the tender age of 23.

Like many parents who suffer through the death of a child, Fred cut himself off from the outside world. Nothing meant what it once had. Including the time while caring for Kim, Patek, one of the most visible sports figures in Kansas City history, went into a dark isolation for more than 10 years. "I was in a shell," Patek said. "When you go through that, you go through so many emotions—hurt, sad, angry, and you don't understand. There's more than what words can explain. The only thing I can tell you is that I was never the same; I was totally different."

It's only through his strong belief in God and the encouragement of Jerri and their oldest daughter, Heather, that Fred didn't go into complete despair. Of course, there was Jordan, Patek's first grandchild. She was born just a few months after Kim died. "She saved my life," Patek said quietly. "She's the one God gave me to keep me going."

Patek is back to talking baseball again—about the letters he received and the countless comments he's heard about how inspirational he was on the field. Despite his many accomplishments during his playing days, Patek is most proud of one thing—the fact that he had carved out a baseball career when so many people said that someone 5'4" couldn't be a major leaguer. "Comments like those were always the driving factor," Patek said. "I was never overconfident, but in my mind I wasn't going to let someone take my job. That's a driving force for any professional athlete, but in my case, I had that working against me. Even though I played nearly 14 years in the majors, that was always in everybody's mind, I thought. They wondered if I could handle 162 games, playing every day. I also got a lot of grief from fans. I got through all of those things because I loved the game deeply and I put a lot of time and effort into it. Not to mention, God blessed me with a lot of speed and a great arm. I was very fortunate."

39 A Sweet Cookie at Second

If Octavio Victor Rojas' parents had their way, their son would have been a doctor. Octavio couldn't stand the thought of that because he wanted to be a baseball player. So Octavio made a deal with his dad to let him pursue baseball. "The only way that my father let me was because I promised him that if I failed, I would turn back and go to medical school," Rojas said. "Luckily, I never had to do that."

That also was lucky for Kansas City fans, considering Octavio "Cookie" Rojas helped solidify a young Royals defense from his second base spot during 1970–77. "I decided that instead of being a doctor, I was going to make a career out of baseball," said Rojas, who was born in Havana, Cuba. "So I tried to learn the game as much as I could."

That desire served Rojas well because he has worked in professional baseball in some capacity every summer since 1956. After spending time with teams in various ways from playing to serving as a general manager, 2015 marked Rojas' 13th season as an analyst for the Miami Marlins on their Spanish telecast.

After joining the Royals as their everyday second baseman in 1970, Rojas went on to become one of the club's best. He made four straight All-Star appearances, teaming with shortstop Fred Patek to form one the best middle infields in the American League at that time. Rojas, who was inducted into the Royals Hall of Fame in 1987, also helped lead the Royals to their first two American League West crowns. Later in his career, he groomed a young Frank White even before White joined the big league Royals. "I first saw Frank White at the Royals Academy," Rojas said. "I broke my ankle in September and I went down to Florida to rehab it. For some reason the organization never got along with the academy. Jack McKeon, who was managing the Royals, asked me to go down and work with Frank. I told him, 'Of course.' We were going to work out together on Sunday, a day that the academy players had off. The night before, I went out to dinner with some people, including Lou Gorman, who was the minor league director. I told him I was going to work out with Frank White, and Lou thought that was great. I went out Sunday and worked with Frank…I wanted to pass along any knowledge I had to Frank while helping the organization."

In 1976 the Royals wanted to start the transition of White taking over second base. So White was playing more at home—on the artificial turf—while Rojas played more on the road. White had more errors that season (18) than he had during any other season in his career. He sought advice from the guy whose job he'd be taking. "Frank always sat with me on the bench and always asked me questions, wanting to learn more," Rojas said. "I told him one time, 'Frank, I'm going to retire before Freddie Patek. I think that you're going to be a good second baseman, especially with Freddie at short. I'm managing in Venezuela this winter. If you want to learn more, come play for me.' He came down and played second base. He had a tremendous dedication. He was a great athlete with tremendous ability. Off and on the field, he was a gentleman and a scholar. He became the best second baseman in the American League for many, many years. I have great respect for Frank White."

A few years later in 1977 as Rojas's career was coming to a close, it was obvious that White was going to take over at second base. Even though White was a Kansas City native and a great story, Rojas was the fan favorite. On the day the Royals honored Rojas, he made a gesture on the field as a show of support for his replacement. "I appreciated all the fans, ballclub, and my teammates very much, including Frank White," Rojas said. "On that day I took my hat off and put it on Frank's head and I took his hat and put it on my head."

By the time he retired, Rojas had played in the first game at Dodger Stadium—and got his first major league hit off Sandy Koufax—and the first game at Royals Stadium. And in addition to the Royals Hall of Fame, Rojas is in the Latino Baseball Hall of Fame. During his eight seasons with the Royals, Rojas hit .268 with 824 hits, 139 doubles, 25 home runs, and 332 RBIs.

Not bad for someone who should've been a doctor. "[Baseball has] been a great career choice," Rojas said, laughing. "I'm still in baseball now, so I think it's absolutely great that I decided to pursue that instead of being a doctor. I don't see how I could be a doctor anyway because I totally faint at the sight of blood."

40 Greinke Trade Nets Cain and Escobar

Zack Greinke had been a great pitcher for the Royals, a Cy Young Award-winning dominating pitcher, but, like everyone who plays this game, he wanted to play on a championship-caliber team. The Royals weren't quite at that point in 2010 when Greinke suggested to general manager Dayton Moore that the club trade some of its top minor league prospects for major league players.

Feeling a need for an impact center fielder and an upgrade at either shortstop or second base, Moore opened trade discussions to help get Greinke to a contender. The perfect suitor ended up being the Milwaukee Brewers, who had an up-and-coming center fielder named Lorenzo Cain, who split time in 2010 between Double A, Triple A, and the majors. Originally, the Brewers were going to send Cain and pitcher Jake Odorizzi to Kansas City in exchange for Greinke. Moore really wanted Milwaukee shortstop Alcides Escobar as part of the deal, though, so he offered to add Royals shortshop Yuniesky Betancourt in exchange for Escobar. "I liked Escobar and Cain mainly for their speed and defense," Moore said. "The Brewers were giving up players of the future in exchange for a front-line starter and Cy Young award winner who could help them get back to the playoffs."

From Day One in 2011, Escobar became Kansas City's shortstop, and it benefited everyone. His .980 fielding percentage in 2015 equaled his career best. Also in 2015, he was an American League All-Star for the first time. Offensively, Escobar is what you could call an anomaly. Just look at 2015. In spite of his .257 batting average, 26 walks, and relatively low .293 on-base percentage, something magical happened to the Royals when Escobar hit in the leadoff spot. They won—a lot. From Opening Day through

Game 5 of the World Series, the Royals were 93–54 with Escobar in the lead-off spot. When he was down in the order? They were 6–11. "Statistically speaking, it doesn't make any sense," said Royals manager Ned Yost, who knew Escobar and Cain from his days managing Milwaukee. "But it works. It works. We find ways to win baseball games…It's just the chemistry of the lineup somehow that is kind of unexplainable to me how it works and why it works, but it does."

Even though everyone knows Escobar's likely swinging at the first pitch, teams kept starting him off with fastballs, and he kept hitting them. During the 2015 American League Championship Series, he set a major league record by leading off his team's half of the first inning with a hit in four consecutive postseason games. Then he led off the bottom of the first in Game 1 of the World Series with an inside-the-park home run against Matt Harvey and the New York Mets—on the first pitch, of course. Escobar became the first player to hit an inside-the-park homer in the World Series since 1929.

Escobar was impressive enough during the ALCS that he was the series' MVP. "For me it's a surprise," Escobar said of the award. "I know I'm playing really good, and my team is playing really good. Together we play. And when I heard the news, I was so happy for that."

Yost was thrilled for him, too. "I used to bring Esky to big league spring training when he was in A ball because I loved to watch him play," Yost said. "For him to get the MVP this year is very satisfying to me. I've always known he was an MVP type of player in these type of situations. I'm excited for him."

Coincidentally, Lorenzo Cain won the 2014 ALCS MVP award. Cain, who's known for his infectious smile and the way he's tormented on Instagram by his close friend Salvador Perez, had a slower route to Kansas City than Escobar. Cain spent the majority of 2011 at Triple A Omaha and didn't make the full transition to the major leagues until 2012. That's understandable, though, for the latest bloomer of all late bloomers. "Many people felt he was major league ready," Moore wrote in his book *More Than a Season.* "He didn't complain at all, but I could tell he wasn't sure what to think of us, and we had to build that relationship."

Cain didn't play organized baseball until he was 16—when he was a freshman in high school—after he failed to make the Madison County High School (Florida) basketball team. But there he was, a little more than a decade later in the middle of the field at Kauffman Stadium, accepting the ALCS MVP award. "To see him on that stage throughout the postseason and to know what he meant to our team in 2014 was incredible," Moore said. "I was happy and proud for him in his personal growth as a player and as a man."

Cain's growth as a player continued in the 2015 season, which was his best offensive season thus far in his career. During the regular season, he had career highs in batting average (.307), hits (169), runs (101), doubles (34), triples (six), home runs (16), RBIs (72), walks (37), and a tie for stolen bases (28).

Greinke remains one of the top pitchers in the majors, which was why the Arizona Diamondbacks signed him to a six-year contract for $206 million before the 2016 season, but his willingness to be traded, Moore's patience, and Yost's history managing Milwaukee all helped give the Royals two key components—Escobar and Cain—to reach back-to-back World Series. "They needed time to develop and grow," Yost said of Cain and Escobar before Game 1 of the 2015 World Series. "Both of those kids were about as skinny as a broomstick. You could tell that they had good actions and good eyes, they were very athletic, and—once they filled out and developed—that they had a chance to be really, really good players. And they both have turned into that."

41 Leo's Comeback

May 28. The date itself isn't very fresh in Dennis Leonard's mind. But when reminded, he can joke about it. "I better stay off my feet that day," he said.

The Royals-Orioles game on May 28, 1983, was one that cruelly altered the rest of his career and three years later reinforced to Royals fans just what type of player and person Leonard was. With Cal Ripken Jr. at the plate for Baltimore, Leonard went through his regular pitching motion. When he landed, though, he says it sounded as if Velcro was pulling apart as his knee gave out. His patella tendon was completely severed.

"I had a problem with my knee before that, but it just happened to blow that day," Leonard said. "Before the pitch I didn't have any unusual pain. When I threw it, I originally thought I got hit by a line drive. As I was going down, though, I heard the umpire call strike. The next thing I knew, my knee was hurting a little bit, and I reached down and felt my kneecap on the outside part of my leg. Until I saw a replay of it later, I never realized my body went the opposite way on my follow-through. I think when I saw the replay, that's when it hurt the most."

Over the next three years, he went through four surgeries and extensive rehabilitation. Leonard, who still lives in Blue Springs, Missouri, was at home during the summer for the first time as an adult, spending time with his wife, Audrey, and their kids and seeing what it was like to barbecue at night while listening to Denny Matthews and Fred White. Most importantly, though, he focused on his rehab, which he'd complete each day with trainer Mickey Cobb before the team arrived at the stadium. Leonard always made sure he was finished before the players—his teammates—got there. Otherwise it was too painful.

In 1985, as the Royals were beating the St. Louis Cardinals in the World Series, he chose to rehabilitate in Florida. As it turns out, Leonard's World Series reception came six months later. On the last day of spring training in 1986, pitcher Danny Jackson twisted his ankle and was forced to miss a start. Leonard, who was scheduled to begin the season in relief, took Jackson's spot on April 12 against Toronto, the fifth game of the season and second at home. And it happened to be a nationally televised Saturday afternoon game. "I remember watching Leo walk in from the bullpen to start that game," former broadcaster Fred White said. "Walks are usually walks, but I've never seen a more determined walk than he had that day."

Leonard did not hold huge aspirations for his comeback performance. "When I went out there that day, I was just hoping not to embarrass myself," he said. "I didn't know what to expect, but I was hoping for five good innings. As the game progressed, I felt good and realized that I just needed a run."

In the eighth inning, the Royals got that run. That's all they—and Leonard—needed. He ended up throwing a complete game, three-hit shutout. It was one of the 103 complete games in Leonard's career, which ended after that 1986 season. After the game, Leonard immediately gave the game ball to Cobb. "When you travel with the team, you regularly get back home around 1:00 AM, and then [it's] 2 or so by the time you get to your house," Leonard said. "Mickey traveled with the team but then was at the ballpark by 8:30 or 9 the next morning to check on me. He was the big inspiration to keep me going. Rehab wasn't painful, but it was boring. As a player you just want to be on the field. Mickey was there, pulling for me to get back on the field.

"I couldn't have dreamed of throwing better that day. I've said this before, but there were about 27,000 people there that day. I'm so appreciative of them for being there and the applause they gave me. That was my World Series."

42 Visit the Royals Hall of Fame

Curt Nelson knows his Royals facts, both well-known and obscure—and everything in between. "Mr. Kauffman's nickname in the Navy became 'Lucky,'" Nelson said. "While he was in the Navy during World War II, he learned how to play cards...and he became *very* good." Nelson continues with the story about how Kauffman won a lot of money playing cards during the war and eventually used that money toward the founding of Marion Laboratories, which in turn helped Kauffman buy the Royals.

Nelson then tells the story of how Hall of Fame outfielder Andre Dawson had been accepted to the Royals Baseball Academy, but his mom insisted that he attend college instead, which he did. A few minutes later he's telling the story about how Dan Quisenberry used some insistence and persistence to get signed by longtime Royals scout Rosey Gilhousen. Indeed, Nelson is a walking, talking Royals reference book. That's a good thing, considering he's the director of the Royals Hall of Fame.

The Royals Hall of Fame takes fans on a journey throughout baseball's history in Kansas City, dating to the late 1800s. But its most vivid story—and the team with the most show-and-tell items—features the Royals. Following a 14-minute Royals dugout theater experience that features comments from some Royals

Oh, How We Miss the Halter Top

The Royals have had a great history of promotions and giveaways. Many of those items are displayed in the Royals Hall of Fame. Some of the more popular ones have been Bat Day, Batting Helmet Day, Seat Cushion Night, a Belt Buckle Day, and a Visor Day. The team even gave way the unforgettable FoamDome in 1982.

But the giveaway talked about the most is one the Royals did for three years in the late 1970s: the infamous Halter Top Day. Albeit brief, the promotion was so popular that fans around baseball still remember stories from it. "You know what I remember about the halter tops," Willie Wilson said, "was that on a really hot day [relief pitcher Dan Quisenberry] would take the hose and shoot the [water] up on all the girls in the halter tops."

An original halter top is on display at the Royals Hall of Fame along with a retro halter top that the team busted out in 2009 thanks to online voting by fans. Fortunately or unfortunately, it wasn't quite the same. There likely won't be another Halter Top Day anytime soon.

legends, visitors learn about the club's history from before Day One of the Royals through today.

Although subject to change, here are some of the artifacts on display:

- Seats from Municipal Stadium
- Gloves used by Amos Otis, Willie Wilson, Jermaine Dye, and Frank White
- Rolaids Relief Man awards won by Quisenberry and Jeff Montgomery
- Gold Gloves won by Frank White and Alex Gordon
- The bat George Brett used when he recorded his 3,000th hit
- And, of course, the 1985 and 2015 World Series trophies

Visitors also can tour a Cooperstown Corner, which is a themed display with artifacts on loan from the National Baseball Hall of Fame. (The display will change periodically.) The Royals

Hall of Fame ends in a room with plaques featuring each member of the Royals Hall of Fame.

Tours of the Royals Hall of Fame are available year-round, though hours vary during the offseason. So it's best to call ahead or order tickets at Royals.com. Including the intro movie, fans should allow more than an hour to take in the Hall of Fame. If you're lucky enough to have Nelson give the tour, it likely will take at least 90 minutes. "I could tell stories all day," he said. "The team has a wonderful history that I think we do a good job of telling here."

43 Brett Becomes First Royal in HOF

January 5, 1999 is a day many Royals fans will remember. It's the day that the first true*—and so far only—member of the Royals found out he was becoming a member of the National Baseball Hall of Fame. Sure, Harmon Killebrew, for instance, played for the Royals and went into the Hall of Fame in 1984, but he wasn't a Royals player. Same for 1985 inductee Hoyt Wilhelm, whom the Royals selected in the 1968 Expansion Draft at the age of 46. (He never played for the Royals. The club traded him in December 1968 to California.)*

You were pretty much a sure thing to gain induction, but what stands out about when you received the call from the Hall of Fame in January 1999?

George Brett: I was a little nervous because you never know what a "lock" is, but I thought Nolan [Ryan] was a lock, I thought Robin [Yount] was a lock, and I thought I had a pretty good chance. You never know for sure, though, until you get the phone call. It's a little weird when the media has your fate in their hands. If you

A Royal Presence in the Hall of Fame

Besides seeing George Brett and Denny Matthews—or, at least, their likenesses—in the National Baseball Hall of Fame, there are other Royals artifacts on display in Cooperstown:

- Jersey worn by Eric Hosmer when he scored the tying run in the ninth inning of Game 5 of the 2015 World Series
- Jersey worn by Ned Yost during the ALCS when he became the first manager to win the first eight postseason games he managed
- Jersey worn by Zack Greinke during his 2009 Cy Young-winning season
- Cap worn by Billy Butler on September 26, 2009, when he became the eighth player in major league history to hit 50 doubles in a season before turning 24
- Helmet worn by Reggie Sanders when he hit his 300th home run on June 10, 2006, becoming the fifth player in major league history to hit at least 300 career homers and steal at least 300 bases
- Jersey worn by Joe Randa when he tied an American League record with six hits and tied a major league record with six runs in a game on September 9, 2004
- Bat used by Brett at the end of the 1990 season when he became the first player to win a batting title in three different decades
- A glove used by Frank White and the bat White used when he delivered his pinch-hit home run in the 1986 All-Star Game
- The "Pine Tar" bat

don't have a good relationship with a certain voter, he might say, "Screw it, I'm not going to vote for him." As a result there are some surprises in the Hall of Fame and some surprises to me of guys not in the Hall of Fame.

Should there be statistical criteria for a guy to get into the Hall of Fame?

GB: I thought there were certain numbers that would make a guy a lock. I thought 3,000 hits would get you in and 300 wins and

500 home runs. But it comes down to this: how good were you in your era? Did you dominate your position for a long time in your league? Did you play the game the way you should play it? And then the media can look at the stats and say that this guy was good for a 10-year period and had a good run on some good teams that got to play in postseason. Others, though, might not have that opportunity, even though they were really good players but not on very good teams.

Standing next to (left to right) Orlando Cepeda, Robin Yount, and Nolan Ryan in 1999, George Brett became the first true Royals player to be inducted into the Baseball Hall of Fame. (AP Images)

When you guys played in the 1970s and '80s, you had a lot of guys who were practical jokers. Former catcher Don Slaught has told a story about how one night in 1983 a bunch of guys, including you and Steve Renko, went to a bar during spring training. You guys played a trick on him where he was drinking some type of liquor while you guys were drinking water—unknown to him.
GB: We did that one time with Kevin Appier, too, when he got sent down to Omaha. We were in Oakland at the hotel bar before he had to leave for the airport the next morning. We took Ape in there and did the old shot trick on him. He thinks we're drinking tequila or vodka or gin when we're really drinking water. He ends up sleeping in and missing his flight to Omaha the next day. I did that to [Bret] Saberhagen one time in spring training, but that goofy son of a gun was tight-roping on the second-floor handrail. I kept telling him to get down because he was going to fall and hurt himself or worse, and then we'd all be in trouble.

We had a great time. In a nutshell I loved playing the game of baseball, but I also loved the life of being a Major League Baseball player and the perks that come with that—the travel, the camaraderie with the guys, and the card games in the clubhouse. I loved every minute of it. I really did. Remembering that story about Don Slaught, that's all part of it and being a part of the team. We didn't haze, but we did have a lot of fun together and we knew what it was like to be on good teams with good teammates.

Does it seem different these days with the younger players?
GB: When we played, there was a lot of discussion about the game afterwards if you lost. I'll never forget sitting around the clubhouse with Hal McRae, who was one of the greatest teammates I ever had because he'd sit around and just talk to you. You could learn a lot of things from him, and he could learn a lot of things from you. We would sit around for an hour and let the traffic leave the ballpark because you couldn't go anywhere fast if you left right after

the game anyway. So we'd sit around in a circle, have a few beers, and wait for the traffic to leave. There's a lot to be learned about the game after the game if you sit around and take the time to visit with your teammates about a situation in the game or how a guy pitched you that night. The game is different now. Are the players having as much fun as we did in the '70s? No. Did we have as much fun as the guys in the '40s and '50s, who were riding trains everywhere together? I doubt it because they'd spend days together on trains while we were spending a couple hours together on a plane. It's definitely different. But I had a lot of fun and enjoyed the era I played in.

44 David Cone

The Royals have had three homegrown Cy Young Award winners. The Royals picked Bret Saberhagen, who won the Cy Young in 1985 and again in '89, in the 19th round of the 1982 draft. Zack Greinke, the Royals' first-round pick in 2002, won the Cy Young in 2009. But neither of them was homegrown in the sense that David Cone, who won the award in 1994, was.

Kansas City selected Cone out of Kansas City's Rockhurst High School in the third round of the 1981 draft. Weirdly enough—and much like Frank White and Lincoln High School—Rockhurst didn't have a baseball team when Cone was a student there. "I was a huge Royals fan growing up," Cone said. "Getting the chance to be on the same team with George Brett was quite a thrill for a KC kid."

Cone's Cy Young year in 1994 was not necessarily the best season of the 17 he played in the big leagues, but it was impressive nonetheless. In 23 starts Cone went 16–5 with a 2.94 ERA. Already established as one of the game's best strikeout pitchers by that time, Cone had 132 strikeouts to go with 54 walks. "Jeff Montgomery and David Cone were two of my favorite guys to catch," said longtime Royals catcher Mike Macfarlane. "They were similar in their competitiveness and in their ability to throw a strike when you asked, whether it was a 2–0 breaking ball or a 3–2 breaking ball, or sneaking a fastball by someone. They could pitch under stressful situations, which gives credence to the performances they laid out and the awards they received throughout their careers."

Cone's Cy Young year was actually part of his *second* stint with the Royals. After coming up with the club in 1986 and pitching in only 22⅔ innings, the Royals traded Cone to the New York Mets in March 1987 for catcher Ed Hearn and two pitchers. General manager Herk Robinson felt the Royals were a catcher away from getting back to the World Series. Owner Ewing Kauffman, however, eventually called it the worst trade in the history of the Royals.

Cone spent the next six seasons pitching for the Mets and then the Toronto Blue Jays. When he had the chance after the 1992 season, he signed again with his hometown team, the Royals. He struggled mightily in the early part of 1993. Things turned around, though, when Kauffman, who was in the last few months of a battle with cancer, called Cone. "When I was 0–5 and Mr. Kauffman was in very bad health, he had the presence of mind to call me and say he didn't regret the move, that he was very happy with me being in Kansas City," Cone said. "That had a profound impact on me. If it wasn't for Mr. Kauffman, I wouldn't have been wearing a Royals uniform." Kauffman passed away on August 1, 1993.

Cone's Cy Young season of '94 was the last time he pitched for the Royals. On April 6, 1995, the Royals traded him *again*. This time he went back to Toronto in exchange for Chris Stynes, Tony Medrano, and David Sinnes.

In three seasons with the Royals, Cone went 27–19 with a 3.29 ERA, 344 strikeouts, and 181 walks. He ended up playing 17 years in the big leagues with five teams. Cone, a five-time All-Star, pitched in the World Series five years—one with Toronto and four with the New York Yankees. His team won all five times.

45 A Glass Half-Full or Half-Empty?

From the time of Ewing Kauffman's death in 1993 until David Glass bought the club in April 2000, the Royals wandered through the desert. They had a board of directors appointed to run the club while searching for a new owner who would keep the Royals in Kansas City, per Mr. K's wishes. Since 2000 Royals fans have been split: they've either accepted Glass as the owner of the Royals or despised Glass as the owner of the club. There isn't a lot of gray area—even with trips to the World Series in 2014 and 2015. With that in mind, are you in the Glass Half-Full or the Glass Half-Empty camp?

Half-Full

Kauffman wanted Glass to buy the Royals, knowing that he'd likely do a good job running it—as he had done for Walmart—and because he'd keep the team in Kansas City. Glass, however, was reluctant to jump in. He wasn't sure how the fans felt about him. "Personally, I think baseball fans in this city should get down and kiss David Glass' butt because when I was covering the Royals in the 1990s and they were going through the ownership questions, no one else stepped up to the plate," said Jeffrey Flanagan, who's covered the Royals for multiple outlets. "They went to every rich person in Kansas City, and no one wanted to take it on...Before purchasing it David stepped back when he felt the town had turned on him, and it wasn't the right time to step in. He continued, though, to help secure an owner. There was Miles Prentice, who didn't have enough money. And God bless George Brett. He's a friend of mine, but that group didn't have enough money. So when those and every other option was exhausted, David Glass stepped in.

"David was nervous about it because he knew the feeling in town was that he and [general manager] Herk Robinson and everyone else involved had wrecked the franchise. That wasn't true; he was trying to save the franchise and he was also battling the George Steinbrenners and everyone else in baseball, trying to level the playing field and make it fair for Kansas City and Milwaukee and these other small markets. Of course, the bigger markets resisted and resisted, and now there is this monstrous gap between Kansas City and New York and Milwaukee and Boston. Don't get me wrong, I'm not saying David Glass is an angel, but he's been unfairly portrayed. He has done a lot of good for baseball in Kansas City."

Half-Empty

Owners own professional teams for various reasons. For some it's ego. For others it's a sense of civic duty. There's no telling, though, if it's to make more money. Glass haters are convinced that in today's economic climate of Major League Baseball, he has to be making money, unlike Kauffman, who second-guessed his decision to buy the club after talking with a reporter about the $20 million of his own money he'd put into the club. "I'll never get that 20 million back!" Kauffman said. "I'll just leave that to Kansas City, the stadium, and all its beautiful surroundings. But this is my only regret about having baseball—I would have done so much more with $20 million for Kansas City."

Fans weary of Glass have complained through letters to Glass, called sports talk shows, and even staged in-game walk outs. One fan, however, took it to another level. Joe Accurso started a grassroots effort to get funding for a full-page letter in *The Star*, encouraging Glass to sell the team. Through his website, no-more-glass.com, Accurso raised $5,100 and took out a half-page ad in August 2012 to run his letter. After thanking Glass for buying the team, the letter states: "I refuse to believe that there is not a way to orchestrate your making a $250,000,000 profit by selling the team to a local ownership group with a long-term view, willing to put

The Glass Family Thanks Royals Employees in 2014

The chant was faint, but the beautiful sound was unmistakable, even through radio and television speakers. *"Let's go, Royals!" Clap, clap… clap, clap, clap. "Let's go, Royals!" Clap, clap…clap, clap, clap. "Let's go, Royals!" Clap, clap…clap, clap, clap.*

Sure, that became somewhat of a rallying cry for Royals fans at Kauffman Stadium throughout the 2014 postseason. Only thing was, this time the chant was being heard from AT&T Park in San Francisco. What's more, it was mainly from a large contingency of Royals' front-office staffers.

Throughout the Royals' lean years, owner David Glass was called all sorts of names that can't be printed in this book—and shouldn't be printed in any publication. With the idea that the Royals couldn't keep players who were on the verge of stardom, the most popular word to describe Glass was usually "cheapskate," along with some reference to Walmart. Well, besides spending more money on the player side of the business in recent years, the Glass family made sure most of the members of the Royals' front office were able to experience the World Series… in San Francisco.

Recognizing the hard, thankless work that people in the front office do, including too many long nights and weekends away from family and friends from March until (now) October, David and Dan Glass paid for a chartered flight, game tickets, and hotel for all almost the entire staff and one of their family members. Of course, they sat in the same section, all clad in blue.

money back into the team to revitalize this once-proud organization in this great city of ours for generations to come."

And the ire is not held to typical fans. Longtime Kansas City television sports anchor Jack Harry used his "Jack's Smack" commentary in June 2013 to encourage fans to "band together" against Glass. "David Glass is milking the fans for every buck he can get," Harry said. "The Royals will receive $52 million in revenue from Major League Baseball beginning [in 2014]. Yet they turn out a lousy product on the field year after year and get away with it. A growing number of us have become skeptical. David Glass as CEO or owner of this franchise has one winning season in 20 years. Maybe it's time to start flying some banners over the ballpark. We need to band together as one voice and do everything humanly possible to convince this man to get out of the way and sell this team. He needs to do it—and the sooner the better for the good of all baseball fans in this city." Harry used "Jack's Smack" multiple times for similar messages about Glass, including a segment in 2012 when he encouraged fans to get involved with no-more-glass.com.

46 Mike Sweeney

For more than a decade from 1995–2007, Mike Sweeney was one of the nicest and most respected Royals players. His .340 batting average in 2002 remains second on the club's single-season list behind George Brett's .390 in 1980. He also had 206 hits in 2000. He's in the top 10 of all-time Royals in games played (1,282), runs scored (700), hits (1,398), doubles (297), home runs (197), and RBIs (837). He was inducted into the Royals Hall of Fame in 2015.

When you think back to your time in Kansas City, what comes to mind?

Mike Sweeney: Hospitality, love, and barbecue. When I came to Kansas City, I didn't know where I was going to live. I was introduced to a man named Bob Reams, who's become like family to me. We hit it off right away. As a rookie coming up from minor league ball, you don't have anything. Bob graciously invited me to live with his family in his home for the last month of the season. So when I say hospitality, that's why. He was the first of many people who opened up their hearts to us.

No. 2 is love. I absolutely loved Kansas City. Growing up in Southern California, I didn't know anything about the Midwest. I felt very welcomed and loved by the fans and the Kansas City community. I met some amazing, Godly people in Kansas City. It's a very special place to me.

And then barbecue. When I first came to Kansas City, I didn't know much about barbecue. Now part of my trips to Kansas City center around barbecue. I started with the hot spots like Gates and K.C. Masterpiece, but now my favorite barbecue on the planet is Jack Stack. I still have it flown in to California. My three favorites are Jack Stack, Oklahoma Joe's, and probably Gates.

What do you remember about your first major league stint?

MS: The thing I remember most is having mentors like Jeff Montgomery, Mike Macfarlane, and Tim Belcher on our team. Not only did they allow me to feel like a major leaguer, but they taught me how to act. They were the big brothers I never had. In turn I was able to pay that forward years down the road. That was also the fulfillment of my dream to be a big league ballplayer.

My first hit was against Paul Assenmacher of the Cleveland Indians. Ironically, I got called up in September and I didn't play much. Going into the last day of the season, I had two at-bats in my big league career. On the last day, I was expecting to get the start. I didn't, but it was a blowout, so I was able to get two at-bats. I hit a line drive off Paul Assenmacher. What a feeling—it was awesome!

How close were you to becoming the American League batting champion in 2002 when you hit .340?
MS: I was leading the league in hitting before the last five games of the season. Due to the altercation that took place between me and Jeff Weaver, Matt Anderson of the Detroit Tigers drilled me in the ribs with a 98-mile per hour fastball. That was his way of saying he had Weaver's back and Robert Fick's back from the fight a couple years earlier. I jogged to first base, but I was in rough shape. We played the Tigers again the next day. I didn't want them to think they got me, so I went out there to play. I went 0-for-8. I could've sat out, but I didn't. We were in Cleveland for the last series of the season, and I was knotted up with Manny Ramirez. Friday I was hurting, but I was going to play. I went 1-for-4, and Manny went 1-for-2 before leaving the game. He got a slight lead on me. I played and went 2-for-8 in the final two games. Looking back, the way it went down, I'd rather finish second like that than sit out and finish first.

Were there any other games or moments that stand out to you?
MS: I remember Joe Randa hitting a game-winning grand slam on the anniversary of his mother's death. I wept that day. I'll never forget hitting a walk-off double against Barry Bonds and the San Francisco Giants on Father's Day with my proud dad in the stands. I remember a straight steal of home at the K against Andy Pettitte.

And I'll never forget Tony Muser telling the story of his first day as manager of the Kansas City Royals. Everyone was lined up on the first-base line. He has butterflies in his stomach, and the national anthem begins. He looks down the line and sees all of his players. Right next to him is his three-hole hitter and first baseman

Jeff King. Tony looks into his eyes and says, "Kinger, how are you doin'?" King looks over at him and said, "Every time I hear this song, I have a bad game." That's one of the best moments and stories I can recall.

47 Visit the Negro Leagues Baseball Museum

Every baseball fan should visit the Negro Leagues Baseball Museum. It's a wonderful place to learn about American history and Kansas City's importance to baseball. A venture to the museum is like a trip back in time with hundreds of photos, along with letters, equipment, uniforms, and statues. The museum, which is not a hall of fame, is continually evolving and seems to get better with every visit. Appropriately, there's a tribute to Buck O'Neil, who was instrumental in the NLBM's early existence.

Horace Peterson III, who was the founder of the Black Archives of Mid-America, called O'Neil with the idea of forming a Negro Leagues Hall of Fame. O'Neil responded with a different idea. "No, we don't need a Hall of Fame because I think the guys who are qualified should be in the Hall of Fame in Cooperstown," O'Neil said. "We should have a Negro Leagues Baseball Museum."

O'Neil was also an original contributor. "Former Monarchs paid the rent. I paid it one month, Lefty LaMarque paid it one month, Connie Johnson paid it one month, and so on," he said. "That's the way we existed until reverend Emanuel Cleaver, who was a councilman at the time, got money for this area [18th and Vine]. That's when we moved across the street and into the same building with the jazz museum."

Kansas City has a longtime connection between jazz and baseball, dating to around the time the Negro National League was born in Kansas City in 1920. In its heyday the 18th and Vine district in Kansas City was hopping with jazz. And after the Monarchs finished their game at nearby 22nd and Brooklyn, the players would head to 18th and Vine to hear the likes of Charlie Parker or Count Basie.

Since the 1990s the two have remained intertwined in a revitalization of the 18th and Vine district through the baseball museum and the American Jazz Museum. Housed in the same building, the two museums are hidden gems in Kansas City. The latter museum has some wonderful artifacts, including a saxophone that Parker played, some of Duke Ellington's original notes, and Ella Fitzgerald's American Express card.

Just a few blocks away is the Paseo YMCA, the setting where eight independent black baseball teams met in 1920 to form the Negro League. It was home to Hall of Fame players such as Satchel Paige and Jackie Robinson, who first played professional baseball for the Monarchs. To make visiting the YMCA and museum an even more enjoyable—and quintessential Kansas City—day, go to nearby Arthur Bryant's for barbecue and then head south to see the site of old Municipal Stadium where the Blues, Monarchs, A's, and Royals all played.

48 The Truman Sports Complex

There's an artist's rendering hanging in a back room of Chappell's restaurant that shows a baseball stadium and a football stadium with a funny-looking half-moon structure between the two buildings. The caption reveals architect Charles Deaton's idea for a rolling roof between what would become the Truman Sports Complex—Royals Stadium and Arrowhead.

Although the rolling roof never came to fruition, even the whole idea of two stadiums seemed preposterous. Throughout the 1960s in cities with Major League Baseball and NFL teams, multipurpose or cookie-cutter stadiums were the rage. Stadiums were sought that could hold both baseball and football, and they were sprouting all over the country: New York (Shea Stadium), Atlanta, Pittsburgh, Philadelphia, Cincinnati, and St. Louis to name a few.

In the late 1960s, the Chiefs and A's were looking for funding for new stadiums. A's owner Charlie Finley had threatened for years to leave if he didn't get one. After going to the first Super Bowl, the Chiefs needed one, too. Chiefs owner Lamar Hunt and team president Jack Steadman didn't want a cookie-cutter stadium, fearing that Finley might move the A's and they'd be stuck with a stadium that didn't fit their needs. After much politicking Jackson County voters approved $102 million in general bonds, $43 million of which would be used for the Jackson County Sports Complex.

With the new Sports Complex being built, many of Kansas City's signature buildings started sprouting. Kansas City International Airport was dedicated in 1972. Crown Center opened in 1973 as did Worlds of Fun. Construction of Kemper Arena began in 1973 for the NBA's Kings and NHL's Scouts, and Bartle Hall opened in 1976. "All of that boom in Kansas City came from the sports complex," Steadman said. "From the point the funding was approved, everything started going crazy around here…all of a sudden, everything started moving in Kansas City in a big way."

That wasn't the only moving. After the bond issue passed in June 1967, Finley moved the A's west. That opened the door for the Royals, of course, but also for the club to build its stadium the way it saw fit. With general manager Cedric Tallis' experience helping to oversee the construction of Anaheim Stadium, which was a cousin of Dodger Stadium, Royals Stadium took bits and pieces of the design from each of those stadiums.

Owner Ewing Kauffman, who put in approximately $7 million initially, had two special additions to the stadium. A 12-story state-of-the-art crown scoreboard and a 322-foot-wide water spectacular, a beautiful feature for which the stadium is still known. The water idea was Muriel Kauffman's. It featured 150 combinations of spray and color effects. Ewing Kauffman, who wasn't a big fan of baseball when he bought the team, felt the fountains would be an added reason for people to go to games. "When the crowd yells, the water shoots up," he said. "The louder they yell, the higher it will go. If they yell loud enough, five jet streams of water will go seven stories high."

Royals Stadium, which was the only baseball-centric stadium built in the major leagues from 1962 to 1991, was scheduled to open in 1972, but a construction strike caused a delay that pushed the opening to '73. (Arrowhead opened on time in '72.) That delay cost Kauffman an additional $2 million.

The construction crew—not necessarily two of the people involved in the strike, mind you—included actor Chris Cooper, who has starred in *The Patriot*, *Seabiscuit*, *The Bourne Identity*, among other movies, and Royals Hall of Fame second baseman Frank White. "I did labor stuff, carried things here and there," White said. "When they poured the columns for the main level, I had this little machine and I'd drive around and smooth out the concrete. On the third floor, I learned how to seal some bathroom floors."

The venue was renamed Kauffman Stadium—in honor of Ewing—in 1993 and completed a renovation in 2009. But the Royals' home remains one the most aesthetically beautiful stadiums in the major leagues.

49 Country Breakfast Feeds on AL Pitching

A player usually doesn't forget his first major league game. Billy Butler definitely won't. It was May 1, 2007 against the Los Angeles Angels of Anaheim. Bartolo Colon, one of the American League's best pitchers at the time, was on the mound. With a veteran's confidence rather than that of a recently turned 21-year-old kid, Butler stepped calmly inside the batter's box for his first plate appearance. He got a hit. "I was absolutely nervous as you should be at that point in your career," said Butler, who went 2-of-4 that day. "I'm still nervous when I go up there. It's one of those things that hopefully never goes away. That's the edge, the fire inside, wanting to do well, and help the team."

Butler, who has one of the purest swings you'll ever see, was born to be a hitter. In his slow Southern drawl (or as much of a Southern accent as you'd expect from someone from Jacksonville, Florida), he'll tell you matter of factly that he first realized he could play this game a long time ago. He was about 12 or 13 when colleges started contacting him. Butler, who was given the nickname "Country Breakfast" by some fans in 2011, eventually signed a letter of intent with one of those interested schools, the University of Florida. The Royals, of course, interrupted those plans when the club selected him with the 14th overall pick in the 2004 draft.

It looked immediately as if the Royals got what they needed. Butler was the Rookie of the Year in the Pioneer League in 2004 and then the California League Rookie of the Year in '05. In 2006 he won the Texas League batting title with a .331 average. The incredible part of the story is that he did those things before the age of 21. "The thing I like about Billy is that he has always been a hitter, so he knows what he's doing," said Frank White, who managed Butler at the Double A Wichita, Kansas, affiliate. "Then you listen to his comments when he comes back to the dugout and you know he follows the sequence of pitches and what the pitchers are trying to do."

One of those moments came early in his career. During his rookie season, the Royals played two series against the Detroit Tigers in a two-week span. In the second series with Butler scheduled to hit, the Tigers changed pitchers. Since they had used so many pitchers during the season, hitting coach Mike Barnett asked Butler if he knew anything about the pitcher. "Yeah, he throws about 92 or 93," Butler responded. "Last time he faced me in Kansas City, he threw me two sinkers in, a cutter away and then he hung a split that I hit back up the middle for a base hit."

In addition to his Yoda-like wisdom of the game that he passed along, White, who managed the Wichita Wranglers from 2004–06, made sure his players had an idea of life in the majors if they made it that far. "I wanted to talk to them a lot about being accountable, picking each other up, knowing how to walk into a major league clubhouse, and respecting the game and the guys before them," White said. "I wanted to teach them that there is a way to do things in this game and that they should carry themselves in that manner."

Butler was one of White's pupils for part of 2005 and all of '06. When Butler first made it to Wichita during his second season of professional baseball, he was a typical young player, trying so hard to continue advancing in the system. His youth and—frankly—immaturity would show up if he didn't like a call by an umpire or if he simply had a bad at-bat. "Oh, Billy and I had a lot of conversations," White said with a laugh. "We'd talk about his body language for instance when umpires would call a strike and how long it would take him to get back in the box between pitches. I tried to give him some ideas of what umpires in the big leagues think about rookies and the way players should ask questions about pitches instead of being so obvious about his displeasure for the

Billy Butler, who hit better than .300 during three of his eight seasons with the Royals, bats against the New York Yankees in 2013. (AP Images)

pitch." Then White paused and thought for a minute about Butler. "Really, he's just an awesome kid," White gushed.

In 2009 Butler became only the fifth player in major league history to record at least 50 doubles and 20 home runs in a season before turning 24 years old. He joined Hank Greenberg (1934), Alex Rodriguez (1996), Albert Pujols (2003), and Miguel Cabrera (2006) when he had 51 doubles and 21 homers—at the age of 23. Then in 2012 Butler was selected as the Silver Slugger Award winner at designated hitter in the American League. He was the seventh Royals player to win the award, joining George Brett (three times), Willie Wilson (twice), Hal McRae, White, Gary Gaetti, and Dean Palmer.

Because of various acquisitions and signings—not to mention the emergence of Eric Hosmer at first base—Butler became almost exclusively the club's designated hitter. In 2013 he appeared in all of the club's 162 games for the first time in his career. Regardless of where he plays, it suits Butler just fine. "I feel like I'm just another person playing this game, but to some fans you're way more than that," he said. "That's what the big leagues does for you. Some people never have a chance to make it to this level, which is why I'll never take it for granted."

Butler struggled throughout the 2014 postseason, going hitless in the American League Division Series against the Los Angeles Angels of Anaheim but then hit .333 (5-for-15) in the World Series. He signed with the Oakland A's as a free agent in November 2014.

50 Matthews Joins Broadcasting Legends

Picture this: enough people to fill Arrowhead Stadium crammed into the space of one of Kansas City's bigger high schools. That was what the scene looked like during Hall of Fame weekend in 2007 in Cooperstown, New York, a town of about 2,200, when the "Voice of the Royals," Denny Matthews, received the Ford C. Frick Award for broadcasting excellence in front of at least 75,000 people on July 29.

Sure, the majority of the fans were there to see Hall of Fame inductees Cal Ripken Jr. and Tony Gwynn. It didn't matter to Matthews; it was something to behold. "When the Hall of Famers walked onto the stage for the induction," Matthews said, "all of them gasped at the size of the crowd. When you hear guys—from the one who had seen the most inductions to this year's inductees—gasp, you know it's a special crowd."

Coincidentally, the previous record crowd of approximately 50,000 was in 1999 with the induction class that included George Brett. In addition to the record crowd of spectators, a record number of Hall of Famers (55) was there, including Brett.

When he thinks back to the weekend's pageantry, the Arrowhead Stadium analogy is very appropriate for Matthews, who was a standout wide receiver for Illinois Wesleyan in the 1960s. He's compared the Hall of Fame festivities to the week of a big football rivalry game. The talk and anticipation begins on Monday, builds throughout the week with the participants going through a wide range of emotions, and then everything culminates with "gameday." "I suppose I was nervous, sure, but it was a good nervous," Matthews said. "The anticipation, adrenaline, butterflies—all of that kept rising during that week."

You couldn't tell. As Matthews has displayed to Royals fans since he went on the air for the club's inaugural game in 1969, he delivered a speech that was silver-tongued, humorous, and appreciated history. After opening with memories of being 10 years old and listening to some of baseball's best broadcasters while lying next to the family's console radio, Matthews told his infamous Guy's snack foods story from 1970.

"We are in Milwaukee. We are coming up on the Fourth of July weekend holiday. So I remember the producer handed me a little card that said, 'Guy's Foods,' so I was supposed to think of a one-liner that would be timely and appropriate and so I said in a burst of brilliance, 'For those of you planning a party, make sure you take along plenty of those good Guy's potato chips.' It was kind of a slow game, and Al Fitzmorris was taking his time between pitches, and I thought, *You know what? That was pretty good. They are a good sponsor, so give it another shot.* And the next line out of my mouth was, 'And fans, while you're in the store, be sure and grab Guy's nuts,' at which point I thought my budding broadcast career was coming to a screeching halt."

The story, as always, brought plenty of laughs.

Matthews closed his speech by reading a letter he received years ago from Margaret Jenkins, a 93-year-old fan from western Kansas. Over the years the letter has reaffirmed to Matthews why he's broadcasting: for the fans. "Through your eyes and your words," Matthews read from the letter, "I feel like I'm sitting at the ballpark watching the game. Listening to the Royals is the highlight of my day. It gives me something to look forward to, so keep up the good work."

It was one of the few times during the 11-minute speech that Matthews got choked up. The other times were when he talked about his dad, George "Matty" Matthews, an All-American baseball player at Illinois State who passed away in 1985, and then when he addressed his three brothers—Steve, Doug, and Mike. "I was teamed with Carlton Fisk and Whitey Ford for the golf tournament on Saturday," Matthews said a few days after the ceremony, "and I talked to Fisk about [being emotional]...He said [the Hall of Famers] would wonder about me if I didn't get choked up."

Although Sunday's ceremony was the highlight for most fans, the weekend was full of activities for the Hall of Famers and award winners. Besides the Saturday morning golf tournament, there were celebration dinners on Friday and Saturday nights and a tour of the Hall of Fame museum with only Hall of Famers and family members after they were paraded through Cooperstown in open trolleys. Each event gave Matthews a chance to see many of the Hall of Famers he's known, mostly American Leaguers, such as Fisk, Yogi Berra, and Harmon Killebrew, who ended his career in 1975 with the Royals.

It also gave Matthews a chance to be 10 again as he met many of the players he admired as a child. Two of the more memorable were Sandy Koufax and Willie Mays. On the bus ride from the Hall of Famers' hotel to the ceremony at the Clark Sports Complex on Sunday, Matthews sat in front of Koufax and next to Mays. "I had heard that Willie was kind of sullen at times, but he turned out to be great and gave me a fascinating conversation during the 20-minute ride," Matthews said. "Among other topics, I asked him how he did as a player against Koufax. He said, 'Well, I hit four home runs against him, and he never threw breaking balls against me. Then one night in San Francisco he threw me a slider, and I hit a home run. The next day I went over and asked Sandy why he threw me a slider. He said he wanted to see if I could hit one.' I wish that ride was longer than a few miles."

Matthews, who isn't one to employ hackneyed phrases on or off the air, asks to pardon this expression to sum up the entire weekend that put his name alongside other great broadcasters such as Harry Caray, Jack Brickhouse, Ernie Harwell, and Joe Garagiola. "It was a once in a lifetime experience," he said. "That cliché is appropriate here. I will never ever experience anything like that weekend again. It was an unforgettable time. It was an honor for me to represent Kansas City fans and the Royals organization."

51 The 1983 Drug Scandal

Wins, losses, and a few bad apples aside, the Royals have been an organization built on class. It started with Ewing Kauffman and trickled down. For the most part, the players haven't acted like jerks or hell-raisers (at least not publicly). So when the news broke in 1983, every Royals fan couldn't help but be stunned.

Four players—Willie Wilson, Vida Blue, Jerry Martin, and Willie Aikens—became involved in a drug scandal. All served jail time during the offseason. Wilson was the only player who remained with the club. He served a 32-game suspension (an arbitrator reduced the season-long suspension originally handed down by commissioner Bowie Kuhn) before being selected as the Royals Player of the Year.

The story of the 1983 scandal has been told countless times. The behind-the-scenes part, however, has not. The Royals were in New York to play the Yankees when the players found out they were being investigated. The Royals player representative was Steve Renko, who received a call at the hotel from Marvin Miller, the executive director of the Major League Baseball Players Association. Miller told Renko they needed to meet. "I went over to the association's office and sat down with Marvin and Don Fehr," Renko said. "They told me that every ballclub had an FBI agent in its town looking into drugs. Marvin said that Kansas City was one of the worst places, which was a surprise to me."

That night Renko called a closed-door meeting with the team at Yankee Stadium. "I told them that if there was anything going on to let it go," Renko said, "because it wasn't going to end well." And it didn't. When the Royals returned to Kansas City after the series with the Yankees, Renko had a note on his chair in the clubhouse. It read: "Go to a pay phone and call Marvin."

"He gave me a list of guys and said to have them call him from a pay phone when they got to the clubhouse," Renko said. "I don't know what Marvin told them, but when they came back from talking to him, they were really somber and just sat in their chairs. It wasn't long after that the roof fell in. It was a rough time. I remember Amos Otis, who wasn't one of the guys who was supposed to call Marvin, was stopped by an FBI agent on the way to his car, and they searched him and his car. Amos went up to Mr. K, ranting and raving. It wasn't a good situation."

The year was a rough one all the way around for the Royals. The 1983 club finished with a 79–83 record, its first losing record (in a non-strike year) since 1974. The record, however, wasn't necessarily an indication that the drug allegations were a distraction. That was the year of Dennis Leonard's season-ending (and nearly career-ending) knee injury on May 28. George Brett broke his toe and was on the disabled list for three weeks. Later in the season, Wilson broke a knuckle. The people affected most by the drug scandal—besides the players involved—were Kauffman, John Schuerholz, and Dick Howser. "Mr. Kauffman was probably hurt by it more than anybody," said broadcaster Denny Matthews. "It wasn't only because this was happening to his franchise, but rather this was happening to his players."

"I think the situation really made Dick mad," said broadcaster Fred White, who was friends with Howser. "He felt that the players involved really let the other guys down, let everyone in the clubhouse down. Dick had a very great sense of honor about wearing that uniform and how you should act in the clubhouse and how the players had each others' backs. So he was angry that a guy in uniform could betray the other guys in the clubhouse with him."

As much of a black eye that the scandal put on the organization, at least temporarily, it might've helped lead the club to the joy of 1985—not to mention the playoffs in '84. Two young pitchers joined the club out of spring training in 1984: Mark Gubicza and Bret Saberhagen. They joined Danny Jackson, who was a September 1983 call up. Had it not been for the drug scandal, they might not have joined the club that early. "We stepped way outside of the box on our thinking with that," said Schuerholz, who was the general manager at the time. "We had no choice but to do that because of the horrible disruption caused in our organization. We knew we had talented young players. But the more we talked about it and evaluated internally what we needed to do to remedy our organization, to fix the organization, and to make our team better, we were drawn to our own talent because they were so talented—Mark Gubicza, Bret Saberhagen, Danny Jackson. They had great ability and a great makeup. Even though they were young of age, they were strong and competitive in spirit. We believed we could comfortably elevate those guys from Double A. We did it, and the rest is in the history books."

Those young pitchers, along with Bud Black and Charlie Leibrandt, would reinvigorate the franchise. "We needed them," said Royals Hall of Famer Paul Splittorff, who was in his final season with the Royals in '83. "We had gotten old, and the club needed to do something. Those guys were young and brash, but they were really good."

52 Tallis Tallies the Royals' Future

Amos Otis won't soon forget Cedric Tallis or his early impression of the club's first general manager. It was in spring training of 1970, the Royals' second-ever spring and Otis' first with the club. Otis, who was 22 at the time, came to the Royals from the New York Mets in exchange for Joe Foy. Even though he had left a World Series champion to join a second-year expansion club, Otis looked forward to the opportunity because he wanted to play in the outfield every day. Shoot, he just wanted to play regularly.

During a spring training game, Otis slid into second base. He couldn't get up. "I found out what kidney stones were all about," Otis said, laughing. "Cedric Tallis came by the hospital and told me not to worry about anything and that center field was mine."

Otis' anecdote speaks volumes about Tallis, who cared about the club's players, had a knack for acquiring talent, and knew what type of people he needed around him to make things work. He wasn't looking for yes men. "Cedric was a great guy for getting the best scouts he could to scout the opposition," said Art Stewart, whom Tallis and Lou Gorman hired from the New York Yankees. "He also was a great listener."

Tallis was an absolutely perfect general manager for the expansion Royals. "Cedric was a character. He was a big bull of a guy," said Bud Blattner, the first "voice" of the Royals. "It is very important that a GM be popular among other general managers. They are kind of a club. He was very, very popular. We were an expansion club, and Cedric could make deals that other GMs could not. He was very astute. We got Cookie Rojas, and nobody could have gotten him for what we got him for. Cedric was liked by the ballplayers, and the manager, and the coaches. He was fun to be around. He was a terrible driver. He would go 90 miles an hour in a 10 miles-an-hour zone. He was one of the few men I know to stand up to [Yankees owner] George Steinbrenner. He enjoyed life to the fullest."

In the Rojas deal Blattner mentioned, the Royals got Cookie from the St. Louis Cardinals for Fred Rico. In the Otis trade, which is likely the best in club history, the Royals also got Bob Johnson, a rookie pitcher, in exchange for Foy. Johnson struck out a Royals-high 206 batters in 1970 and then was part of a six-player deal in December that brought Fred Patek to Kansas City from the Pittsburgh Pirates.

Other Tallis-led deals included John Mayberry for Jim York and Hal McRae for Roger Nelson and Richie Scheinblum. In addition to those Royals Hall of Famers, Tallis also brought in dependable pitchers Steve Mingori and Marty Pattin in smaller deals. (It's probably best at this time to overlook the deal that sent Lou Piniella to the Yankees for Lindy McDaniel. But in all fairness, he did get Piniella from the Seattle Pilots for Steve Whitaker and John Gelnar.) Additionally, some of the players whom the Royals drafted and/or came up through the organization under Tallis include Paul Splittorff, Steve Busby, Dennis Leonard, and George Brett. In 1971 *The Sporting News* selected Tallis as baseball's executive of the year.

Tallis joined the Royals as the club's first general manager in 1968 after spending the previous seven years with the Los Angeles-California Angels as business manager and then vice president of operations. His main legacy there was overseeing the team's move to Anaheim and into a new stadium. Kansas City was attractive because of the prevailing thought that the Royals would move into a new stadium, which they did in 1973.

The Tallis regime, of course, wasn't perfect in Kansas City. Like most around the organization except for Ewing Kauffman, Tallis was openly against the experimental Royals Baseball Academy.

He opposed it so much that he held it against the Academy's top graduate, Frank White, who reached the majors in 1973.

In 1974 Tallis left the Royals to join the Yankees where he handled the rebuilding of Yankee Stadium. Then from 1980–82, Tallis served as the team's general manager. In 1983 the Tampa Bay Baseball Group hired Tallis as its managing director in an attempt to get a major league team (most notably the Minnesota Twins) to move to Tampa, an ultimately unsuccessful effort.

Tallis spent 43 years in professional baseball. On May 8, 1991, he suffered a heart attack and died in Tampa at the age of 76. But in many ways, Tallis still lives on with the Royals. The three people who followed Tallis as general manager—Joe Burke, John Schuerholz, and Herk Robinson—all worked in some capacity with Tallis. And current general manager Dayton Moore learned from Schuerholz with the Atlanta Braves.

As each year passes, it becomes easier to forget what an incredible impression Tallis left on this organization. But 10 of the Royals Hall of Fame players have direct ties to Tallis. "He was a fierce competitor," said Jack McKeon, whom Tallis hired to manage the Royals in 1973, to the Associated Press upon Tallis' death. "People don't give him as much credit as he should get. He was very much responsible for putting that Kansas City franchise together, and they had successful results in a short time."

53 Holland Cruises in '13

The Royals enjoyed something in 2013 they hadn't experienced in years: a dominant closer to finish off meaningful games. Sure, there was that Joakim Soria fella. He was great for the better part of five seasons, even saving 42 games in 2008—just shy of the single-season team record at the time of 45. He then added one to his total in 2010 when he saved 43. But completely out of Soria's control was how the team did when he wasn't on the field. The Royals finished 75–87 in '08 and 67–95 in '10.

Greg Holland, the Royals Pitcher of the Year in 2012, made the most of every save opportunity, saving a club-record 47 games in 2013. Nearly as impressive was the Royals record when Holland pitched. In his 68 appearances the Royals went 61–7. That includes two games early in the season when he entered the game with the Royals trailing. On May 12 the Royals lost 4–2 to the New York Yankees. About two weeks later on May 25, the Royals were in the midst of 7–0 loss to the Los Angeles Angels of Anaheim when Holland entered the game.

Besides his 47 saves, which were second in the American League to Baltimore's Jim Johnson's 50, Holland had a gaudy 1.21 ERA in 67 innings. Equally impressive was his strikeout-to-walk ratio, which featured a club-record for strikeouts by relievers with 103 to go along with 18 walks. His walks plus hits per innings pitched (WHIP) was 0.866, which was lower than the best seasons for Dan Quisenberry (0.928 in 1983) and Jeff Montgomery (0.989 in 1989) and just a notch higher than Soria's best (0.861 in 2008).

After he gave up one run in 15 innings and converted 11 of 12 save opportunities and helped keep the Royals in the wild-card chase, Holland was selected as the Major League Baseball Delivery Man of the Month for September. It was the second time Holland received the honor in 2013, showing that he could be well on his way to adding the Royals closer legacy of Quisenberry, Montgomery, and Soria.

Holland was even more dominant in 2014, when, as the last member of the "H-D-H" bullpen of Kelvin Herrera, Wade Davis, and Holland, he saved 46 games with a 1.44 ERA. During the post-season Holland saved six games, including all four in the American

League Championship Series, in eight appearances with a miniscule 1.13 ERA.

The Royals picked Holland in the 10th round of the 2007 MLB Amateur Draft out of Western Carolina University. He made his major league debut three years later with 15 appearances in 2010. En route to being selected as the club's top pitcher in 2012, Holland went 7–4 with 16 saves in 67 innings (67 games). He struck out 91 and walked 34. "Obviously, I've been somewhat successful, but winning ballgames is the main objective," Holland told Fox Sports Kansas City. "[You] can't really let things like that—records and stuff—enter your brain because you're thinking about the wrong things."

Late in the 2015 season, Holland's season came to an end because of elbow problems. He had Tommy John surgery in September, missing the club's run to the championship.

54 Monty Spells Relief

Jeff Montgomery forgets things quickly, and that's a good thing. "The biggest asset for a closer is a short memory," he said. "If things are going well, you don't need anything to boost you that day. If things are bad, you sure don't need anything to bring you down. You have to go out day after day and pitch to your strengths."

In reality Montgomery has a sharp mind that retains a lot of information. After all, the guy was a computer science major at Marshall University. Then the Cincinnati Reds picked him in the ninth round of the 1983 draft. Montgomery went on to pitch 12 years for the Royals and consistently got the three hardest outs in

Jeff Montgomery saved 304 games during his 12 years with the Royals.

a game more effectively and more often than anyone else in Royals history.

With a short memory and four top-shelf pitches, Montgomery became the Royals' all-time career saves leader with 304. "The way you pitch in the fifth, sixth, or seventh inning is going to be different than the way you pitch in the eighth and ninth inning," Montgomery said. "Please don't let anyone ever tell you that pitching the ninth inning is easier than pitching the sixth or seventh inning. I've tried both, and it's not. It's amazing, and I've never been able to figure out why it is, but those last three outs are the toughest."

The Royals acquired Montgomery from the Reds in exchange for Van Snider in February 1988. After making 14 appearances for Cincinnati (none in a save situation), Monty didn't appear in a uniform other than the Royals, a span of 12 years and 686 appearances. When asked about memorable outings, two significant ones stand out to Montgomery: his last save of 1993—which tied him with Dan Quisenberry as the club's single-season saves leader with 45—and career save No. 300 about six years later.

Montgomery had come close to saving 40 games before '93. He had 33 in 1991 and then 39 in '92. But in 1993—the last time before 2013 that the Royals won at least 84 games and the year before the strike-shortened season of '94—Montgomery tied for the American League lead with 45 to go with a 2.27 ERA and he won the Rolaids Relief Man award. At one point during the year, Monty converted 24 consecutive save chances.

Six years later and one night after blowing a save against the Baltimore Orioles, Montgomery demonstrated his short memory on August 25, 1999, racking up his 300th career save. After giving up two hits in the two-run game, Montgomery induced a groundball out from Albert Belle for his 300th save. The 37-year-old Montgomery, who at the time battled a hip issue, became the 10th player to reach 300 saves and the first to get all of his saves with one club.

55 Whitey Herzog

The manager, who had the most wins in the Royals' history from 1979 until Ned Yost took over the top spot in 2015, was Dorrel Norman Elvert Herzog…a.k.a. Whitey. Herzog took over the reins during the 1975 season when the organization needed a spark. By the end of the 1978 season, Herzog had guided the Royals to three straight American League West crowns. By the end of his final season with the Royals in 1979, Herzog's teams had won 410 games and compiled a .574 winning percentage.

What comes to mind when you think back to your days with the Royals?

Whitey Herzog: When we finally broke the ice, won a division title, and played the New York Yankees in 1976, I really felt good about that. We lost a tough playoff with the Chris Chambliss home run in the ninth inning of the fifth game, but I thought we had a tremendous year. It was rewarding for the fans of Kansas City because it was the first time they had won anything in Major League Baseball.

Our best team was in 1977. We started off 33–33, but ended up 102–60. We won 24 out of 25 during one stretch from August 31 to September 25 and won the division by seven games. [The Texas Rangers won 94 games.] We had the Yankees down two games to one, but we had some problems and ended up losing again in the ninth inning of the fifth game. It was a tough thing to lose.

Free agency had started, so each year the Yankees kept getting better by spending money for players like Reggie Jackson. They kept adding more power to their team. The Royals' policy at that time was to not sign any free agents. So by 1978 when we faced them again in the playoffs, they were a little bit better because they had added Rich "Goose" Gossage, which gave them him and Sparky Lyle in the bullpen.

What was the key to getting over the hump in '76?

WH: When I got here in June of 1975, we were about 15 games out of first place, behind Oakland. We ended up winning 91 ballgames and finished seven games out. We figured that we were going to have a pretty good run in 1976. Going into spring training, my players felt that way. We thought we had a great chance of winning. I stepped into the Royals job at a wonderful time. George Brett was a rookie, having a tremendous year. John Mayberry hit 34 home runs that season. Frank White and Al Cowens were on the bench, so I put both of them in the lineup, which was like making a major trade to get two stars without giving up anybody. White became an outstanding second baseman. Freddie Patek at shortstop was a tremendous player. With Mayberry, White, Patek, and Brett on the infield, we really had a great infield. Then, Cowens became great in right field; Amos Otis was an All-Star in center; then our left fielders of Tom Poquette, Jim Wohlford, and Joe Zdeb did a super job.

To me the biggest acquisition at that time was getting Darrell Porter before the 1977 season in a trade with Milwaukee. He was a tremendous ballplayer for us. Not only did he throw everybody out at catcher, he was a tough out at the plate. He did a lot of things on the ballfield to help us win that the average fan didn't notice.

Which season was more disappointing, 1976 or 1977?

WH: I don't think 1976 was a disappointment. It was a tough loss, but no one gave us much of a chance to do much that year anyway.

The 1977 team was the best team I've ever managed. Even though we won three pennants and a World Series in St. Louis and played some good defense, the 1977 Royals team was the best team I ever had. We had the Yankees down two games to one. That was a playoff we should have won.

It's amazing today to think the small-market Royals and large-market Yankees had a great rivalry back then.
WH: We played a balanced schedule back then and we could handle the Yankees pretty well during the season. I had a lot of left-handed pitching, and then Steve Mingori coming out of the bullpen pitched very well against New York. During the season we'd end up winning a bunch of the ballgames against them. But they had the best starting pitcher in baseball at that time, Ron Guidry, so in a five-game playoff series, he'd pitch twice against us. Then with Goose Gossage and Sparky Lyle in the bullpen, if they brought in one of them, they'd win. We were fortunate that we had great playoffs, but we lost three straight to them. After finishing three games out in 1979, I got fired, so I learned to never finish in second again.

You spent 10 successful years in St. Louis after leaving Kansas City. Of course, one of those years was 1985. Was it more difficult to lose a World Series to a franchise to which you were so connected?
WH: That World Series was great for the state of Missouri. It was a World Series where we didn't score any runs. The Royals pitching staff was outstanding. We only scored 13 runs in seven games. We should have won the World Series in six games, though, because we were leading 1–0 when we had that famous call at first. We self-destructed after that. If the runner had been called out at first—everybody knew he was out—the series would have been over.

56 All-Star Game Hosts

After 13 frustrating years with the Kansas City A's and a little more than four years with an infant—albeit improving—Royals franchise, Kansas City was proving to be a baseball town. Fans got a chance to display that affection on a national scale with a pair of events in 1973. Royals Stadium opened with its distinct and spacious design, artificial turf, and 12-story-tall scoreboard. Later that season on July 24, that new stadium and a city full of excitement for baseball, hosted the Major League Baseball All-Star Game. It was the second All-Star Game in Kansas City. (The first was at Municipal Stadium in 1960.) "Everywhere I went that year, people were excited for the new stadium and the fact that the All-Star Game was being played there," said Royals Hall of Fame outfielder Amos Otis. "On top of that, we were playing pretty good baseball that year. We were in second place at the break, so baseball excitement was all over the city."

Fellow All-Star representative John Mayberry agreed. "I'd go get my haircut or go to church or go to lunch with Buck O'Neil and Satchel Paige, and they'd talk about how excited they were," said Mayberry, a Royals Hall of Famer. "The whole town was really fired up."

As luck would have it, in the days leading up to the big game, it rained. And rained. And rained. It rained so much for a few days that officials were concerned whether the artificial turf would be dry enough to play. Even if the field was playable, the state-of-the-art scoreboard was struck by lightning during the storms and wasn't working. "Suddenly, just a few hours before the first pitch, the clouds rolled away, the grounds crew got the field squeegeed off, and it was a gorgeous night for baseball. You wouldn't have known that for four or five days and nights leading up to the game the rain was about as bad as it could've been," broadcaster Denny Matthews said. "Then about 45 minutes before the game, they got the scoreboard fixed. That was a wonderful turn of events."

It's a good thing because the 40,849 in attendance were in for a treat. The game featured 22 future members of the Baseball Hall of Fame—three managers, and 19 players—including Willie Mays, who was making his 24th and final All-Star Game appearance. The future of Hall of Famers were: Hank Aaron, Johnny Bench, Bert Blyleven, Rod Carew, Rollie Fingers, Carlton Fisk, Jim "Catfish" Hunter, Reggie Jackson, Mays, Joe Morgan, Brooks Robinson,

The 2012 All-Star Game

Kauffman Stadium and Kansas City hosted the 83rd All-Star Game. It marked the first time since 1973 that the All-Star Game was played in Kansas City. "It's about time is the first thing I'd say," legendary golfer and Kansas City native Tom Watson said. Kansas City received the distinction of hosting the 2012 game to commemorate the renovations to Kauffman Stadium. Billy Butler was the lone Royals player chosen to play in that game. He went hitless in two forgetful at-bats, as the AL took a tough 8–0 loss during a game in which former Royal Melky Cabrera earned MVP honors.

Even if Butler's All-Star Game appearance wasn't memorable, his non-appearance the night before will never be forgotten by Royals fans. Yankees second baseman Robinson Cano, the captain of the AL Home Run Derby squad, said that if Butler was an All-Star selection, he'd pick Butler for Monday's derby. Well, Butler did get the All-Star nod, but Cano didn't select him. And he heard about it, getting vehemently booed for two nights.

In contrast, every time Butler was shown on the Kauffman Stadium video board during the Home Run Derby and the All-Star Game, Royals fans went nuts. "I definitely feel like I get great support every night at the ballpark whenever we're here. That was something special," Butler said. "That was beyond anything you can expect. I was very grateful for everything the fans did for me the past couple days."

Nolan Ryan, Ron Santo, Tom Seaver, Willie Stargell, Don Sutton, Joe Torre, Billy Williams, Carl Yastrzemski, Sparky Anderson (National League manager), Whitey Herzog (American League coach), and Dick Williams (AL manager). And before the game, which marked the 40th anniversary of baseball's first midsummer classic, several members of the original 1933 All-Star teams were at the game, including Carl Hubbell, Lefty Gomez, Lefty Grove, and Charlie Gehringer.

Otis, Mayberry, and Cookie Rojas represented the Royals. Besides being the first appearance for the 23-year-old Mayberry, he started the game unexpectedly and played all nine innings in place of the selected starter, Dick Allen, who hurt his leg a few days earlier. "When I found out I was going to start, my heart skipped a beat," Mayberry said. "To be around those veteran greats and to have Willie Mays walk up to me before the game and start talking to me and the love they showed me as a young kid put me on top of the world."

Otis received enough votes to start the game along with fellow outfielders Bobby Murcer and Reggie Jackson. Murcer, also a center fielder, had more votes than Otis, so Murcer would start in center field. *Usually.* "Murcer walked up to me before the game and said, 'This is your town. You play center field,' which I thought was very admirable," Otis said appreciatively, even 40-plus years later. "We became good friends after that."

One highlight of the game, won 7–1 by the National League, was a monstrous home run by one of those future Hall of Fame players, Bench. In the fourth inning, Bench crushed a Bill Singer pitch over the left-field concourse. The estimated 480-foot shot remains the longest homer ever hit at Kauffman Stadium, according to the Royals. At the time there was a concession stand behind the section of seats, and the ball hit the roof of that stand.

Although Bobby Bonds, who hit his own blast of a home run, was selected as the game's Most Valuable Player, the AL star was

Otis, who went 2-for-2 with a stolen base and drove in the AL's lone run. (He's also the only AL player who got at least two hits in the game.) "Even though that game was in Kansas City, I wasn't nervous at all," Otis said. "It was just an honor for me to play against my idol [Hank Aaron] and to be on the same field with so many Hall of Fame players. To be able to do that in front of my hometown fans made it even more special."

Rojas, who replaced Carew at second base, walked during his lone plate appearance. Mayberry went 1-for-3 with a double and a walk. "When you think about a career, you can't really think about one game," Mayberry said. "But that one day, that one game, was one of the best moments in my life."

Otis made five All-Star teams, but he started only the '73 game. "Playing in the 1980 World Series is the highlight of my career," Otis said, "but right behind that is the 1973 All-Star Game. It's not because I started or because of the game I had; it's because it was in Kansas City."

57 Eat at Chappell's: A Bar, Restaurant, and Museum

As Jim Chappell walks around the restaurant, you'd swear he's running for office. He stops by a table of old friends and chats for a few moments before going to a table with six young business folks. And then he visits with a young family, handing Styrofoam baseballs with his likeness emblazoned in maroon to the two children.

It's funny that Chappell comes across as a politician. He's dabbled in politics, and his office walls are jammed with photos of him posing with a who's who of local and national politicians. And this restaurant began as a political and sports bar. Instead of politician, though, Chappell is the owner, host, and tour guide of this restaurant that bears his name. Chappell's (pronounced like the place of worship—not like some fancy joint that could be found on the Champs-Elysees) is at 323 Armour Road in North Kansas City, approximately 20 minutes from Kauffman Stadium.

Since opening in 1986—and quickly dropping the political aspect, thankfully—Chappell's has become one of the best sports museums in the Midwest. It also happens to house the greatest collection of Royals memorabilia outside the Royals Hall of Fame.

"I moved to Kansas City in 1968 between the A's leaving for Oakland and the first season for the Royals," Chappell said. "So I've been a fan since Day One and during that time I've been able to collect some things that Royals fans always enjoy seeing when they come in."

Among the Royals-related items inside the restaurant: Paul Splittorff's rookie jersey; a Dick Howser game-worn (and autographed) jersey from 1985; Bo Jackson's jersey; home plate from Municipal Stadium; a Howser-signed lineup card from the game on August 8, 1985; and countless autographs, photographs, pennants, steins, and original bobbleheads from 1969 and the early '70s. Besides the Royals memorabilia, though, it's been common throughout the years to see former Royals at the restaurant. On any given day, one might see Dennis Leonard, Fred Patek, George Brett, John Wathan, Willie Wilson, or Frank White to name a few. That's not to mention the players who have been there for various radio broadcasts and Royals alumni meetings. "This is a great place. I'm really impressed," said Texas Rangers announcer and Royals Hall of Fame pitcher Steve Busby, who was at the restaurant for a radio show while visiting Kansas City with the Rangers. "The varied exhibits [Chappell] has in here are incredible. I could spend days in here, looking at this stuff. A lot of this stuff jogs my memory as a kid and watching a lot of these guys play not to mention guys from my era and after. It's really a fantastic place."

Chappell's is one of those places where you could visit hundreds of times and be fascinated by a new photograph or trinket each time—even if it's been in the same place for years. It might be Tom Watson's putter; the signed photograph of baseball legends Jackie Robinson and Satchel Paige posing in Monarch uniforms; a bat signed by Brooks Robinson; the 1973 Oakland A's World Series trophy; Paul Hornung's Heisman Trophy; or baseballs signed by the likes of Babe Ruth, Lou Gehrig, and Ty Cobb. Then there are the football helmets on the ceiling. Chappell said there are thousands of helmets and somehow he can lead you to the one from your college or favorite NFL team. "You can walk around Chappell's and find memorabilia for just about any sports and definitely every local team. You name it, it's here," Leonard said. "On the flip side, if you want a good meal, you go to Chappell's. Besides the artifacts and food, though, Jim Chappell is always courteous and polite—a fun guy to be around."

Chappell's has gained national attention and popularity. *Sports Illustrated* selected the restaurant a few years ago as one of the top 10 sports bars in America. So did the *Chicago Tribune*. Even non-Royals celebrities have made sure they've stopped by Chappell's during trips to Kansas City. Dave Winfield, Marcus Allen, artist LeRoy Neiman, and country singer Vince Gill have eaten here along with other regulars such as Hank Bauer, Len Dawson, Joe Montana, and Chiefs founder Lamar Hunt, who used to take his guests on tours of the restaurant. "When I opened I didn't know anybody outside of North Kansas City would have any idea this place existed," said Chappell, who graduated from Drury University, the same alma mater as Royals President Dan Glass. "I never thought that people, especially celebrities, would seek it out."

But they have. So whether it's an early dinner stop on the way to Kauffman Stadium or a work lunch (though you might need an "extended" lunch to walk around the restaurant), Chappell's is a must for any Royals fan. "If you want to see incredible sports memorabilia in the Kansas City area, this is the place to be. And the food is great here, too," Patek said. "This is a landmark. It's worth your while to spend time just walking around to look at the things on the wall and read the different articles. This place is unique."

58 Colborn's Unlikely No-Hitter

Three Royals have thrown no-hitters: Steve Busby, Bret Saberhagen, and Jim Colborn. Wait, *Jim Colborn*?

Colborn's no-hitter, though, was the first thrown by a Royals pitcher at Kauffman Stadium. A 20-game winner with the Milwaukee Brewers in 1973, he had a career record of 61–62 in eight seasons when the Royals acquired him as part of the five-player trade that brought catcher Darrell Porter to Kansas City in exchange for Jamie Quirk, Jim Wohlford, and Bob McClure before the 1977 season. Colborn was an innings eater who had thrown at least 200 in his previous four seasons with the Brewers, including 314⅓ in '73. (By comparison James Shields threw 228⅔ innings in 2013.) Colborn was a solid pitcher; he just didn't necessarily have electric stuff—let alone no-hitter stuff.

He was now pitching, however, for a club that was coming off its first American League West title and was in the midst of its only 100-win season (102–60). So he had a defense behind him that could salvage a no-hitter along with an offense that could score runs. "There's no doubt it was one of the best teams in baseball, even though we didn't get to the World Series," Colborn said. "We won more than 100 games, but maybe we just didn't have the experience to get through that last inning in the playoffs against the New York Yankees. It was a loose, good-natured group with great guys such as Amos Otis, John Mayberry, George Brett, Fred Patek, Frank White, Dennis Leonard, and Paul Splittorff. We all came together pretty well—even the coaches. It was really a fun group to be around."

When Colborn took the mound on Saturday, May 14 at then-Royals Stadium against the Texas Rangers, he didn't feel particularly good. He was coming off two bad outings, a 6–3 loss to the Chicago White Sox on May 4 and a 5–3 loss to the California Angels on Monday. In both games he'd given up nine hits.

Colborn didn't follow his normal routine that day. That's a no-no for most starting pitchers. As a favor to a friend, he made an appearance at a kids' baseball clinic that afternoon, and that might have had a weird benefit. "I seemed to have very peak concentration for some reason before the game," Colborn said. "I remember shagging balls in the outfield during batting practice, and it looked like they were moving in slow motion. Other than that my stuff wasn't any different. I was very relaxed from going to that clinic and I had really sharp focus."

Texas was a strong offensive ballclub with the likes of Claudell Washington, Bert Campaneris, Mike Hargrove, and Toby Harrah, but they couldn't find an answer for Colborn. They didn't get their first base runner until the fifth when Colborn hit Harrah. By that time he was gaining more confidence. "In about the third inning," he said, "I looked up and noticed they didn't have any runs or hits and I said to myself somewhat sarcastically, *It's about time you did something.*"

Texas had only one other base runner in the game when Jim Sundberg (a future Royals player) led off the top of the sixth with a walk. In the top of the seventh with the Royals leading 4–0, Campaneris blooped a ball toward center field. Al Cowens, playing center, charged in and caught the ball at his knees. "You could see the determination he had in going after it," Colborn said. "When he caught it, I thought to myself that they were trying extra hard out there to see a no-hitter."

The Royals added two more runs in the eighth and went on to win 6–0. Coincidentally, Colborn's battery mate was Porter, the player who joined him in the trade from Milwaukee. Porter was one of five Royals with two hits that night. He had a double and a triple, scored once, and had one RBI.

Did the no-hitter and his new pregame routine give Colborn confidence five days later against the White Sox? "It completely messed me up," he said. "It was so outside of the concept I had of myself that I changed my routine. Normally I'd rest and focus on the start during the day of a start. Because of the no-hitter, I thought I didn't have to do that. So my next start was in Chicago, and I went out, walked around the streets of the city, and I don't think I ever really got myself focused." In the bottom of the first with two outs, the Sox's Jorge Orta (who would end his career with the Royals) homered. Colborn lasted only two and two-thirds innings as he gave up five hits and six runs. Chicago won the game 8–3.

Colborn went 18–14 that season for the Royals. His 20-win season was the only other time in Colborn's 10-year major league career that he finished with a winning record. After eight appearances in 1978 (including three starts), the Royals traded Colborn to the Seattle Mariners for Steve Braun.

59 Battle Royales

Many fans might look at the early part of the 2015 season, when the Royals were having some…um…issues with a few opponents, ending in minor skirmishes, and forget about some of the more

Ganging Up on Gamboa

This wasn't a fight among players, per se, but the Royals bench cleared, ready to help one of its own on September 19, 2002, in Chicago.

After yelling insults at Royals first-base coach Tom Gamboa all night, shirtless 34-year-old William Ligue Jr. and his 15-year-old and equally shirtless son, William III, stormed the field at Comiskey Park in the seventh inning, threw the 54-year-old Gamboa to the ground, and started punching and kicking him. Along with the Royals in the dugout, the bullpen rushed in from right field to help Gamboa. Several players jumped on the fans, and punches were exchanged.

Although there's no question the Ligue "men" were yelling at Gamboa, they contended that Gamboa made an obscene gesture and "got what he deserved." *Stay classy, Chicago White Sox fans.* Security took Ligue and his son off the field in handcuffs while trainers attended to Gamboa, who had blood streaming from his forehead. Gamboa, though, was smiling and laughing as he got more treatment in the dugout. But Gamboa suffered permanent hearing loss in his right ear because of the incident. The following season he was moved to bullpen coach and then he was let go after the 2003 season. He didn't coach in the major leagues again.

After being charged with three counts of aggravated battery and one count of mob action, Ligue apologized to a grand jury on October 11, 2003. He and his son amazingly got off with just 30 months of probation without any prison time. They, however, would find their way back into trouble. The elder Ligue was sentenced to five years in prison in 2006 for breaking into a car, which was a violation of the probation he received for attacking Gamboa. The younger Ligue served time for a 2010 drug charge.

heated battles throughout the Royals' history. The club has certainly had its share of base-brawls throughout its history, most notably one in Oakland before the Royals clinched their first division title. Dennis Leonard was on the mound for the Royals in September 1976, when a pitch "slipped" out of his hand and hit Don Baylor of the A's. *Big mistake.* "I really did try to hit him because they had hit two home runs off us, but I kind of lost the

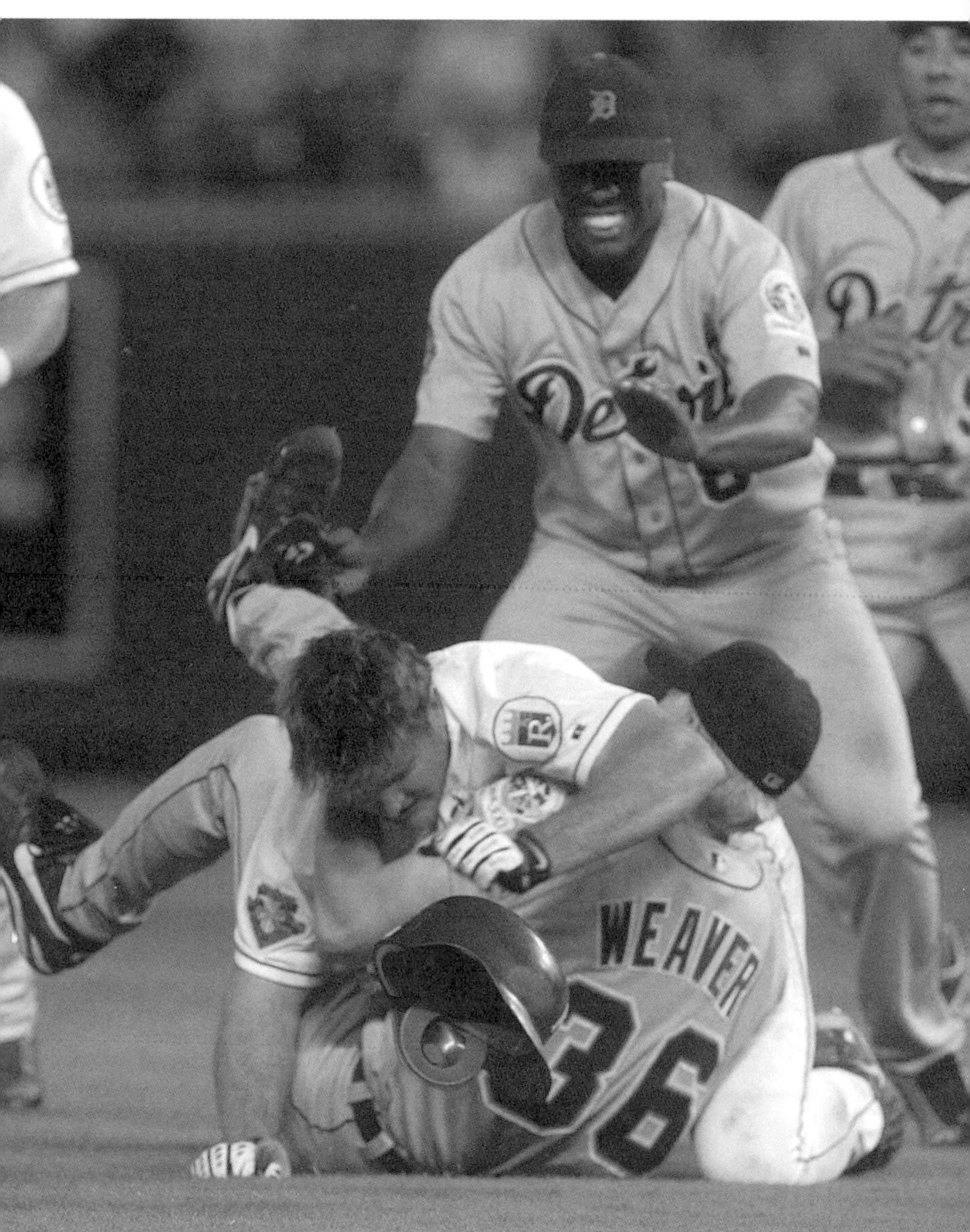

Though known as one of the nicer guys in sports, Mike Sweeney tackles Detroit Tigers pitcher Jeff Weaver on August 10, 2001, one of several notorious brawls in Royals history. (AP Images)

grip a little bit and hit him between the shoulder blades," Leonard said. "I don't think he would've come out toward the mound, but the home-plate umpire jumped in front of Baylor and I think that kind of incited him a little bit, and he started looking at me. Immediately I realized that hitting him might not have been a good career decision."

Catcher Buck Martinez tried to get in front of Baylor to block him from going toward Leonard, but Baylor picked up Martinez and moved him out of the way. Sensing he was in trouble, Leonard ran toward the dugout—the A's dugout. "That was not the smartest thing I'd done in my career, either," Leonard said, laughing. "The next thing I know, there's all of this green and gold—a whole line of them—starting with Gene Tenace, who was wearing his catcher's gear. He swung and missed when I ducked. The next thing I know, Phil Garner grabbed me, and I found myself on the bottom of a big pile. All hell broke loose after that. I got thrown out of the game." Said Amos Otis: "That fight went on for what seemed like forever. That night was a mess."

Later in the game, a mini-melee commenced near the Kansas City bullpen. Fans were coming down to take swings at Kansas City players—namely Doug Bird, Tom Bruno, and Hal McRae, who was swinging at fans with an umbrella.

As bad as that night was, though, it didn't compare to the brawl between the Royals and the Rangers in Texas in May of 1977. And once again Leonard happened to be pitching for Kansas City. This fight actually began brewing in Kansas City earlier. Leonard hit a Texas batter, and then Bert Blyleven hit Royals catcher Darrell Porter. When the series shifted to Texas, further chaos would ensue.

With Bump Wills on third base, Leonard threw a pitchout, looking for a possible squeeze. Porter got Wills in a rundown before he was tagged out near third base by George Brett. Porter and Wills exchanged pleasantries and then went at it—and at it. The fight lasted about 15 to 20 minutes. "Willie Horton, who was wearing a nylon jacket under his jersey, kept coming back to the pile," Leonard said. "I'm not sure what prompted George to do this, but I saw him grab a hold of Horton by the shirt and rip it off. That wasn't smart. Willie's eyes just shot out. He was not happy. All of that was ugly. There were fights everywhere."

In July of 1987, the Royals and Cleveland Indians fought in back-to-back games. On the first night, Cleveland pitcher Ken Schrom threw a pitch near the head of Willie Wilson. After Wilson flew out, he rounded first and then went after Schrom, clearing the benches. On the next night, Royals starter Danny Jackson threw his first pitch of the first inning behind Brett Butler. After a warning from the umpires, Jackson's next pitch went over Butler's head. Butler charged the mound, punched Jackson, and the teams jumped out of the dugout.

And, of course, who could forget the competitive—but usually genteel—Mike Sweeney tackling Detroit pitcher Jeff Weaver at Kauffman Stadium in August 2001? The skirmish began when Sweeney got ready to bat in the sixth inning and asked umpire Mike Fichter to have Weaver move the resin bag from a distracting spot on the top of the mound. Weaver, according to Sweeney, then said something profane. Sweeney threw his batting helmet at the pitcher and rushed the mound. Numerous punches were thrown as the benches and bullpens cleared, resulting in a 12-minute delay. (Another fight occurred during the same game with Sweeney and Tigers catcher Robert Fick getting into it.) In terms of being memorable during pennant-winning seasons, however, the ones in 1976 and '77 were two of the worst in team history.

60 Blattner Hires Denny Matthews

As the first radio "voice" of the Royals, Buddy Blattner was the first link between the team and its fans. By the time the Royals hired Blattner, he was established as one of the great radio broadcasters, doing local and national work. As with Cedric Tallis, Blattner was working for the then-California Angels before joining the Royals. Besides serving as the Royals' first broadcaster through 1975, Blattner also happens to be the main person responsible for the Royals hiring an unknown kid—at least not known outside Bloomington, Illinois—named Denny Matthews before the 1969 season. Blattner, who lived in Missouri most of his adult life, passed away in 2009 at the age of 89.

What made you want to leave the Angels and join the expansion Royals?

Buddy Blattner: Cedric Tallis was a friend of mine and he resigned as the stadium director of the Angels to become the GM of the Royals. He then met with Ewing Kauffman about what was going to happen next and he suggested that I become their lead announcer. They contacted me, and then I talked to Gene Autry, who was a wonderful boss in California. It was tough to leave, but I wanted to get back to the Midwest. I knew so many of the gentlemen involved in the Royals organization. The Royals became competitive from the get-go with a cast of characters such as Lou Piniella. Then, it was a joy moving into the new ballpark in 1973. It's still a very beautiful spot. During my stay we didn't win a pennant, but we were a competitive and an interesting club.

Besides being a terrific first "voice" for the Royals, you're responsible for Denny Matthews getting the job as the No. 2 guy, which eventually led to him taking over for you. Why did you hire someone so inexperienced?
BB: That's one of the reasons I chose Denny Matthews to be my partner: he had no experience whatsoever. People shook their heads when I picked him because he had done a couple college games, but that was about it. What he had done, though, was a Chicago game—I don't remember if it was the Cubs or White Sox—and he did it live at the stadium. After seeing his resume and hearing his tape, I invited him to my house in St. Louis. We sat down in the bar room and had a chat. I told him what I would expect. He very much liked baseball. He was a reasonably good athlete. He had an utterly fantastic memory. He would say, "Do you remember that game in Milwaukee two years ago in July?" No, I didn't remember it; I barely remember being in the town. He had a talent for remembering.

But you weren't concerned about his lack of broadcasting experience?
BB: For one thing, that meant he didn't have any bad [broadcasting] habits to break…I didn't try to mold him at all. I just told him certain things that I thought he should do. Denny was quick. He would make a mistake, realize it, but just keep going on. I said, "Denny, if you make a mistake and you know it, just say 'oops!' You're going to have hundreds of thousands of people who are listening, and that's all they have to do. If you just keep going without recognizing the mistake, they'll think you didn't even realize you made a mistake. That's bad. There's nothing wrong, with the thousands of words you'll say during the season, to occasionally misspeak." From there on out, he'd meld it in when he made a mistake. People love you when you point out you made a mistake.

One of his biggest mistakes was when he delivered the infamous line for Guy's Foods: "When you're in the store, be sure to grab Guy's nuts." He was convinced his career was over.

BB: I had a local show presented by Guy's Foods, and Guy Caldwell thought Denny's mistake was funny. But I told Denny that things like that happen. All you do is say something and let it go. Then everybody laughs. Denny learned quickly that there are people that rely on your broadcast every day. This gives them three hours that they enjoy.

Fans are looking for you to come into their homes, caress them with a broadcast. Denny always appreciated and understood that. It was a joy for my wife, Babs, and me to see this young man grow up. He was a college, rah-rah kid when he got to Kansas City. He didn't force himself on people. He was quiet, in the background. He would ask certain questions, but he knew what to do and he did it. I loved him for that.

61 Visit Municipal Stadium and Eat at Bryant's

It's hard to believe that this is actually the place. It looks so different now—just a smattering of newer homes and a stone and metal sign that reads, "Monarch Manor." It's quiet on this summer afternoon. There's no construction on this swath of open space. But Lincoln High School—where Royals Hall of Famer Frank White used to stand atop the football field's bleachers with his friends to catch a glimpse the baseball action—does sit a couple hundred yards away. White's childhood home also is just a few blocks away as is the 18th and Vine District. And the aroma of Arthur Bryant's has made its way up here. If you didn't stop to look, it would be easy to miss the nondescript brick walkway of the "Monarch Plaza" with some nondescript black and white photos of former baseball and football players. But this is the site—22nd and Brooklyn—of the old Municipal Stadium, the Royals' original home.

This is where it all began for Major League Baseball in Kansas City in 1955, when the Philadelphia Athletics moved west and called this place home. Although professional baseball had been played at this site for decades, the combination of the stadium's location, Major League Baseball coming to Kansas City, and the forethought of Charlie Bryant to move Arthur Bryant's just up the road to 17th and Brooklyn in 1958 helped put the restaurant on a national map. So grab a beef sandwich and french fries from Arthur Bryant's and head to the site of old Municipal Stadium to imagine what it was like when Major League Baseball began in Kansas City.

Known for its vinegar and paprika-tasting sauces, Bryant's is one of the most famous barbecue restaurants in the country. Luminaries including Steven Spielberg, Jack Nicholson, Bryant Gumbel, and presidents Harry Truman and Jimmy Carter have sampled the brisket burnt ends, ribs, and fries. While playing at Municipal Stadium, both the A's and the Royals made regular visits to Arthur Bryant's—*even during a game*. Pitcher Moe Drabowsky would order ribs from Bryant's (or have equipment manager Al Zych do so). Bryant's was located for many years at 18th and Euclid Streets—four blocks away from the stadium—before it moved to 1727 Brooklyn. But the unpretentious décor—Formica tables, fluorescent lighting, and bottles of sauce placed in the windows—remains intact.

In April 1955 Kansas City joined the ranks of Major League Baseball thanks largely to a poor team in Philly and a Chicago businessman named Arnold Johnson, who didn't intend on becoming a major league owner. Several years before moving the A's, Johnson wanted to purchase Yankee Stadium from his friends, Del Webb and Dan Topping. But the two men insisted that Johnson also buy their Triple A stadium, Blues Stadium, in Kansas City. Johnson acquiesced and, unwittingly, pushed Kansas City toward becoming a major league city. After unsuccessful attempts by Connie Mack, his family, and several Philadelphia businessmen to keep the Athletics from moving, Johnson changed his tune in the winter of 1954 and purchased the Athletics for a reported $3.5 million. The only major piece left in Kansas City was preparing Municipal Stadium, which also had been occupied by the Monarchs of the Negro Leagues.

In 22 weeks the stadium essentially was rebuilt. A second deck was added, and Johnson purchased the old Boston Braves Field scoreboard for $100,000 and put it in right-center field.

During that 1955 season, the Kansas City Athletics drew a whopping 1,393,054 fans, a far cry from the 304,666 in their final season in Philadelphia. The attendance in '55 was the largest ever in the history of Municipal, including the Royals' four seasons there. "The desire for us to go to the ballpark wasn't as strong in Philadelphia as it was in Kansas City," said Art Ditmar, who led the A's in wins in 1955 and '56 with 12 each season. "The new Municipal was great, but it was greater having people in the stands."

New home or not, the change of cities didn't make a big difference to the Athletics' opponents. It still was the team that went 51–103 in '54. "Sure, we felt confident that we could beat them," said Hank Bauer, who was a key player for the Yankees during 1948–59 before finishing his career with the Kansas City A's in 1961.

For the A's, though, it was a brand new experience. They responded by beating the Detroit Tigers on Opening Day. They won 62 more times that season while losing 91. The team finished sixth in the American League (out of eight teams). They never finished above .500 and they lost 90 games or more in nine of their 13 seasons.

There, however, were some memorable moments and characters led by the eventual top man, Charlie O. Finley, who bought 51 percent of the club in December 1960. An insurance broker by trade, Finley was a true hands-on—and eccentric—owner. His antics included using a mule as team mascot, a mechanical rabbit that brought baseballs to the home-plate umpire, sheep in right field, and a petting zoo. "I liked to hit fungos to our right fielder before the game and hit them as far as I could to see if I could hit some sheep," joked Drabowsky, the opening day pitcher in 1965 who pitched for both the A's and the Royals. "I felt sorry for the shepherd who had to tend to the sheep. He wore a toga, and his head was wrapped up. Imagine how hot that was. He used to get something like $10 per game to tend to those sheep. On doubleheaders he thought he should've gotten $20, and he told Charlie that. During the next doubleheader, I noticed that he wasn't there. We never saw the shepherd again. I guess Charlie didn't think he deserved $20."

Some of the other players who played in Kansas City include Norm Siebern, Charley Lau, Reggie Jackson, Satchel Paige, and Bert Campaneris, who played all nine positions in one 1965 game. After a failed attempt to move the team to Dallas five years earlier, Finley closed shop at Municipal and moved the Athletics to Oakland following the 1967 season.

Two years later, the anti-Finley, Ewing Kauffman, bought the expansion Royals. They occupied the same Municipal Stadium—and ordered the same Arthur Bryant's—for four years and quickly won over the hearts of the forlorn Kansas City fans.

62 From Cy Young Award to Free-Agent Bust

Before you laugh, gasp, or roll your eyes after reading the next sentence, keep in mind that not everything that happened while he was with the Royals was his fault. Here you go: Mark Davis has been a longtime pitching coach in the Royals' farm system.

During his playing days, Davis came to Kansas City a year after he won the National League Cy Young Award with 44 saves and a career-best 1.85 ERA for the San Diego Padres. Yet during his two-plus seasons with the Royals from 1990–92, Davis compiled a 9–13 record with seven saves in 95 games. To many people he remains one of the biggest busts in Royals history. "Overall I just didn't pitch consistently," he said. "You put more pressure on yourself when you're not doing well. Plus coming to a new team and getting the contract that I signed added to me pressing a little."

Oh, yes, a mention of Mark Davis with the Royals usually isn't made without referencing his $14-million contract. He was baseball's fourth $3 million man with the first, future Hall of Famer Kirby Puckett, signing a contract a few weeks earlier. "I'd always just played the game of baseball because I enjoyed it," Davis said. "When I was [with the Royals,] I felt like I had to justify what I was making instead of just pitching. I was afraid to fail. The game became more of a business. I didn't make that adjustment as well as I needed to. I'm saying that looking back, of course. As a player you don't realize you're putting pressure on yourself."

Davis, who's kept a home in the Phoenix/Scottsdale area since 1983, signed with the Royals largely to move his family to the Midwest. It also didn't hurt that the Royals were coming off one of their best seasons. They won 92 games in 1989, their highest win total since 1980. Bret Saberhagen won the AL Cy Young in '89, meaning the club would feature each league's Cy Young winner in 1990.

Instead of playing better, though, the Royals won their lowest number of games—75—since 1970 and finished sixth in the division. Much of the fans' ire was directed toward Davis. "That bothered me a lot at the time," Davis said. "Although I probably tried to do too much at times, I couldn't have done any more."

The Royals traded Davis to the Atlanta Braves during 1992. He then played for the Philadelphia Phillies and Padres before three surgeries to his elbow and shoulder sidelined him for most of 1994 and all of '95 and '96. He came back and pitched in 19 games for the Milwaukee Brewers in 1997. He went to spring training in 1998 with the Arizona Diamondbacks but realized quickly that he didn't have his stuff anymore. He finished his career with 96 saves and 1,007 strikeouts.

Davis was the pitching coach in Surprise during 2006–10. He was the organization's minor league pitching coordinator in 2011 and then returned to coaching in Surprise in 2012. "I don't think what you do in a career means that you can or cannot teach," Davis said. "I've gone from the top of the baseball heap to the bottom of the baseball heap, which I can use as a teaching tool. Going through some things and having the surgeries and learning to throw again has given me more ammo to help guys."

Although that proverbial 20-20 hindsight can remind a person of roads not taken, Davis doesn't have any regrets about signing with the Royals in 1989. "I could've been the same type of pitcher anywhere else," he said, "or I might've done better somewhere else. But if I would've picked another place for different reasons, it would've bothered me because I would've wondered later why I didn't go where I really wanted to be, Kansas City. You're sent different places in the path of your life, and Kansas City was the right place for me to go."

63 Missed Opportunities: 1994 and 2003

When looking at the Royals' barren playoff years between 1985 and 2014, there have been two seasons—excluding 2013—when it seemed as if the club might have a legitimate shot of reaching the postseason: 1994 and 2003. Of course, it didn't happen either season. One was out of the Royals' control; the other wasn't.

1994: The Strike

Some Royals from the 1994 team will tell you that the club would have been headed for the playoffs if it hadn't been for the strike that wiped out the season. "Tonight would have been Game 3 in Kansas City, and I'd have rather been pitching that game," David Cone said when he received the Cy Young award at the end of October 1994. "I don't think it's too far-fetched to think the Royals had a legitimate shot to be there."

It's easy to understand the optimism. Prior to the season-ending players' strike, the Royals had a 14-game winning streak under manager Hal McRae. Bob Hamelin won the Rookie of the Year award—the first for the Royals since Lou Piniella in 1969—and Cone's Cy Young campaign included a 16–5 record and 2.94 ERA. The club's rotation also featured Tom Gordon (11–7 that year), Kevin Appier (7–6), and Mark Gubicza (7–9). The Royals finished the season with a 64–51 record. They would not finish with a winning record until 2003.

2003: Quick Start Fades Away

With Tony Pena at the helm, the Royals got off to a hot start in 2003, winning their first nine games and holding to first place in the division for 107 days. They began to fade, though, in late

August and couldn't hold on. They finished the season with an 83–79 record.

"Everything clicked. We had a great manager with Tony Pena. We had a great minor league system," said Mike Sweeney, who hit .293 with 83 RBIs that year. "We had a group of players who loved each other. It was like we had bought a new house and put in new furniture, but coming down the stretch we went to bed. We ran out of gas and didn't finish the race. We limped toward the finish line instead of sprinting to the finish line."

The Royals season also may have featured some smoke and mirrors, benefitting from feasting on a historically bad divisional opponent, the 43–119 Detroit Tigers, whom the Royals went 14–5 against. In addition to the boost provided by a woeful Tigers team, the Royals did have several notable performances that year—particularly early in the season. The year featured Dos Carlos—second baseman Febles and center fielder Beltran, who hit. 307. Pitcher Runelvys Hernandez started 4–0 before finishing 7–5, and closer Mike MacDougal didn't give up an earned run in his first nine games before finishing with 27 saves.

Pena was selected as Manager of the Year, and Angel Berroa was the Rookie of the Year in 2003. It also represented the last time the Royals finished above .500 until 2013.

64 The Damon-Beltran-Dye Outfield

For a brief period around the turn of the century, the Royals outfield was one of the best in all of baseball. Beginning in 1999 the Royals started a 25-year-old Johnny Damon in left field, a 22-year-old Carlos Beltran in center, and a 25-year-old Jermaine Dye in right. That season the trio led every other outfield in the big leagues with 552 hits, 110 doubles, 24 triples, 304 RBIs, and 41 assists. They were second in runs with 309.

The oldest of the group by a little more than two months was Damon, whom the Royals picked in the first round (35th overall) of the 1992 draft. By the time he made his debut in 1995 at the age of 21, the Royals thought they were looking for their next superstar. As Ken Brett once said: "There's nothing as damning as unlimited potential." Damon faced that along with the tag of being the next George Brett. "Johnny was a victim of other people's expectations," former broadcaster Fred White said.

Damon responded, though, with decent numbers during his early career, gradually improving offensively. By his last season in Kansas City in 2000, he was batting .327. Defensively? Well, that was a different story. He was good with the glove, but pretty much anyone could (and would) run against Damon's arm. He, though, gradually got better there.

Beltran was a Royals second-round pick in 1995 who made his debut in 1998 at the age of 21. In his first full season in 1999, he hit .293 with 194 hits, 22 home runs, and 108 RBIs, which garnered him the Rookie of the Year award. Once Beltran came up and took over center field, Damon moved to left, which was a better fit.

The Atlanta Braves drafted Dye in the 17th round of the 1993 draft. He came to Kansas City in 1997 as part of the deal that sent Keith Lockhart and Michael Tucker to Atlanta. He went to his natural position of right field where he won a Gold Glove in 2000 after fighting through injuries during his first two years in Kansas City.

Unfortunately, reality began to set in that the small-market Royals weren't going to sink enough into salaries to keep all three. Before the 2001 season, Damon was part of a three-team trade that brought Angel Berroa, A.J. Hinch, and Roberto Hernandez

Carlos Beltran, who robs Jason Varitek of an outfield hit in 1999, was part of a star-studded outfield also featuring Johnny Damon and Jermaine Dye. Sadly, the Royals would trade away all three players. (AP Images)

to Kansas City. Six months later Dye was part of a three-team trade that brought Neifi Perez to the Royals. Alas in June 2004, another three-team deal sent Beltran to the Houston Astros while the Royals received Mark Teahen, Mike Wood, and John Buck. "When I first came up as a Royal, I felt like I wanted to end my career as a Royal, but this game has changed so much," Beltran told Fox Sports Midwest. "Right now it's a big business, and I knew if we didn't get something done, I was going to be traded."

Damon went on to win two World Series rings, one as one of the leaders of the "idiots" for the Boston Red Sox and another with the New York Yankees. Dye, who had been on one of Atlanta's losing World Series teams before joining the Royals, won a ring and a World Series MVP with the Chicago White Sox in 2005. Known for his clutch postseason heroics, Beltran played in the postseason for Houston, the New York Mets, and St. Louis. He went to his first World Series with the Cardinals in 2013. "I look back and I remember the times I was here when Johnny was in left field and Jermaine was in right field," Beltran said. "One of those years we led the league in assists, but the problem here always was they couldn't keep everyone together. I really enjoyed my time. I was able to be around so many good ballplayers and good friends, and we still stay in contact."

65 "Big" John Mayberry

The booming, gregarious voice is the same. So is the infectious laugh. But as much as anything else, the love of baseball is still there for "Big" John Mayberry, who was one of the first great sluggers for the Royals in the early 1970s. After being acquired in a trade with the Houston

Astros, Mayberry spent six seasons with the Royals from 1972–77. He belted 25 home runs and drove in 100 runs during his first season in Kansas City. Mayberry averaged 24 home runs during his career with the Royals. His best campaign came in 1975 when he became the club's first 30-home run hitter, knocking out 34 homers and driving in 106.

What do you think of Fred White's assertion that opposing pitchers probably feared you more than any other hitter in the Royals' lineup during the 1970s?
John Mayberry: I worked hard to be a feared hitter. I was labeled a power hitter when I first stepped foot in Kansas City, at 6'3", 230 pounds. To hear opposing pitchers and [people around the organization] give me that type of respect is really gratifying.

You ended up having the Royals' last home run at Municipal Stadium and then the club's first homer at then-Royals Stadium during a cold April night against the Texas Rangers. Take us through that fifth-inning blast off of Bill Gogolewski into the right-field fountain (which wasn't working yet).
JM: I didn't realize I hit the last one at Municipal until a few years back. I did like hitting that first home run in Royals Stadium because it was a brand new stadium, and it was going to last for a long time. The only thing I thought about all winter and all of spring training was being the first one to hit a home run at the new Royals Stadium. Before the season all the guys worried about playing on the new artificial turf. Not me. I just wanted that homer. People asked me about it on Opening Day before the game, but I didn't hit until fourth in the lineup, so I didn't know if I was going to be able to do it or not.

How was it different hitting in Royals Stadium versus Municipal?
JM: Royals Stadium was a real spacious stadium. I really didn't start hitting home runs on a consistent basis at Municipal until the

second half of the season. The first half of the season, I struggled a little bit. I was 23 years old. Bob Lemon was our manager. I wanted to stay in the big leagues so bad that I started pressing a little bit. After I got settled down after about June 1, I was getting really comfortable with Municipal. Right field there wasn't as spacious as right field in Royals Stadium. I also think the ball carried a little better at Municipal Stadium than it did at Royals Stadium. I pulled the ball most of the time, so I was getting comfortable with Municipal's right field. I hit nine home runs in the month of September in 1972.

You began your Royals career playing for Bob Lemon, a manager who's often termed a "player's manager. What was that like?
JM: I'll always remember Bob Lemon because he's the one who really got me over the hump. Before him I kept going from the minors to the majors and back down again. When I got to Kansas City, he called me into his office during my first spring training with the Royals. He said, "John, the job [at first] is yours if you can prove that you can do it." That's all I needed to hear...I've never heard any of the guys say anything bad about Bob Lemon. He was a baseball man to the full degree.

Describe the camaraderie among the Royals teams of the 1970s and 1980s.
JM: We had tremendous chemistry in the clubhouse. We knew each other very well. Our families knew each other, our kids played together, we went out to eat together. Then when we went out to the field, we were all on the same page. That made a big difference. That's why we had a lot of fun not only on the field, but off the field as well. I'm just glad that I was a part of it.

66 Sweet Lou

Lou Piniella had a pretty good idea—and a downright hope—that either Seattle or Kansas City would take him in the 1968 Expansion Draft. After all, guys like him—guys who played just four games in 1964 for the Baltimore Orioles and six games in '68 for the Cleveland Indians—weren't likely to be protected. Turns out he landed on both expansion teams.

The Seattle Pilots selected Piniella with the 28th overall pick in the draft. About a week before the season on April 1, 1969, the Royals traded John Gelnar and Steve Whitaker to the Pilots in exchange for Piniella. "Lou always had an explosive nature and he had some run-ins with [Pilots manager] Joe Schultz during spring training," said Lou Gorman, the Royals farm director who moved to Kansas City from the Baltimore organization. "We had Lou in the Baltimore farm system, traded Buster Narum to Washington for him, and we always felt Lou had a lot of potential. Back then he not only could hit, but could play center field, too."

It turned out to be one of the best trades in Royals history. It gave the club its first Rookie of the Year, not to mention one of its best characters of all time. From the outset Piniella didn't disappoint. In the franchise's first game in 1969, Piniella led off the bottom of the first with a double and then scored the club's first run on a Jerry Adair single. He got hits in his first four at-bats and went 4-for-5 in the game.

By the end of the season, Piniella was batting .282 with 139 hits, 11 home runs, and 68 RBIs. It was good enough to win the Rookie of the Year award. Piniella, who could be considered the first "star" for the Royals, went on to have four more very good seasons, including an All-Star selection in 1972. That was the only time he received such an honor.

Besides being a .286 hitter in 700 games for the Royals, Piniella gave the club a bona fide character. Stories about Piniella and his temper with the Royals of the early '70s are legendary. His nickname—"Sweet Lou"—facetiously poked fun at his less than sweet demeanor. "In the outfield [at Municipal Stadium] close to left-center, there was a light standard, which had a door at field level," said former pitcher Tom Burgmeier. "When Piniella would make an out and get mad at himself, he would go into that room at the bottom of the light standard, and we'd suddenly hear: Boom! Boom! Boom! along with some yelling. Lou was in there with a bat or a 2" x 4", hitting the wall. Then he would come out, ready to play. You knew whenever he made an out, he was going to do something crazy and you'd better be on the lookout. Sure enough, this one game he struck out and came back to the dugout all excited. So he kicked the water cooler, breaking the pipe in the process, making water shoot everywhere! In a panic he started yelling, 'Oh, no…somebody help me, somebody help me.' Of course, we were too busy laughing to help."

Former pitcher Al Fitzmorris had another great Pinella story from spring training in 1970 when Charlie Metro was the manager. "We came to the ballpark, and Metro was mad," Fitzmorris said. "He started yelling, 'That's it, I've had it with you people! I caught some guys out after curfew.' I knew I was doomed because I was one of them. He kept talking: 'I want a check from everybody right now for $100.' I wrote the check for the last $100 to my name, and Lou turned to me and said, 'I don't know what to do, I don't have a checkbook.' I said, 'Lou, you may not believe this, but you can write a check on anything. Just put the name of your bank, who it's to, the amount, and sign your name and date it.' So, Lou got a brown paper bag, cut it into the size of a check, wrote on it, and took it to Metro. Metro came out of his office, screaming mad.

He didn't know what to do so he started ripping up everybody's checks."

After the 1973 season, the Royals traded Piniella to the New York Yankees for Lindy McDaniel. Many longtime Royals fans consider it to be the worst trade in Royals history.

67 Bad Trades

Every team has made its share of bad trades, and the Royals are no exception. In fact, to many Royals fans, it sometimes feels as if the bad trade ship has sailed through Kansas City way too many times. Here are five bad trades that may have altered—or did alter—the future of the organization. Instead of attempting to rank them in order of worst to first, they're in chronological order. (That might be the only time that logic was associated with some of these doozies.)

December 7, 1973

Lou Piniella and Ken Wright to the New York Yankees for Lindy McDaniel

Throughout his pitching career, McDaniel was a dependable workhorse. When he signed with the St. Louis Cardinals in 1955, he went straight to the big club, bypassing the minors. By the time he retired in 1975, he had made 987 appearances, second at the time only to Hoyt Wilhelm. Over 21 seasons pitching for five teams, McDaniel compiled a 141–119 record with 172 saves. Unfortunately, fans in Kansas City didn't get to see the real McDaniel. In two seasons with the Royals, he went 6–5 with two saves in 184⅔ innings.

The problem was that McDaniel came to Kansas City at the expense of the club's first Rookie of the Year, Piniella. After spending his first five seasons with the Royals, Piniella went on to play his final 11 seasons with the Yankees. He retired after the 1984 season with a .291 career batting average and 1,705 hits in 1,747 games.

March 27, 1987

David Cone and Chris Jelic to the New York Mets for Ed Hearn, Rick Anderson, and Mauro Gozzo

This trade is often argued as the worst in the organization's history and the beginning of a downward spiral for the team. Less than six months after he was part of a ticker-tape parade, celebrating the Mets' World Series win over the Boston Red Sox, Hearn joined the Royals in exchange, mainly, for pitcher and hometown product Cone. Things unraveled quickly. Hearn played in only six games in 1987 before injuring his shoulder. Then he appeared in seven games in '88. His injury, along with Cone's subsequent success in New York, led Royals owner Ewing Kauffman to call the deal the worst in the history of the Royals. "With the team we had in '87, we were one piece—me—away from being back to the 1985 level," Hearn said. "I think about that all the time...But I've never had feelings of guilt about the trade. You can't control what you can't control. [General manager] John Schuerholz had no idea, and I had no idea that [my injury] would happen. Only the good Lord knew."

On a side note, as if once wasn't enough, the Royals got another chance to trade Cone in a deal that was more head-turning and perhaps less forgivable. On April 6, 1995, the Royals sent Cone, the reigning Cy Young winner who signed with Kansas City as a free agent in December 1992, to the Toronto Blue Jays in exchange for Chris Stynes and minor leaguers David Sinnes and Tony Medrano. None of three made a major impact for the Royals.

Royals owner Ewing Kauffman deemed the trade of David Cone, who returned to Kansas City as a free agent in 1993, to the New York Mets before the 1987 season as the worst deal in franchise history.

December 11, 1991

Bret Saberhagen and Bill Pecota to the Mets for Gregg Jefferies, Keith Miller, and Kevin McReynolds

The people who don't feel this was a bad trade generally point to the fact that Jefferies, Miller, and McReynolds were serviceable—even solid. After all, in his one season with the Royals, Jefferies batted .285 with 172 hits and 75 RBIs. McReynolds batted .247 and .245 during his two seasons with Kansas City, and then Miller had a good first season with 118 hits, 38 RBIs, and a .284 batting average before falling off in the next three seasons. That's all well and good.

But during his last season with the Royals in 1991, Pecota hit .286 with 114 hits and 45 RBIs in 125 games—pretty comparable to, if not better than, McReynolds and Miller. And then there's Saberhagen, who had spent eight seasons with the Royals and won two Cy Young Awards with them. After leaving the Royals, Saberhagen went 57–39. Can you imagine if Saberhagen had remained with Kansas City to anchor a rotation that included David Cone, Mark Gubicza, Kevin Appier, Tom Gordon, and Jose Rosado, among others? On second thought, don't imagine that scenario. It will be bad for your long-term health.

July 25, 2001

Jermaine Dye to the Oakland A's (via the Colorado Rockies) for Neifi Perez

A stretch of bad trades in the early 21st century left many fans ready to give up on the organization. But the realization hit that a small-market team like the Royals couldn't—or wouldn't—keep prized players. That became apparent with the January 2001 trade of Johnny Damon but then was hammered home when Dye was sent to Oakland in a three-team deal that brought Perez to Kansas City. Dye struggled during his first two seasons in Kansas City (1997 and '98), but then he busted out in '99 with a .294 batting average,

27 home runs, and 119 RBIs. The next season he was an All-Star selection as he batted .321 with 193 hits, 41 doubles, 33 homers, and 118 RBIs. He became too good and too expensive. He went on to play eight very good seasons with the A's and Chicago White Sox. In Perez the Royals got a marginal middle infielder whom they placed on waivers in November 2002.

June 24, 2004

Carlos Beltran to the Houston Astros (in a three-team trade) for Mark Teahen, Mike Wood, and John Buck

Once again a player got too good for the small-market team, and the team had to trade him before a big contract. The Royals were part of a three-team trade that brought Teahen, Wood, and Buck to Kansas City for the homegrown Beltran, who was a Rookie of the Year in 1999. As of the end of the 2013 season, Beltran has been an eight-time All-Star selection, Gold Glove selection, and Silver Slugger winner. The other three? They are all nice guys, but none of them are still on a major league roster.

Honorable Mention:

- Cecil Fielder to the Blue Jays for Leon Roberts
- Dan Miceli and Jon Lieber to the Pittsburgh Pirates for Stan Belinda
- Brian McRae to the Chicago Cubs for Derek Wallace and Geno Morones
- Johnny Damon and Mark Ellis to the A's (via the Tampa Bay Devil Rays) for Roberto Hernandez, A.J. Hinch, and Angel Berroa (Note: Although Damon wasn't likely to sign again with the Royals and Berroa was the Rookie of the Year, Ellis went on to become a solid defensive second baseman for more than a decade.)
- Jose Bautista to the Pirates (via the Mets) for Justin Huber

68 Good Trades

As with most other teams, the Royals have had their fair share of really good—if not great—trades. Here are seven of the best trades that helped shaped the organization. (Note: they are listed in chronological order.)

April 1, 1969

Lou Piniella from the Seattle Pilots for Steve Whitaker and John Gelnar

This is one the Pilots (now better known as the Milwaukee Brewers) eventually wished was a bad April Fool's prank. This trade, which happened one week before the opener in 1969, gave the Royals their first Rookie of the Year. In '69 Piniella batted .282 with 139 hits and 68 RBIs en route to the honor. He went on to bat .286 with 734 hits in five seasons with the Royals. (And then, as you might've read in the previous story, became part of one of the club's worst trades. But we digress.)

Whitaker, an outfielder whom the Royals selected with their 23rd pick of the 1968 Expansion Draft from the New York Yankees, played in 69 games for the Pilots in '69 and batted .250. He played in 16 games the next season with the San Francisco Giants. Gelnar, a pitcher whom the Royals purchased from the Pittsburgh Pirates, went 3–10 with a 3.31 ERA in 39 games for the Pilots in 1969. He pitched two more seasons for the Brewers.

December 3, 1969

Amos Otis and Bob Johnson from the New York Mets for Joe Foy

It could be argued that this is *the* best trade in Royals history. Otis was a mainstay in the outfield for 14 seasons with Kansas City.

During his career with the Royals, A.O. hit .280 with 1,977 hits, 193 home runs, 992 RBIs, and 340 stolen bases, to go with three Gold Gloves and five All-Star selections. Even the Johnson part of this trade was solid. In 1970, Johnson's only season with the Royals, he went 8–13 with four saves and a 3.07 ERA in 40 appearances. Almost a year to the day that the Royals acquired Johnson, they shipped him to Pittsburgh on December 2, 1970, along with Jackie Hernandez and Jimmy Campanis in exchange for Bruce Dal Canton, Jerry May, and Fred Patek.

Foy, who was a solid third baseman (mainly) for the Royals in '69, played only two more seasons in the big leagues—with the Mets in '70 and the Washington Senators in '71—before being released.

December 12, 1972

Hal McRae and Wayne Simpson from the Cincinnati Reds for Roger Nelson and Richie Scheinblum

McRae spent 14 full seasons with the Royals as an outfielder and designated hitter. He was a .293 hitter in Kansas City with 1,924 hits and 1,012 RBIs. He was a three-time All-Star and two-time Royals Player of the Year (1974 and 1982). Simpson made 16 appearances in a Royals uniform, going 3–4 with a 5.73 ERA.

Nelson's best seasons were behind him. Incidentally, his best happened to be in 1972 when he went 11–6 with a 2.08 ERA, which still ranks as the lowest single-season ERA in club history. He won seven games during the rest of his career, which included a final stop in Kansas City in '76. Scheinblum, who hit .300 in 134 games for the Royals in '72, had a couple more seasons, including a second stint with the Royals in '74.

May 17, 1985

Lonnie Smith from the St. Louis Cardinals for John Morris

Many Royals point to the acquisition of Smith as the final piece that helped the team win the 1985 World Series against the

Cardinals. Smith, who spent parts of three seasons with Kansas City, solidified left field for the Royals in '85. Offensively, Smith had 115 hits and 40 stolen bases in 120 games that season. Morris, the Royals' first-round draft pick in 1982, played seven years in the big leagues with the Cardinals, Philadelphia Phillies, and California Angels. He was a career .236 hitter with 145 hits and eight homers.

February 15, 1988

Jeff Montgomery from Cincinnati for Van Snider

This trade provided a dose of steadiness to the Royals for a dozen seasons. Monty, who was elected to the Royals Hall of Fame in 2003, was a three-time All-Star selection and the Rolaids American League Reliever of the Year in 1993 when he recorded 45 saves. That put him atop the club's single-season chart tied with Dan Quisenberry. (Greg Holland broke that record in 2013 with 47.) By the time he retired, Montgomery saved a club-best 304 games. Snider, who had been in the Royals minor leagues for six seasons, played a total of 19 games in the major leagues. He struck out 18 times and hit .200.

December 19, 2010

Lorenzo Cain, Alcides Escobar, and Jake Odorizzi from the Milwaukee Brewers for Zack Greinke and Yuniesky Betancourt

The club received future American League Championship Series MVPs Cain and Escobar, along with an important piece of the James Shields and Wade Davis trade, for former Cy Young winner Greinke.

December 9, 2012

James Shields and Wade Davis from the Tampa Bay Rays for Wil Myers, Jake Odorizzi, and others

The news in December 2012 shocked every baseball insider and every fan. The Royals acquired James Shields, an All-Star starting pitcher; Wade Davis, a solid pitcher; and reserve infielder Elliot Johnson (the player to be named later) from Tampa Bay in a monstrous deal that sent Wil Myers, Jake Odorizzi, Mike Montgomery, and Patrick Leonard to the Rays. It was the biggest trade in general manager Dayton Moore's tenure—and one of the most notable in franchise history.

Most "experts" felt Moore had been bamboozled—or simply lost his mind. How else could it be explained that he traded Myers, the *Baseball America* 2012 Player of the Year, for Shields, who was signed through only 2014? "To be clear: I'm with what seems to be the industry consensus, that the Royals are reaching too far and too early and giving up too much," wrote *The Kansas City Star* columnist Sam Mellinger. Former *Star* columnist Joe Posnanski was a little bolder in his assessment of the trade: "I despise the Royals' trade of late Sunday night. Despise. Deplore. Deride. Disapprove." As things turned out, Shields ended up being the ace, veteran pitcher the Royals needed, and Davis became one of the most dominant relievers in baseball history, as the pair helped lead the Royals to the 2014 World Series. Although Shields was gone in 2015, Davis was a masterful closer throughout that postseason.

Honorable Mention:

- Larry Gura from the New York Yankees for Fran Healy
- Buddy Black from the Seattle Mariners for Manny Castillo
- Charlie Leibrandt from the Reds for Bob Tufts
- Jay Bell and Jeff King from the Pirates for Joe Randa, Jeff Granger, Jeff Wallace, and Jeff Martin
- Ervin Santana from the Angels for Brandon Sisk
- Johnny Cueto* from the Reds for Brandon Finnegan, John Lamb, and Cody Reed

- Ben Zobrist* from the Oakland A's for Sean Manaea and Aaron Brooks

* Cueto and Zobrist were acquired by general manager Dayton Moore within two days of each other in 2015. Both turned into key players for the Royals during the club's 2015 World Series championship run.

69 Wade Davis

It's no hyperbole to say that in 2015 on one of baseball's biggest stages, Wade Davis delivered one of the most memorable relief outings in Royals history. It was in Game 6 of the American League Championship Series against the Toronto Blue Jays, and the contest was tied in the eighth inning after Ryan Madson gave up a two-run home run to Jose Bautista and then walked Edwin Encarnacion. Royals manager Ned Yost called on Davis.

Davis not only got the last two outs of the eighth inning, but also had to stay warm through a 45-minute rain delay before returning for the ninth. The Royals had been uncertain about whether he should continue—an hour would pass between his last pitch in the eighth inning and his first pitch in the ninth—but they allowed Davis to make the call.

Kansas City had taken a 4–3 lead in the bottom of the eighth when Lorenzo Cain scored from first on a single. Not surprisingly, Davis wanted to be on the mound. "As long as I felt loose," Davis said afterward, "I felt I was coming back out, especially after we scored."

As Yost pointed out after the game, injured closer Greg Holland, who anchored the bullpen during Kansas City's postseason run in 2014 and for most of the 2015 season, told Yost to let Davis loose. "Don't worry about nothing," Holland said. "Wade wants to go to the World Series."

Davis did not look as sharp in the ninth, allowing a hit to the first batter and a walk to the second. A few steals later, Davis faced a situation that included runners at second and third and one out. One strikeout later Davis faced Josh Donaldson, who went on to be selected as the American League MVP. Davis won the at-bat, inducing a ground-out to Mike Moustakas at third, and the Royals won the game and advanced to the World Series for the second straight season. "Unbelievable," Moustakas said. "That's so tough to do. Wade's been phenomenal, and for him to come back and do that after a delay—unreal."

As general manager Dayton Moore wrote in the book, *More Than a Season*: "After the celebration, I was sitting with Wade in the trainer's room, and we were talking about the moment. The thing that struck me was how poised he remained. Sure, he was very happy that we won, but he wasn't patting himself on the back. With his calmness we could've just as easily been talking after a spring training game. He said, 'That's my job, and I was fortunate to help the team.' That quote from that moment will stick with me."

The game cemented Davis' legacy with the Royals, showcasing all the same elements that allowed him to record a regular season ERA of 0.94 in 69 appearances in 2015, a slight improvement over his 1.00 ERA during 71 outings in 2014. During 2014 Davis didn't allow a run for 20 appearances and didn't give up an extra-base hit for 43 appearances. Davis upped his performance even as he shifted late in the season to a different role, going from eighth inning set-up man to ninth inning closer. Holland had struggled throughout the season due to elbow issues that would eventually require Tommy John surgery, so the Royals eventually shut him down and tabbed Davis to replace him.

Oakland A's catcher Stephen Vogt was a teammate of Davis when both played for the Tampa Bay Rays, and Vogt spoke with *The New York Times* in July—when Davis would pitch in his first All-Star Game—about what made Davis so effective. "His stuff just explodes out of his hand," Vogt said. "He's just got such a good mix. You don't know what's coming. With a lot of relievers, their stuff is so good, but it's fastball or wipeout slider. With him he can throw you a cutter, he can throw you a 2–0 curveball for a strike, he can throw you a four-seam fastball. You just never know. You can't sit on anything because he's got 98."

Davis has starter's stuff with a closer's mentality.

When the Royals acquired him following the 2012 season, little hubbub ensued. The centerpiece of the trade was starting pitcher James Shields, a former All-Star who had logged six straight seasons of 200-plus innings. By comparison Davis had a 4.22 ERA over 64 starts in parts of three seasons for the Rays and had spent the 2012 season in the bullpen. Many saw him as an add-on to the trade. Moore has long contended that wasn't the case; the Royals felt Davis could make an impact for Kansas City. "We felt that he could start," Moore said. "He'd successfully started in the past, and we needed a starter. In 2012 he was dominant in the bullpen, so we knew that if it didn't work out as a starter, he could be a dominant reliever."

The Royals planned to start Davis and they did for a while. Davis started 24 games in 2013. Between those starts and seven relief appearances, he turned in a 5.32 ERA. Then came spring training in 2014, when reliever Luke Hochevar, who was going to be a set-up man for Holland, hurt his elbow, requiring Tommy John surgery. "As Ned and I discussed it, we decided that our best option would be moving Wade Davis into Hoch's spot," Moore wrote in *More Than a Season*. "No one—and I mean no one—could've predicted how dominant Wade would be."

And that trend continued, whether he was setting up for Holland or striking out the league MVP in the clinching game of the 2015 ALCS. "He just makes hitters look like complete fools," Hochevar told *The Kansas City Star* in July 2015. "He can do whatever he wants."

70 The Art of Scouting

The Royals have always emphasized scouting and player development. It's one of the reasons why they won their first division in 1976, just their eighth season of existence. It seems fitting and appropriate that Art Stewart, the longtime scout and senior advisor to general manager Dayton Moore, was inducted into the Royals Hall of Fame in 2008. He was the first person from the scouting/player development side to be inducted. "It's a great personal honor," Stewart said, "but the biggest thing is that the Royals organization is recognizing scouting and player development. Scouting is the life and bloodline of any organization."

Stewart is a dying breed, a true baseball man. He knows the game, knows what it takes to succeed, and tells wonderful stories. He was even mentioned in baseball's most infamous book, *Ball Four*. Stewart also has the most important qualification for being a baseball man: he's devoted his life to the game. After spending 16 years with the New York Yankees, Stewart started with the Royals in 1969. During his Royals career, Stewart has been involved with signing some of the organization's best players such as Kevin Seitzer, Kevin Appier, and Mike Sweeney. "In scouting you never become a millionaire," Stewart said, "so your biggest satisfaction is seeing guys when they're young, and they go on to become great players." Stewart's own baseball career started in Chicago, where he was a shortstop who could run and throw—at least by his admission. Even though he lived just three miles from Wrigley Field, Stewart grew up as a White Sox fan, particularly of their Hall of Fame shortstop, Luke Appling. Stewart was good enough that he seemed destined to be a professional player. The Brooklyn Dodgers and Detroit Tigers offered him class D contracts out of high school. (At the time, the minors consisted of Triple A, Double A, Single A, B, C, and D.) Each contract was for $75 a month.

The problem was that Stewart's dad had died when Art was four years old, and Art's mom was working multiple jobs to keep the family's home. The $75 offer to play baseball would have helped the family if Stewart wasn't already making $100 a month playing semipro baseball. "It killed me at the time, but I had to reject the offer," Stewart said. "I had to do that. As it ended up, I ended up in the big leagues anyway. And I probably had more longevity going this way."

In the early 1950s, Stewart was playing and managing that semipro team, the Chicago Yankees, that had enough talent to win Illinois state championships and play in national tournaments. As a result the New York Yankees noticed Stewart and offered him a job as a Midwest scout. "I was still playing and I didn't want to get involved in anything like that," he said. "They told me I could run the club and still play for a few years before taking over the Midwest for them."

And that's exactly what happened. During the next 16 years, Stewart saw the ultimate team dynasty. The Yankees went to the World Series 10 times while Stewart was there. In 1969—a few years after CBS bought the Yankees and the atmosphere became more corporate—Lou Gorman and Cedric Tallis of the Royals contacted Stewart about being a Midwest scout for the expansion Royals. "I probably never would've left the Yankees had they not sold to CBS," Stewart said. "But the thing that convinced me to come here was when [Gorman and Tallis] told me about Mr. [Ewing] Kauffman's background, how he wanted a family atmosphere, and how they were hiring the best baseball guys to win quickly. The more I thought about that—and not knowing what was going to happen with the Yankees—the timing was right. This sounded like a great opportunity, and I've never regretted it."

Besides Seitzer, Appier, and Sweeney, Stewart also has signed the likes of Mike Macfarlane, Tom Gordon, Johnny Damon, and Carlos Beltran. Of course, one of his top signings—and one of the club's biggest prizes and most unique players—was Bo Jackson. "Bo was the greatest athlete and player with ability that I've ever seen, and that includes Mickey Mantle as a kid," said Stewart. "Bo had the most unbelievable talent. We don't know how great he would've been if not for his injured hip. George Brett said it best when he said that, 'You have to get to practice early to see Bo because you might see something that you've never seen before.'"

The true baseball man, Stewart can be seen today at Royals home games, keenly observing each player. "As long as I have that feeling that I'd like to find another Bo Jackson, I want to keep going," he said. "This has been a great organization with a lot of good people in a great city with great fans. I just love this city so much and I keep loving the Royals."

71 The 1968 Expansion Draft

Throughout expansion draft history, teams—even those picking in the same year—have gone with different philosophies. That was the case with the Royals and the Seattle Pilots in the 1968 American League Expansion Draft. The day after the San Diego Padres and

Montreal Expos went through their expansion draft in the National League, the Royals and Pilots were essentially selecting from the bottom of the barrel of the established teams in their respective leagues.

In the American League draft, the Pilots went after established major league players while the Royals targeted young talent. "Cedric Tallis, Lou Gorman, and Joe Gordon allowed me to sit in with them on draft day," said Buddy Blattner, the first "voice" of the Royals. "So much homework went into it, and it was done in a systematic way. The Royals drafted according to the best available talent, not by position. Seattle went by position, and they were hurt. The Royals came out in fine fashion, actually becoming a team that was competitive right from the very word 'go.'"

Seattle won a coin flip that determined who'd pick first and fourth and who'd pick second and third. The Pilots went second and third. The Royals most desired Joe Foy, a third baseman from the Boston Red Sox. They gambled, though, that the Pilots wouldn't pick him second or third and selected Baltimore Orioles pitcher Roger "Spider" Nelson, who was 4–4 in his first season-plus in the big leagues. Nelson ended up spending four seasons with the Royals (plus three appearances in 1976 after he left and came back).

The gamble paid off. After Seattle took Don Mincher and Tommy Harper, the Royals selected Foy with their second pick. Foy had a good season in '69, but then he was traded to the New York Mets for Amos Otis—in an absolute coup of a trade—before the 1970 season.

Rounding out the top 10, the Royals selected players who were vital to their success in 1969: pitcher Jim Rooker, outfielder Joe Keough, pitcher Steve Jones, pitcher Jon Warden, catcher Ellie Rodriguez, pitcher Dave Morehead, first baseman Mike Fiore, and first baseman Bob Oliver, who played right field on Opening Day.

Other notable selections, most of whom made contributions in '69 and beyond, were: pitcher Wally Bunker (the Royals' 13th

The 1968 American League Baseball Expansion Draft

Pick	Player	Selected from	Selected by
1	Roger Nelson	Baltimore Orioles	Kansas City Royals
2	Don Mincher	California Angels	Seattle Pilots
3	Tommy Harper	Cleveland Indians	Seattle Pilots
4	Joe Foy	Boston Red Sox	Kansas City Royals
5	Ray Oyler	Detroit Tigers	Seattle Pilots
6	Jim Rooker	New York Yankees	Kansas City Royals
7	Jerry McNertney	Chicago White Sox	Seattle Pilots
8	Joe Keough	Oakland Athletics	Kansas City Royals
9	Buzz Stephen	Minnesota Twins	Seattle Pilots
10	Steve Jones	Washington Senators	Kansas City Royals
11	Chico Salmon	Cleveland Indians	Seattle Pilots
12	Jon Warden	Detroit Tigers	Kansas City Royals
13	Ellie Rodriguez	New York Yankees	Kansas City Royals
14	Diego Segui	Oakland Athletics	Seattle Pilots
15	Dave Morehead	Boston Red Sox	Kansas City Royals
16	Tommy Davis	Chicago White Sox	Seattle Pilots
17	Mike Fiore	Baltimore Orioles	Kansas City Royals
18	Marty Pattin	California Angels	Seattle Pilots
19	Bob Oliver	Minnesota Twins	Kansas City Royals
20	Gerry Schoen	Washington Senators	Seattle Pilots
21	Gary Bell	Boston Red Sox	Seattle Pilots
22	Bill Butler	Detroit Tigers	Kansas City Royals
23	Steve Whitaker	New York Yankees	Kansas City Royals
24	Jack Aker	Oakland Athletics	Seattle Pilots
25	Wally Bunker	Baltimore Orioles	Kansas City Royals
26	Rich Rollins	Minnesota Twins	Seattle Pilots
27	Paul Schaal	California Angels	Kansas City Royals
28	Lou Piniella	Cleveland Indians	Seattle Pilots
29	Bill Haynes	Chicago White Sox	Kansas City Royals

pick), third baseman Paul Schaal (14), pitcher Dick Drago (16), pitcher Al Fitzmorris (20), pitcher Moe Drabowsky (21), shortstop Jackie Hernandez (22), pitcher Tom Burgmeier (24), and second baseman Jerry Adair (26). "I am extremely proud of our entire organization," owner Ewing Kauffman said. "Everybody worked hard and made some wise decisions. I feel we got the nucleus of a

Pick	Player	Selected from	Selected by
30	Dick Bates	Washington Senators	Seattle Pilots
31	Dick Drago	Detroit Tigers	Kansas City Royals
32	Larry Haney	Baltimore Orioles	Seattle Pilots
33	Dick Baney	Boston Red Sox	Seattle Pilots
34	Pat Kelly	Minnesota Twins	Kansas City Royals
35	Steve Hovley	California Angels	Seattle Pilots
36	Billy Harris	Cleveland Indians	Kansas City Royals
37	Steve Barber	New York Yankees	Seattle Pilots
38	Don O'Riley	Oakland Athletics	Kansas City Royals
39	John Miklos	Washington Senators	Seattle Pilots
40	Al Fitzmorris	Chicago White Sox	Kansas City Royals
41	Wayne Comer	Detroit Tigers	Seattle Pilots
42	Moe Drabowsky	Baltimore Orioles	Kansas City Royals
43	Jackie Hernandez	Minnesota Twins	Kansas City Royals
44	Bucky Brandon	Boston Red Sox	Seattle Pilots
45	Mike Hedlund	Cleveland Indians	Kansas City Royals
46	Skip Lockwood	Oakland Athletics	Seattle Pilots
47	Tom Burgmeier	California Angels	Kansas City Royals
48	Gary Timberlake	New York Yankees	Seattle Pilots
49	Hoyt Wilhelm	Chicago White Sox	Kansas City Royals
50	Bob Richmond	Washington Senators	Seattle Pilots
51	Jerry Adair	Boston Red Sox	Kansas City Royals
52	John Morris	Baltimore Orioles	Seattle Pilots
53	Mike Marshall	Detroit Tigers	Seattle Pilots
54	Jerry Cram	Minnesota Twins	Kansas City Royals
55	Jim Gosger	Oakland Athletics	Seattle Pilots
56	Fran Healy	Cleveland Indians	Kansas City Royals
57	Mike Ferraro	New York Yankees	Seattle Pilots
58	Scott Northey	Chicago White Sox	Kansas City Royals
59	Paul Click	California Angels	Seattle Pilots
60	Ike Brookens	Washington Senators	Kansas City Royals

fine team. Our scouting was excellent. This is something I looked forward to for a long time."

Two additional picks, who didn't make a huge impact, were pitchers Don O'Riley (19) and Hoyt Wilhelm (25). O'Riley was a Kansas City native and product of Northeast High School. He pitched for the Royals during 1969–70. The Royals traded Wilhelm to the California Angels two months later for Ed Kirkpatrick and Dennis Paepke.

Overall, the draft lasted six hours, 45 minutes. The Royals picked 16 pitchers (12 right-handers), two catchers, seven infielders, and five outfielders.

Bunker, who was the Royals starter on Opening Day, remembers more about that '69 team than anything else. "I just remember how much fun we had," he said. "I don't remember much about pitching on Opening Day. Games except the World Series don't really stand out because they're just games. You win a few, you lose a few. But we had fun because we knew we weren't going to win the pennant, which took a lot of pressure off. It was just a great group of guys that enjoyed being around each other."

Out of the four expansion teams, the Royals were the most successful in 1969 and beyond. The Pilots finished 64–98, moved to Milwaukee, and became the Brewers in 1970. The Expos and Padres finished with identical records of 52–110.

72 Hit a Round at Mac-N-Seitz

Kansas City has several indoor baseball facilities, but one has become most famous because it's run by former Royals teammates. So, grab your bat and hack some swings there and you likely will run into some former and even current Royals.

Mac-N-Seitz

13705 Holmes Road, Kansas City, MO

While they were still playing for the Royals, Kevin Seitzer and Mike Macfarlane started talking about what they were going to do when

Seitz Could Pitch, Too?

Besides suiting up for the Royals, Kevin Seitzer played with the Milwaukee Brewers, Oakland A's, and Cleveland Indians. Royals fans remember him for his great hitting ability. During his six years with Kansas City, he had a .294 batting average, including his rookie season in 1987 when he hit .323 and led the American League in hits with 207. In addition to his prowess at the plate, Seitzer played every position on the field during his 11-year major league career except catcher. That includes pitcher—well, sort of.

While Seitzer was with Oakland in 1993, the A's were playing the Indians, who were wearing out the A's pitchers, leading by eight runs in the ninth inning. With two outs in the last inning, Oakland pitcher Kelly Downs got Cleveland's Carlos Martinez to chase a 2–1 fastball. Downs verbally made sure that Martinez knew he missed badly. The benches cleared. Among other players, Downs and Martinez were ejected.

At the suggestion of pitching coach Dave Duncan, Oakland manager Tony La Russa sent in Seitzer to face Martinez's replacement, Glenallen Hill, with a 2–2 count. "I threw one pitch, and he looked at it. He probably couldn't believe how slow it was when it got to home plate," Seitzer said with a laugh. "It's in the record book because I got credit for striking out a guy that I never faced, and I threw one pitch. I'm the only person in the history of baseball to do that."

their careers were finished. That led to the suggestion of starting an indoor baseball facility. In 1996 the two opened Mac-N-Seitz, which has grown to include busy year-round lessons and clinics. On any given day, the group gives about 60 to 70 lessons for baseball and softball players. "We're trying to put a positive mark on both the kids and their parents, trying to help them become better ballplayers but also helping them understand how to deal with the success and failure of this sport," Macfarlane said. "At the same time, we're trying to get the younger athletes to understand that they don't need to specialize in one sport at the age of 12 or whatever. Play everything you can and then when you're a junior in high school pick one sport if you want. But you're only a kid once. Enjoy it."

Besides indoor batting cages, Mac-N-Seitz features a full-size indoor infield, pitching mounds, and a running track. "We have great instructors, great employees who work for us," Seitzer said. "It's been a real blessing to pour into kids and to see them be able to reach their dreams of playing at the next level. It's very rewarding."

73 George Toma: The Nitty Gritty Dirt Man

Name 10 groundskeepers in professional sports. Oh, okay, how about five? Unless you're a grassophile, there's only one name that will to come to mind: George Toma. He's been called the "god of sod" and the "nitty gritty dirt man" (which is actually the title of his autobiography). Since 1957 he's been a fixture in Kansas City sports as the groundskeeper at Municipal Stadium for the former A's and then the Chiefs and Royals at both Municipal and the Truman Sports Complex. He's also prepared the field for every Super Bowl as well as a couple of Olympic stadiums and various colleges and universities. Toma was so good at what he did that when manager Tony La Russa was asked about his memory of playing for the A's in Kansas City, he said, "The first thing that comes to mind is the ballpark and George Toma. I had never seen a field so beautiful in all my life. The pride and the craftsmanship that he and his crew displayed was incredible." Toma splits his time between Kansas City and Florida.

Royals groundskeeper George Toma, who always was in demand for the biggest sporting events, touches up the grass before Super Bowl XXVII in 1993.

You grew up in Pennsylvania around the coal mines. Did you actually want to become a groundskeeper one day?
George Toma: I thought first when I was young that I'd want to be a male nurse, but I faint with the sight of blood. When a player gets hurt on the field, I go the opposite way.

Even though the A's, Chiefs, and Royals loved you and your fields, one player who wasn't a fan of coming to Municipal was Mickey Mantle.
GT: Sometimes we would do things that we'll call "groundskeeping by deceit." Mickey Mantle didn't care for [Municipal] because I kept center field hard, and it was hard on his legs. One of my best buddies and a guy who served as a coach for the Twins during spring training was Harmon Killebrew, who played with the Royals. I used to keep third base like concrete. The trainer would tell me, "You're going to get my third baseman killed down there" because Harmon could hit that ball, but he was a little slow. So we'd make it hard to make sure the ball would get through the infield. Groundskeeping by deceit.

Did you doctor the pitcher's mound or a part of the infield a certain way?
GT: Guys like Steve Busby always wanted a little hole next to the rubber, so he could push off. In the batter's box, there used to be a special hole for George Brett and a special hole for Amos Otis and for Hal McRae. You could say we did a lot of cheating because we moved the batter's box back about 10 inches. If we got caught, I'd blame it on my son, Chip. Everything went great until the Royals traded Buck Martinez to Milwaukee. The first time they came to town, manager George Bamberger came up to me and said, "George, I don't want any of that stuff, moving that batter's box."

We could do a lot of things. At Municipal Stadium we had a Butternut clock on the left-field tower. It had two dots...We would send Bobby Hofman into the scoreboard before the game and then we'd get the other team's signals. If those two dots were on, it was a fastball. If one dot was on, it was a breaking pitch, or they could look down the third-base line to Charlie O's pen. If the lantern was on, that was a fastball. If the lantern was off, it was a breaking pitch. All of that was just part of the game back then.

What was your most memorable moment working in Kansas City?
GT: Every day that I went to work, I felt I had the best job that anybody ever had. You might hear a lot about George Toma, but there's no George Toma without the people I worked with.

74 Boston Strong

This isn't a story an author wants to include in any book, particularly a sports book. Such a creepy scenario seems straight out of a Stephen King or Dean Koontz novel. But on Monday, April 15, 2013, the far-fetched horror story played out near the finish line at the Boston Marathon as two bombs went off a little more than four hours after the start of the race. Hundreds were seriously wounded, and three were killed. In addition to the marathon, as is tradition in Boston on Patriots' Day, the Red Sox played a day game a few miles away at Fenway Park.

The Sox would hit the road after the game before returning for a weekend series against the Royals, scheduled to start Friday night. As the week played out, the nation—even rival Yankees fans—embraced Boston, rooting for the city and its team.

The Royals arrived in Boston on Wednesday night, following a quick two-game split in Atlanta against the Braves. After a surreal off day in Boston on Thursday, as both law enforcement officials and journalists hunted for clues and answers, the Royals and Red Sox waited for their Friday night game. It didn't happen.

Lester No-Hits the Royals

Perhaps one of the greatest feel-good stories of the early 21st century happened in Boston on May 19, 2008, at the expense of the Royals. That night, Jon Lester, who missed the end of the 2006 season after he was diagnosed with a rare form of non-Hodgkin's lymphoma, no-hit the Royals in a 7–0 victory. "I looked up in the ninth, and you're trying to keep your emotions in check and I went to say something to [pitching coach] John Farrell, and he was being a big baby next to me," said manager Terry Francona. "It made me feel a little bit better."

Lester, who won the final game of the 2007 World Series for the Red Sox, struck out nine Kansas City batters and walked only two—Billy Butler (in the second) and Esteban German (in the ninth). The closest call of the night happened in the fourth when Jose Guillen lined a ball toward right-center. Center fielder Jacoby Ellsbury made a diving catch. "At first I didn't think [Lester] was really feeling it until the third, fourth, fifth inning when he started going," said Royals second baseman Mark Grudzielanek. "Then his breaking balls and everything else started coming along for him."

The loss began a 12-game losing streak for the Royals, who'd had trouble with Lester before that night. On July 18, 2006, shortly before his season ended because of the lymphoma, Lester and Jonathan Papelbon combined for a one-hitter against Kansas City.

The 2008 performance was the fourth no-hitter thrown by a Boston pitcher since 2000. Lester followed Hideo Nomo (2001), Derek Lowe (2002), and Clay Buchholz (2007). But none was as big as Lester's. "His story is a good story as it is," said Boston third baseman Mike Lowell. "But to add a no-hitter to it, it adds something great to the story."

Late Thursday night and into Friday, the FBI and local police departments went on an incredible chase for the two suspects. One suspect was killed. The other escaped, prompting the metropolitan Boston area to do something not seen in a major U.S. city: complete lockdown. Public transportation was shut down, businesses and schools were told to close, and residents were urged to stay inside. As the manhunt continued well into the afternoon, the Red Sox realized their only option was postponement of the series opener with Kansas City. Later that evening, the second suspect was captured, bringing the first chapter of the five-day saga to a close.

The Royals and Red Sox would play as scheduled Saturday in what promised to be one of the most emotional moments in Fenway Park's incredible history. It didn't disappoint. "A 25-minute ceremony preceded Saturday's game at Fenway Park," wrote Royals beat writer Bob Dutton for *The Kansas City Star*, "that shifted smoothly from touchingly symbolic to gently moving before concluding with a touch of defiant pride." With both teams lined up during the pregame ceremony, heroes—police, first responders, and race participants—from the bombings were honored. An emotional video montage of the previous days, including photographs of the victims, played. And then David Ortiz addressed the crowd, ending with an emphatic: "Stay strong!"

"It was electric," said Lorenzo Cain of the ceremony. "To go through that and see everybody getting into it and what this city went through, just to be a part of it was amazing." Cain homered for the Royals in the ninth inning, but it was not enough for Kansas City, who led 2–1 until Daniel Nava hit a three-run homer against Kelvin Herrera in the bottom of the eighth.

Perhaps appropriately this one time, the Red Sox beat the Royals 4–3. "Today was different because we haven't been through what we've been through this past week," Ortiz said after the game. "Driving around and looking around at people's faces, it was a very emotional day here just looking at those guys that were injured by those bombs going off and watching the news nearly every day. It was painful, very painful. Today I could see people opening their chest and letting it go."

Kansas City and Boston, though, played a doubleheader the next day with the Royals sweeping both games, 4–2 and 5–4.

75 Soria Sails to Saves Record

Major League Baseball's Rule 5 Draft might be the most intriguing draft in sports. In essence it's a club's chance to protect its young players and minor league prospects. Depending on how old a player was when a club first signed him, the organization has four or five years before it has to worry about protecting him in the Rule 5 Draft. If another club picks a player in the major league phase of Rule 5, it pays $50,000 for that player. Then he has to stay on the big league roster for the entire season. If he doesn't, the player's original club can buy him back for $25,000. So an organization has to be sure a player is worth the big league roster spot.

During the December 2006 Rule 5 Draft, the Tampa Bay Rays were rumored to be selecting a pitcher from the San Diego Padres organization with the first overall pick. Instead the Rays picked Ryan Goleski from the Cleveland Indians and traded him to the Oakland A's for $100,000. Things didn't work out, and the A's sent Goleski back to the Indians. The pitcher that everyone assumed Tampa would take fell into the lap of the team picking second, the Royals. That pitcher was Joakim Soria. "He throws three above-average pitches, and his mound presence was outstanding," Royals general manager Dayton Moore said. "He was almost too good to be true when we saw him."

Before then, Soria, who missed the 2003 season after Tommy John surgery, hadn't pitched higher than Single A. The Los Angeles Dodgers signed Soria after the 2001 season, but he pitched for their two rookie teams before signing with the Padres. Two days after the Royals drafted Soria, he went out and threw a perfect game—only the third in Mexican League history.

Growing up in Monclova, Mexico, a city about 255 miles southwest of San Antonio, Soria says he likely would've become a dentist just like his brother. But Soria loved baseball, which he started playing when he was about five years old. As with a lot of boys in the early 1990s, especially those who were pitchers, Soria's heroes came from the Atlanta staff—Greg Maddux, Tom Glavine, and John Smoltz. His other favorite was Mariano Rivera, the dominant New York Yankees closer. Whether by coincidence or admiration that turned into imitation, many people compared Soria to Rivera. The two are roughly the same build—6'3" and 185 pounds for Soria and 6'2" and 185 pounds for Rivera. And both boast gaudy career earned run averages—2.57 for Soria and 2.21 for Rivera. (Of course Rivera's ERA comes with about 450 more saves.) Soria, however, isn't one to make any personal comparisons to a future Hall of Fame player. "Let's not do that," he said with an embarrassed laugh. "That's not fair to him. He's the big guy."

In 2008, though, after leading the Royals with 17 saves a year earlier, Soria became Kansas City's own "big guy." He pitched 17 games in '08 before giving up any runs. He ended the season with 42 saves and a 1.60 ERA. He was the first Royals pitcher since Jeff Montgomery in 1993 to save at least 40 games. (Monty tied the club's then-saves record with Dan Quisenberry in '93 with 45.)

Soria and Montgomery shared several traits. Soria, who doesn't blow hitters away with speed, used four pitches—fastball, slider, change-up, curveball—at any point in the count. Not a fireballer either, Montgomery threw four pitches effectively and kept hitters off balance by using any of the four pitches at any time during the count. "One of the biggest keys for someone like Soria, similar to me, is that you have to get away from the mind-set of doing it by the book," Montgomery said. "You're not the typical pitcher. You're trying to get possibly the three toughest outs of the game."

Soria did that as well as anyone in baseball. In 2010 Soria saved 43 games and boasted a 1.78 ERA for Kansas City. In both years—2008 and 2010—with more than 40 saves, Soria was an American League All-Star selection. It was during 2008 when "The Mexicutioner" became a popular phrase on T-shirts. Like many storied closers, he now had a clever nickname. Soria, however, discouraged it because he said the connotation brought to mind the gun violence in his native Mexico.

Soria saved 28 games in 60 appearances during 2011. During spring training in 2012, however, Soria had Tommy John surgery for a second time in his career. The Royals didn't exercise their $8 million option on Soria for 2013, and he signed with the Texas Rangers. Soria saved 160 games and posted a 2.40 ERA for the Royals during 2007–11. When he left Kansas City, he ranked third behind only Montgomery and Quisenberry on the club's all-time saves list.

The Royals brought Soria back, signing him to a contract for the 2016 season.

76 Denny and Fred

"Fred, do you still like the DH?"

"Yeah, I do. Here's where I've always been on the DH. Whether I like it or don't like it, doesn't matter, but I think it needs to be the same in both leagues. What I don't like is the inference that American League baseball is not good baseball because of the DH. American League baseball is fine. Baseball is good with or without it. Where I'm going with that question—and I know I'm sawing an old piece of wood—is the idea that the balance in baseball has been tipped way too much now in favor of offense. The pitchers are going to have to get a little something back."

"I agree, but you know I really get tired of people saying, 'Well, the DH, that's American League baseball.' That's an inference that the American League is not good baseball. That's patently false."

"The DH is just a small part of the problem that pitchers have. I think the caliber of pitching in the big leagues is made to look a little worse than it really is because of the small strike zone, the DH, and things like that. They're just going to have to do something to get out of that mind-set that all people want to do is see offense. That is not true. A good baseball game is not all offense…it never has been and never will be. Unfortunately, that's the direction the 'leadership' of baseball has taken this game in the last 10 to 15 years."

"The DH is far from being the biggest problem in the equation."

"I agree with that. The biggest problem is the strike zone."

"I think it's a good game either way. I don't care if they have the DH or not; I wish it was standard in both leagues."

"I really wasn't talking about the DH; I just threw that out there to get the discussion going."

This was an on-air discussion between Denny Matthews and Fred White, the longtime radio broadcasters for the Royals during a game on April 26, 1998. And we mean "longtime." The 1998 season marked the 25th year Matthews and White were on the air together, making them the longest-running broadcast crew in the American League at the time. They did approximately 4,050 games together, meaning they logged about 12,150 hours of play-by-play with each other. In the National League, they were surpassed only by Jack Buck and Mike Shannon (and by only two years) of the St. Louis Cardinals. Marty Brennaman and Joe Nuxhall also celebrated their 25th anniversary together in 1998 with the Cincinnati Reds.

Beginning in 1973, Denny and Fred—as they'll forever be known to listeners—described the most significant moments in Royals history from the first division title in 1976 through the 1985 World Series. Their combined style, which could be described as laid back, came from their similar childhood backgrounds. Both were from smaller towns in central Illinois and tended to root for the Cardinals as boys. They also grew up listening to the same radio broadcasters: Harry Caray, Jack Brickhouse, and Bob Elston. "Our relationship is very easy," Fred said. "This might sound strange, but we weren't fast friends. We certainly weren't enemies; we were just two guys who worked together and got along together. Things grew out of that. That was always good enough for us."

Away from the microphone, Fred and Denny were like the *Odd Couple*. Denny is somewhat reserved, but Fred enjoyed crowds. Denny records a sporting event and knows in advance when he is going to watch it. Fred, by his own account, wasn't very mechanical, but he liked to cook. Denny is a lifelong bachelor while Fred was happily married. "It was obviously 25 great years working with Fred," Denny said. "Fred worked hard, he had a great sense of humor, and he's easy to be around…Fred and I always got along and seldom had a cross word. We would argue and debate things, which was normal, but we never crossed swords. We disagreed about some things, but that happens to everybody. We got along great."

In a business that tends to breed egos the size of the Truman Sports Complex, Fred and Denny had anything but. Fred was one of the first people who called Denny on the February 2007 day when Matthews found out he received the Baseball Hall of Fame's Ford Frick Award. "This is as much about you as it is me," Matthews told White after Fred's initial congratulations. "I couldn't have done this without you."

Unfortunately, that 25th season in 1998 happened to mark their final season together because Fred's handshake contract was not renewed. (He and Matthews were playing golf together when he got the news.) The news stunned Royals fans and nearly incited a listener riot. To many people Denny and Fred were the only two broadcasters they associated with the Royals. They were friends and family—the ones you enjoy being around and hearing tell stories.

The firing of White brought in Ryan Lefebvre in 1999. And eventually after the Royals realized the mistake of parting ways with Fred, he accepted a front-office position as the director of broadcasting services and the director of alumni. And he filled in occasionally on the radio for a couple of seasons. On May 14, 2013, White announced he was retiring from the Royals after 40 years with the club. The next day White died of complications from melanoma. He was 76. Very few people knew he was sick. "I was stunned," Matthews said the day White passed away. "I just talked with him two weeks ago at the stadium, and we had a great conversation with a lot of laughs. Nothing seemed out of the ordinary. He looked fine and sounded fine. I can't believe it.

"There are so many things I'll miss about Fred, but one will be his sense of humor. We shared humorous moments on and off the air. I think that's what helped us stay together for 25 years and part of what fans enjoyed about our broadcasts. We also had a lot of respect for each other. If we hadn't, we wouldn't have been able to work together as long as we did."

77 Ape Goes Wild

When talking about the greatest Royals starting pitchers of all time, certain names roll off the tongue: Steve Busby, Mark Gubicza, Zack Greinke, Dennis Leonard, Bret Saberhagen, and Paul Splittorff, to name a few. One name that is sometimes overlooked is Kevin Appier. But he remains in the top 10 in career ERA (3.49), wins (115), shutouts (10), and games started (275) and he's the career leader in strikeouts (1,458).

Appier put together some impressive single seasons: 2.46 ERA in 1992, 186 strikeouts in 1993, 196 strikeouts in 1997, and 207 strikeouts in 1996. Also in '96 Appier became the 11th American League pitcher since 1911 to strike out four batters in one inning. He did that on September 3. Perhaps his most impressive single season was 1993 when he won 18 games and registered one of the lowest ERAs in club history, an AL best 2.56. That year he finished third in the Cy Young voting to Jack McDowell and Randy Johnson. "I definitely had my best stuff then," he said, "but I got smarter over the years. But my best physical stuff was in those years."

During that 1993 season, Appier, who had an unorthodox delivery but an incredible workhorse mentality on the mound, threw 33 consecutive scoreless innings, which remained a Royals record until Greinke threw 38 scoreless innings from September 18, 2008 to April 24, 2009. One of Appier's best starts of the season and his career—and one of the more disappointing Royals outcomes of all time—was on July 27 at home against Texas. He threw a no-hitter for six innings until Rafael Palmeiro hit a home run. That was the only hit the Rangers got against "Ape," but it was enough. In spite of the one hit and Appier's 11 strikeouts in the complete game, the Rangers won 1–0. "Take away that one hit, and it's definitely the best game I've ever pitched," Appier said. "He hit a pretty good slider down. He just put a good swing on it."

Appier, whom the Royals selected in the first round of the 1987 draft, remained one of the best pitchers in the league. In 1995—his only year as an All-Star—Appier won 15 games. He followed that up with 14 wins in '96. But after only three starts in 1998, Appier had to have shoulder surgery. It was the second surgery in a year on his throwing shoulder. During the offseason leading into '98, Appier fell on the porch steps at his house and required the first surgery. The Royals traded Appier in July 1999 to the Oakland A's for Jeff D'Amico, Brad Rigby, and Blake Stein.

Although the Royals struggled while Appier was their ace, he won a World Series ring with the Angels in 2002. With an aging arm and shoulder, Appier signed as a free agent with the Royals in August 2003. He pitched in six more games during the rest of '03 and '04. Appier, who was a three-time Royals Pitcher of the Year, was inducted into the Royals Hall of Fame in 2011.

78 Birdie Infuriates the White Rat

As with a lot of teams in the 1970s, the Royals had some characters—guys who could provide some comic relief, whether intentional or not, when things weren't going so well. One of those was pitcher Doug Bird, whom the Royals drafted in their inaugural season of 1969. Manager Whitey Herzog's instructions to "Birdie" were clear: don't throw a strike with an 0–2 count. *Ever.*

Herzog was so adamant about it, in fact, that he fined Bird $100 every time he threw one.

When the Royals were in Anaheim playing the Angels, Bird had a hitter down 0–2. The next pitch—thrown near the strike zone—became a base hit. "Here comes Whitey out of the dugout, and he got all over me," Bird said more than 30 years later. "I just didn't believe in wasting pitches."

During the top of the next inning, Herzog was ejected from the game for arguing. With a smirk from fate, Bird went ahead 0–2 against the leadoff batter in the bottom of the inning. Making sure to avoid Herzog's fine, Bird threw the next pitch high. *Way high.* It nearly hit Royals announcers Denny Matthews and Fred White in the radio booth. "Oh, boy," Bird said, laughing, "I could hear Whitey in the runway screaming at me, but he couldn't come out because he had been ejected from the game."

In addition to being one of the team's more colorful characters, Bird was an important part of the Royals' success. Pitching on three division-winning teams from 1976–78, Bird won 29 games in that span plus the pivotal fourth game of the '76 American League Championship Series against the New York Yankees. "We were a young expansion team with guys who either came up through the minors or were offshoots from other teams," Bird said. "I don't think—being that young—we realized at the time how good we were."

Bird, who pitched for the Royals during 1973–78, still ranks on several of the Royals' all-time top 10 lists, including appearances and win-loss percentage. He has the lowest number of walks-per-nine innings in a season, and his 1.41 ratio led the American League in 1976.

The Royals used Bird in different roles from reliever to starter to closer. Think of a pitching role, and chances are the Royals put

Bird in that situation. "I liked the short relief because I got more games," Bird said. "Starting, you sit around for four days, even though I was more of a starter when I came up after being short relief. Whitey tried everything. He wasn't afraid to experiment."

Bird's final appearance for Kansas City came in relief in Game 3 of the 1978 playoffs. With the Royals leading 5–4 in the bottom of the eighth inning in New York, Bird gave up a two-run homer to Thurman Munson. The Yankees won that game 6–5 and then the decisive fourth game. The Royals traded Bird to the Philadelphia Phillies for Todd Cruz on the final day of spring training in '79. "That was hard," Bird said, "mainly because I didn't expect it at all."

Five seasons and four clubs later, Bird retired. In 11 big-league seasons with the Royals, Phillies, Yankees, Chicago Cubs, and Boston Red Sox, Bird won 73 games and saved 60. But his allegiance remains with the Royals. "Since I came up through the Royals organization, I'm partial to them," Bird said. "I loved playing in Kansas City. The fans were great. Plus, we had a good ballclub that was entertaining."

79 Lonnie Smith: The Catalyst in '85

There are several reasons why the Royals won the 1985 World Series—a great pitching staff that featured a future Cy Young Award winner in Bret Saberhagen, who won 20 games in 1985; a lights-out closer in Dan Quisenberry, who saved 37 games that season; stars George Brett, Hal McRae, Frank White, and Willie Wilson; role players who stepped up in key situations; "the call" in Game 6 of the World Series; and manager Dick Howser, who knew just how to blend all of the key pieces.

But White says there's one overlooked key to the Royals winning the 1985 World Series—the mid-May acquisition of left fielder Lonnie Smith from the St. Louis Cardinals in exchange for fellow outfielder John Morris. "We were a good team, but we didn't have the winning feeling until Lonnie came over," White said. "He was an aggressive player; a hard-nosed guy…He was the missing piece for that '85 season."

It might seem odd to say that of a player whom a teammate nicknamed "Skates" because of his occasional clumsiness in the outfield. But during his 17 years in the big leagues, Smith played in the World Series five times. He was a three-time champion with three organizations in a six-year span: the Philadelphia Phillies (1980), St. Louis (1982), and Kansas City (1985). "It wasn't anything I did," Smith said. "It was being blessed to be in the right place at the right time. I was able to get the job done when needed, which is what I brought with me to Kansas City."

Smith, who also played on two World Series teams in the early 1990s with the Atlanta Braves, brought consistency to a Royals outfield that needed some. During the early part of the season, Wilson was the mainstay in center field with Dane Iorg, Lynn Jones, and Darryl Motley handling most of the duties in left field, and Motley, Iorg, or Pat Sheridan in right. When Smith arrived the Royals had been a little better than average during the first 33 games of the season. But it wasn't until two months later, July 23 to be exact, that the Royals moved up to second place in the division. They didn't stop there. "When I came to Kansas City, they already had all the right ingredients to win," Smith said. "Without me, it was a team more than capable of performing at a high level. It was a matter of getting everybody together, performing and playing hard."

By the end of that regular season, with Smith, who stole 40 bases, in the lineup for 120 of 129 games, the Royals went on to finish the season 91–71, good enough to edge out the California Angels by one game in the American League West.

During that postseason run, the Royals faced elimination against the Toronto Blue Jays (down three games to one) before battling back. That set up an unforgettable World Series against cross-state rival St. Louis. Smith became the first player in World Series history to face the team that traded him in the same season. "Really, I was hoping we'd play them," said a chuckling Smith. "Not because I was upset about the trade, but because I felt we were capable of beating those guys. It wasn't going to be easy, but I thought we could beat them. Plus, it was amazing to have both teams from Missouri playing each other. That's as big of a deal as the Yankees and Mets playing in the World Series."

After the Royals lost the first two games against the Cardinals at home, Kansas City won Game 3 in large part because of a two-run double by Smith and a two-run home run by White. After losing the next night and facing elimination in yet another series, the Royals won Game 5 in St. Louis before coming home for two of the most memorable wins in Royals history.

Has Smith ever given his ex-Cardinals mates a hard time about beating them? "No, not at all," Smith said. "The Cardinals were a bunch of guys that I loved and respected—just like I did the other players on the Royals. There was no need to give them a hard time when the pain is there from losing."

When Smith thinks about the 1985 season and all of the unforgettable images, a particular one comes to mind. "It's always that last out with Darryl catching the fly ball," he said. "Until that last out is made, you don't realize what's just happened. So my most enjoyable image is the last out and then enjoying the time on the field with all of the guys. I'll never forget that."

80 Quirk's Intriguing Home Run

To say Jamie Quirk helped push the Royals into the playoffs wouldn't be such an incredible statement on its own. After all, Quirk, the California native, appeared headed for football—with a scholarship to play quarterback at Notre Dame—until the Royals intervened by drafting him in the first round in 1972. He turned into a dependable player during his three stints with the Royals: 1975–76, 1978–82, and 1985–88, which were just a few seasons of his 18-year big league playing career.

But Quirk may have helped the Royals the most when he was playing for the Cleveland Indians. During the 1984 season, the Royals were in an American League West pennant race with the Minnesota Twins. Meanwhile, Quirk lived much of '84 out of his suitcase. He started the year in spring training with the St. Louis Cardinals. After they released him, he signed with the Chicago White Sox, who sent him to their Triple A team in Denver for most of the season. He played three games with the big league White Sox before being sent back down to Denver.

With less than a week left in the regular season, the Indians acquired Quirk from Chicago. (Coincidentally, one of Cleveland's remaining series was against the Twins.) Before reporting to the Indians, though, Quirk attended Paul Splittorff's retirement party in Kansas City. When Quirk left that night, he made a prediction. "I was kidding around with the guys," Quirk said, "and I told them that I'd help them win the division."

On Thursday the 27th, an off day, the Royals were headed to Oakland for the final series of the regular season. Kansas City held a one-and-a-half game lead over Minnesota. While at an airport, some Royals had a radio tuned to the Minnesota-Cleveland game.

In the top of the ninth inning, Quirk went into the game as the Indians catcher. In the bottom of the inning, Quirk stepped up to the plate with two outs, nobody on base, and the game tied at three. Announcer Fred White, who was listening to the game with George Brett, one of Quirk's close friends, turned to Brett and said: "You don't suppose he's going to do that, do you?"

"Why else would he be there?" Brett replied. "Of course he's going to do it." And he did. Facing Ron Davis, Quirk hit the longest home run of his career into the upper deck at Cleveland's old Municipal Stadium. "No, I wasn't thinking about the Royals at the moment, but I definitely was after the game," Quirk said. "I guess it made for a great story line."

Quirk's game-winning home run, for all intents and purposes, knocked the Twins out of contention, and the Royals clinched the division the next day. That was Quirk's only at-bat with the Indians. "So probably my biggest hit for the Royals," he said, "was when I wasn't even a member of the Royals."

81 Royals Baseball Academy

Royals owner Ewing Kauffman, who was way ahead of his time in just about everything he did, wanted to launch an experiment. Though he didn't have a baseball background when he founded the Royals, Kauffman quickly became knowledgeable about the game and felt there had to be a way to find players other than the traditional outlets of the early 1970s: the draft and trades. So one of his projects, though it never really caught on, was called the Royals Baseball Academy.

The most noteworthy graduate of the Royals Baseball Academy, defensive whiz Frank White, makes a play during the 1977 playoffs against the New York Yankees. (AP Images)

Kauffman and the academy's director, Syd Thrift, believed that you could take a great athlete, particularly a guy with speed, and turn him into a baseball player by basically having a school where the focus was fundamentally sound baseball. "In terms of baseball, learning fundamentals is the most important thing in the world for young players," said Thrift, who passed away in 2006. "They even have to understand what a baseball does in flight. They have to understand the baseball bat—what it can do, how to hit with two strikes, and so on. Look at it this way: if you have a tough subject in school and you've really prepared well for the final exam, you've drilled yourself over and over. You have no fear. But if you've been sloughing off, you're going to have a problem. There's poor execution in the major leagues today because players haven't been drilled over and over in the fundamentals."

Players were sent to Florida, where the Royals built a complex near Sarasota, with five fields, dorms, and a swimming pool. Players attended classes at nearby Manatee Junior College and then worked on the fundamentals of baseball. Players weren't allowed to have cars there, and they all had to be single—at least most of them. Thrift traveled around the country, holding tryout camps from which he handpicked players for the academy. One of the players he found turned into not only the academy's greatest success story, but also one of the best players in Royals history—Frank White.

White was married and working as a sheet metal clerk at Metals Protection Plating Company when he decided to try out for the academy. Thrift, who was very proud of the fact he discovered White, was so enamored with him that he convinced Kauffman to bend the rules about marriage for this one player. "Frank did things so easily and with such grace," Thrift said. "I used to get on him about taking charge because he was a great athlete, but he was so laid back."

Another graduate of the academy who has become well known as a player and manager is Ron Washington. "Syd Thrift signed me from a tryout camp in New Orleans," Washington said. "The first tryout, Syd sent me home early. But then he called and invited me back with three other guys." Washington was the only one signed out of the 156 who showed up at the New Orleans tryout. "[At the academy] we learned baseball on the chalkboard and then took it to the field," Washington said. "We went to school in the morning and learned fundamentals day after day after day. When it was time to play a game, we executed."

The academy seemed to work for a few years. Unfortunately, though, there was a division between Kauffman and some of his front-office people, including general manager Cedric Tallis and manager Charlie Metro, and the academy folded after four years. But not before 12 other players made it to the major leagues, including U.L. Washington and Jeff Cox.

"I was 16 years old and had just graduated from high school [in 1970] when they signed me," Ron Washington said. "I learned perseverance through the baseball academy. It taught us not only how to play the game, but also how to be men and how to deal with adversity. The knowledge that I give to the kids today, I learned at 17 years old with Kansas City. Some of these kids don't have it yet. Mr. Kauffman did a great job of trying to do something for kids that might not get drafted."

82 Attend Royals Fantasy Camp

Have you ever wondered what it'd be like to be in the batter's box against Dennis Leonard or Jeff Montgomery? Or to pitch to George Brett or John Mayberry? Or to be in the outfield alongside Jermaine Dye and Willie Wilson? With the annual Royals Alumni

Fantasy Camp held each winter at the Royals spring training facility in Surprise, Arizona, you could find out.

Fantasy Camp is set up much like a shortened version of major league's spring training. After the first day, which consists of clinics and live batting practice—basically a quick chance to loosen up the muscles—the alumni coaches hold a draft. And then the games begin. The campers' teams go against each other before the experience concludes with three-inning games of campers vs. alumni.

The only similarity among the campers—besides being Royals fans—is that everyone is at least 30 years old. Other than that people of all sorts—and every sort—of background attend the camp: photographers, preachers, writers, firemen, policemen, insurance agents, salesmen, land developers, doctors, software developers, teachers, undercover FBI agents, and so on. And they come from all points throughout the United States. "Because of the wide range of ages and athletic abilities, you'll see all sorts of things you don't normally see on a baseball field," said former Royals pitcher Jaime Bluma, who makes an effort to be a coach as often as his schedule and the alumni lineup will allow. "There was a guy playing in the field a few years ago—and I won't tell you his name, occupation, or where he's from—who went chasing after a foul ball in the first inning and didn't show back up until the fifth inning... Another year, we had a family doctor who was 72 years old. Great guy and fun to be around. He was in the outfield and after innings it was taking him awhile to get back to the dugout, so we finally told him, 'Unless you're due to hit, don't even worry about coming to the dugout when we're hitting.'"

The Royals alumni cap the number at 72 campers along with 18 to 20 former players, which means three former players coach a team of 12 campers. Some of the coaches who frequently attend include Brett, Montgomery, Wilson, Leonard, Mayberry, John Wathan, and Al Fitzmorris. Other former players have included: Willie Aikens, Steve Balboni, Dye, Jim Eisenreich, Mark Gubicza,

If You're Not Camping, There's Always BP

The Royals know that the large price tag precludes many fans, even the biggest die-hards, from attending Royals Fantasy Camp. So in the early 2000s, they started Royals BP Day, a drastically scaled-down version of Fantasy Camp. (Cost for BP Day is about one-tenth of Fantasy Camp.) Twice a season the Royals alumni hold four-hour batting practice sessions at Kauffman Stadium. Each Royals BP Day is limited to 40 participants and has 10 former Royals players. "Although it's not the same experience as going to Arizona, everyone who does this has a blast," said former pitcher Jaime Bluma. "It's not only a cost factor but also traveling to Arizona and taking five days off work. Some people just can't do that. This way it's at Kauffman Stadium, and you're taking only half of a Saturday to be a part of something really cool."

The campers, who receive a T-shirt and shorts, go through four stations: batting practice in the cages behind the Royals dugout, infield practice, shagging fly balls in the outfield, and, of course, live batting practice on the field.

David Howard, Brian McRae, Mike Macfarlane, Fred Patek, Joe Randa, Bret Saberhagen, Kevin Seitzer, Mike Sweeney, Jerry Terrell, and Frank White. In 2014 first-timers Jason Kendall and Cookie Rojas will be among the coaches.

The week costs about $4,000, and that includes hotel, breakfast, lunch, two personalized uniforms to keep, clubhouse locker, autograph session with the alumni, baseball cards, team photo, and a camp video. A typical day consists of breakfast at the team hotel, a morning game, lunch at the complex, an afternoon game, and then a chance to hang out in the clubhouse. "I attended the Royals Fantasy Camp from 2004 to 2006," said Chris Reaves, who lives in the Kansas City area. "During those three years, I built up lasting friendships that I carry on to this day with not only other campers, but also several Royals alumni. During these camps the Royals staff and alumni treated us as if we were major leaguers and made us feel like we were one of the guys. At the time I thought playing baseball with a bunch of ex-Royals players would be the highlight, but instead it turned out that the camaraderie and inside the clubhouse stories and friendships are what make this camp the ultimate fantasy for any baseball fan."

The late Fred White was instrumental in the camp from its early days until his death in 2013. "Being around it I see guys having more fun than they ever thought they'd have in their life," White said. "They're reliving their boyhood while getting on the field with former major league players, playing games, maybe pulling a hamstring. There's a reason they call it fantasy camp; it's because guys are living out their fantasies."

83 Boys Will Be Boys: Royals Pranksters

The Royals have had some characters throughout the years: practical jokers, guys who loved to play pranks on teammates, or just goofballs. Although the stories are endless, here are a few of the oddest.

Tom Burgmeier on Moe Drabowsky

TB: We had a stuffed monkey with a noose around its neck, and if you had a bad game, someone would hang that monkey in your locker. We were on a losing streak, and that monkey was hanging in someone's locker. This particular night the security guard was standing there, and Drabo asks to see the guard's gun. Not thinking about it, he hands the gun to Drabo, who decided to shoot the monkey! The bullet went through the monkey and a couple of suitcases behind it.

Another time, Drabo, stark naked after the game, grabbed a 20-gauge shotgun, went into the shower, and yelled, "Alright, you sons of bitches" and boom—fired the shotgun in the shower!

Fred White on Carl Taylor

FW: Carl Taylor got so frustrated after a game in Baltimore—when he ended the game hitting into a double play or striking out—that he burned his uniform in the clubhouse. He decided that was it; he was quitting. I remember also being on the bus one time, and Taylor, who was Boog Powell's stepbrother, was having trouble finding a seat, so he yelled out, "Why don't some of you people stand up and let a real ballplayer sit down." A voice replied, "Good idea, Carl, but you're already standing."

Steve Mingori on Al Hrabosky

SM: The first time I met Al Hrabosky, we went to dinner with his wife and my girlfriend on the Plaza. There was a rose there with thorns. He picked it up and ate all of it, including the thorns. I couldn't believe it. He later asked me if I'd help him with his change-up, which I did. It was funny, though, because he'd go [behind the mound] for his fist pump and his mad stare, and he'd stomp up to the mound. And then he'd throw a change-up.

Jerry Terrell on Amos Otis

JT: Amos was a practical joker, but [trainer Mickey Cobb] and I got him back one time. Amos couldn't stand that I was a little, skinny guy, but I kept telling him that I outweighed him. He'd say I didn't, and we'd go back and forth. Finally, he said, "Let's go to the scales." What he didn't know was that Mickey and I cooked up a plan. Mickey had those small circle weights and he took two five-pound weights and put them in my back pockets. Amos got on the scale and he was something like 185. I got on and I was 189. He got so mad. "There's got to be something wrong with the scale. Somebody's messing with it," he said. I told him to adjust it however he wanted to. Well, bottom line each time, no matter what he did, I was three to five pounds heavier than Amos. He'd go into [equipment manager] Al Zych's room and start grabbing candy bars and watermelon—anything to add weight. This went on for 30 days. Thirty days! It got to a point where I was putting two 10-pound weights in my pockets. After 30 days he was up to 197 pounds. Mickey convinced me that we needed to tell Amos. So, we got on the scale one more time. Amos weighed 197. Then, I got on…175. He couldn't believe it! Mickey held up the weights and said, "Are you looking for these, Amos?" That was the longest prank I was ever involved with. To this day Amos looks at me and asks, "Got any weights in your pockets?"

Denny Matthews on Bo Jackson

DM: Bo was big into hunting and he'd take his bow and arrows to the clubhouse. When no one was in there or at least not in danger, he'd shoot that thing in the clubhouse as target practice. Even though he wasn't going to hurt anyone, I don't think that went over too well.

Mark Gubicza on his close friend, Bret Saberhagen

MG: He was a practical joker, but a couple of his jokes backfired on him. Bo Jackson was wearing a suit, and Sabes threw a grape or a strawberry that got on Bo's suit. Bo was upset. He wasn't a good guy to have upset at you. He was willing, ready, and able to make Sabes part of the wall. Luckily for all of us, he didn't.

Another time, I was pitching on a terribly hot Sunday afternoon. I finished the game, and Sabes came up to throw a big bucket of ice water on me. It missed me and hit Jose Martinez, our first-base coach. Jose lost it. He wanted to get a hold of Sabes. I think it just shocked Jose so much. Sabie had a blast and he wasn't selective in his craziness. That's for sure.

John Wathan on the Cleveland Indians

JW: We were sitting around in Cleveland after a game one time, having some beers and we didn't have a ride back to the hotel. There was one of those Pushman golf carts right outside the clubhouse with some beer kegs on it. We decided we would take that back to the hotel. So we drove through the streets of Cleveland on that golf cart, hauling beer kegs. I think we might have lost a keg on the way back. We pulled into the hotel and paid one of the bellmen to drive the cart back to the stadium.

84 Jim Sundberg and the 1985 Pitching Staff

There were several keys for the 1985 World Series-winning Royals. One was the addition of 11-year veteran catcher Jim Sundberg, whom the Royals acquired in a six-player, four-team trade with the Texas Rangers, Milwaukee Brewers, and the New York Mets in January of 1985. To land Sundberg, who was known for his defensive abilities rather than his bat, the Royals sent catcher Don Slaught to Texas and pitcher Frank Wills to New York. After winning six consecutive Gold Gloves, "Sunny" spent two seasons with the Royals. He never hit better than .245 with the Royals but masterfully handled a young pitching staff.

What were the attributes of that great 1985 starting rotation?

Jim Sundberg: We had three left-handers, and they were all different. Danny Jackson, for instance, was an extreme power pitcher with a sinking fastball and hard slider. Bud Black used three to four pitches, and then Charlie Leibrandt was a finesse guy who moved his fastball around. Then on the right side, you had Bret

Saberhagen and Mark Gubicza, who were both power guys. Sabes probably had the best fastball I ever caught. It was an accelerator. It gave the impression that it popped at the end. Gubie had a hard sinker and a hard slider. They all competed internally against each other, but they all pulled for each other. It's also the only time in my major league career when the entire staff remained intact the entire season.

Was anyone on that staff hard to catch?
JS: Danny Jackson was one of the hardest guys for me to catch in my career because of his explosive fastball. He wasn't quite sure if he'd cut it or sink it, so that was tough because I had to set up and be ready to go in either direction.

What were the dispositions of the starting pitchers?
JS: The temperaments of the pitchers were very different. Danny was probably one of the more intense guys I've caught and he could get very angry between innings and be hard on himself. Gubie might get mad at other guys. But keep in mind that Jackson, Sabes, and Gubie were all young guys with great confidence and poise on the mound. Sabes was very happy-go-lucky. Pressure didn't affect him. In the seventh game of the World Series, he was so good that I came in after the first inning and told the guys in the dugout that he was throwing so well that if we got one run, we'd win. Those last four innings—with our big lead and how well he was pitching—were probably the most fun I ever had on the field, just knowing we were going to win.

What's the best World Series slide you've ever seen?
JS: [Laughs.] I would say mine in '85 in the sixth game. It's interesting because there's part of me wondering if Dick Howser was going to pinch run for me. I was the winning run at second with the bases loaded. I remember thinking that I wanted a big lead

and to get a good jump. As the play happened, I saw [St. Louis Cardinals catcher] Darrell Porter move in front of the plate, so that caused me to slide headfirst to the back side of the plate. It was the fastest I ran at that age. [Laughs.] It was fun. Lonnie Smith and Buddy Biancalana met me at the plate, and I jumped up in their arms. Of course, Dane Iorg got a bloody nose because guys were pounding on him so much after he hit those two runs in.

That trip to the postseason in 1985 was the only one in your 16-year career. Can you put that experience into words?
JS: You never know if you'll get that chance. Some incredible players never get that opportunity. It was remarkable. I remember that as we continued to win, the pressure for me was released. The most pressure to me was just trying to get to the postseason. Once we got there, it was easier to play. Once we beat Toronto in the playoffs and were headed to the World Series, I felt like a 10-year-old giggly kid with the honor of being one of the two teams left playing. The greatest thrill was playing in the World Series, and the greatest fun was the last four innings of the seventh game against St. Louis. That World Series ring that you get on Opening Day of the following season is what you play this game for. The bonus check is nice, but you play for that ring.

As the final fly ball in Game 7 was headed toward Darryl Motley, what was going through your mind?
JS: It was suspended animation. The ball goes up, and you know that as soon as it's caught, the game is over. The ball was hit so high that George [Brett] ran to the mound as the ball was in the air, and I started to run out there. Once it was caught, it's just mass chaos. It's such a tremendous feeling. The cover of *Sports Illustrated* was of six or seven of us celebrating at the mound. I have that framed in my home office, and it's just a wonderful feeling and memory.

85 The McRaes and Other Royal Families

Even though it's taken on a cheesy image, giving a Hallmark flair to *Field of Dreams*, baseball has the ability to strengthen the bond between fathers and sons. And when it comes to a professional baseball family tree, the Royals have some pretty deep roots. More than a dozen former Royals have had a close relative in professional baseball. The Royals have had some unique situations with a father managing his son, brothers playing together, and two managers who are parts of three-generation baseball families.

Perhaps the most well-known pair is Hal and Brian McRae. After Brian grew up around the Royals from his early elementary school days with his dad, Hal, the Royals selected Brian in the first round of the 1985 draft. Thirty-eight games into Brian's first full season with the Royals in 1991, Hal McRae became manager of the Royals. "I didn't like playing for him at first because I wasn't established here," Brian said. "In every big league city, people wanted to talk about us. I felt it was a lot of undue focus on me when I hadn't done anything yet."

After a couple seasons, Brian McRae was a legitimate big league outfielder. Then it was time to have some fun with Dad. And it was time to enjoy life together as a family year-round for the first time. "I was a father more than a coach or a manager," Hal said, "which [Brian] preferred, and it worked out better that way. We remained friends because of that. Looking back on it, it was a thrill of a lifetime. How many people get to manage in the big leagues, and play in the big leagues, play in the World Series, and manage his son? That's quite a bit."

With Hal McRae's playing career ending just three years before Brian's started, several players had a chance to play with both

One of several family connections in Royals history, Hal McRae managed his son and outfielder, Brian, for four seasons.

McRaes. One was George Brett, who was good friends with Hal. When both arrived in Kansas City in 1973, they added an intensity to the club that helped lead it to supremacy in the American League West. Brett learned much of that all-out style from his dad and three brothers. One of his brothers, Ken, was a longtime major league pitcher, including time with George and the Royals during 1980–81. "We were taught by our father that when you go out there to play baseball, you give 100 percent. You don't let your team down," Brett said. "I knew that I would've gotten a call from all of my brothers if they ever saw, if they ever heard, or if someone ever told them that I wasn't hustling."

Two former Royals managers—Bob Boone and Buddy Bell—are part of a small fraternity who have had three generations of players in the big leagues. Bell had three sons in professional baseball. The most notable was David, an important part of the San Francisco Giants' 2002 World Series team. Middle brother Mike spent several years in the minor leagues and played briefly with the Cincinnati Reds. Bell's youngest son, Rick, spent a decade in the minors with five organizations, including Kansas City's Omaha affiliate. Buddy's dad, Gus, spent 15 years in the big leagues. Then, of course, there's Buddy, who played 18 seasons and won six Gold Glove awards. "I don't ever remember not wanting to be a major league player," Bell said. "I wouldn't have the same desire, maybe, if I didn't have a father who played, but as far back as I can remember, this is what I wanted to do."

Bob Boone played catcher for the Royals from 1989–90 and managed them from 1995–97. His father, Ray, was a two-time All-Star who played for six teams, including the Kansas City A's in 1959. Bob's sons, Aaron and Bret, also became All-Stars, making the Boones the first baseball family to send three generations to the All-Star Game.

The Royals' baseball family tree isn't limited to the field. Broadcaster Ryan Lefebvre's dad, Jim, enjoyed a long career in the

All in the Family

Several other Royals have had another family member in professional baseball. Here are some of the more memorable ones. Tenure with Royals is indicated in parentheses.

- **Jeremy Giambi** (1998–99), whose brother, Jason, had a long major league career.
- **Chris Gwynn** (1992–93), whose brother, Tony, had a Hall of Fame career with the San Diego Padres.
- **Whitey Herzog** (manager 1975–79), whose grandson, John Urick, played in the New York Yankees and Philadelphia Phillies farm systems.
- **Dane Iorg** (1984–85), whose brother, Garth, played for the Toronto Blue Jays for nine years.
- **Jason Kendall** (2010), whose dad, Fred, played in the big leagues before serving as the Royals bullpen coach (2006–07).
- **Joe Keough** (1969–72), whose brother, Marty, and Marty's son, Matt, played in the major leagues.
- **John Mayberry** (1972–77), whose son, John Jr., made a name for himself with the Phillies.
- **Lindy McDaniel** (1974–75), whose brother, Von, played with him for the St. Louis Cardinals.
- **Marty Pattin** (1974–80), whose son, Jon, played in the San Francisco Giants and Anaheim Angels organizations.
- **Gaylord Perry** (1983), whose brother, Jim, pitched for four teams during a 17-year big league career.
- **Steve Renko** (1983), whose sons, Steve III, spent 12 years in professional baseball with six affiliated organizations, and Todd, played one year in the Angels organization.
- **Danny Tartabull** (1987–91), whose dad, Jose, spent nine years in the major leagues, including time with the Kansas City A's.
- **John Wathan** (1976–85), whose sons, Derek and Dusty, both played in the minor leagues with Dusty playing for the Royals during the 2002 season.

majors as a player, coach, and manager. Ryan Lefebvre had a great career at the University of Minnesota as a three-time All-Big Ten pick before spending one season in the Cleveland Indians' farm system. "Watching him deal with reporters in the manager's office after games indirectly has influenced my broadcasting career," Lefebvre said, "because I've never been intimidated behind a microphone or a television camera."

Traveling around the majors as a broadcaster, Lefebvre's had a chance to talk with players who've had fathers in the major leagues. He says the experience of growing up with a major league player as a father was similar for him and many of the players. "Dads who play baseball generally don't push their sons toward the sport like other fathers do with their kids," Lefebvre said. "Like any other kid, you grow up wanting to be like your dad. It just happens that, for some of us, our dad played Major League Baseball."

86 Letterman's Biancalana Hit Counter

Two months before Biancalana's stellar 1985 World Series, he started to become somewhat of a folk hero and cult legend in mid-August, thanks to David Letterman. As Pete Rose closed in on Ty Cobb's career hits record, Letterman, always a fan of interesting last names, brought out a "Buddy Biancalana Hit Counter" on his show to display Biancalana's chase of Rose and Cobb. "The attention of the baseball world will shift then to another historic record chase," Letterman said. "And with this Buddy Biancalana Hit Counter, you can chart the Royals' veteran utility infielder's march to immortality." And then after adding a hit to Biancalana's total, giving him 12, Letterman joked: "Only 4,181 hits to go. Good luck, Buddy, keep up the good work." (For the record, Letterman wasn't giving Biancalana enough credit. Biancalana was around 50 career hits when Letterman introduced the counter.)

Throughout the rest of the season, Letterman brought out the hit counter periodically and told everyone how Rose and Biancalana did the previous day. After the season Biancalana, being a good sport, appeared in studio with Letterman. Because of those two months, Biancalana will always be a hero and a legend to some fans. "That definitely got me a lot of notoriety at a time where my play wasn't. It was a wonderful experience," said Biancalana, whom the Royals picked in the first round of the 1978 draft. "There's nothing wrong with some publicity, and I certainly got it."

Although he was batting only .194 with three home runs while playing in parts of four major league seasons at the end of '85, Biancalana entered "the zone" during the World Series, hitting .278 and going without an error at shortstop as the Royals defeated the St. Louis Cardinals. "The World Series was a fabulous experience for me, as people can imagine, but taking it to a different level [was] that was the best baseball I had ever played," he said. "I reached a level of concentration that I never experienced prior to that time. I don't know how I got there except that for the first time I acknowledged fear—the fear that I experienced prior to Game 1 of the World Series. I'll never forget sitting on my chair in front of my locker prior to the game about a half-hour before ABC wanted us on the foul line. I started thinking, 'Oh my, this is really intense.'"

At that moment Biancalana figured he could put on his street clothes and go watch the game on television or he could grab his glove, walk down the runway, and take the field. "Fear can be our greatest ally or our greatest enemy," he said. "On the other side of fear are tremendous strength, power, freedom, creativity, and all sorts of other good stuff. Since that time I've tried to figure out how to cultivate that."

After back problems cut his playing career short in 1989, he went through a divorce, health problems, and some other personal situations, but Biancalana bounced back. He served as a minor league infield coordinator and a manager in the Tampa Bay Rays and Philadelphia Phillies farm systems. Then in 2006 he and Steve Yellin co-founded PMPM (Perfect Mind, Perfect Motion) Sports. They also co-authored a book, *The 7 Secrets of World-Class Athletes.* "We're able to teach by design what an athlete learns by chance when he's playing his best," Biancalana said. "The only reason an athlete has a slump, assuming he has good mechanics, is a breakdown in the mind-body connection. With PMPM we're going to the source of the mind-body connection. We're able to set up the conditions systematically for the best motion an athlete has in him."

That symbiosis started with his play during the '85 World Series. "One of the keys for us that year was how we had several come-from-behind wins," he said. "This might sound strange, but late in several games at home when the other team was changing pitchers, that 'Do Wah Diddy Diddy' song was played throughout the stadium, and that got us fired up. The energy that song gave off seemed to trigger something that allowed us to come back and win a lot of games."

It also didn't hurt that the Royals had George Brett, Hal McRae, Frank White, Willie Wilson, and Dick Howser aboard. "Playing between two [Royals] Hall of Famers with George and Frank can only make you a better player. As crummy of a player as I was, who knows how bad I could've been had I not had those two guys?" Biancalana said with a laugh. "And we had a great leader in Dick Howser, who managed flawlessly in the World Series. He was a fiery guy who never panicked. Panicking is not conducive to successful baseball."

87 Visit FanFest

The concept shouldn't seem so novel: doing something for the fans. Well, pardon the expression, but in 2008 the Royals hit a home run with their fans with the introduction of an annual FanFest during the winter, shortly before spring training. Since then it's gone through some experimenting and some growing pains, but FanFest has nearly everything a Royals fan could want—and more. "We thought it could be great for the fans," said Royals general manager Dayton Moore in 2008, "but this is incredible."

There are autograph sessions with current and former Royals—including club Hall of Famers—game-used memorabilia, Royals merchandise, interactive games, special exhibits, on-stage interviews, and other entertainment. Along the way there's a good chance of running into some of the front-office folks, including owner David Glass and Moore, who can be seen walking around the festivities, chatting with fans.

Usually during the weekend, the Royals honor their previous year's award winners at the major league level. (Usually that's in the form of a banquet the night before FanFest and then recognition on the stage during the weekend.) Besides all of that, though, FanFest is a chance for more than 10,000 Royals fans to get out of the winter doldrums, if only for a few hours, and get excited about the upcoming baseball season. Excluding 2012 when the event was not held due—the Royals say—to that upcoming summer's All-Star Game FanFest, the first five Royals FanFests were held at the Overland Park Convention Center. In 2014 it was moved to the more spacious Bartle Hall in downtown Kansas City, Missouri. That move increased the amount of room from 60,000 square feet to more than 360,000 square feet. In most years the Royals FanFest has been a two-day event.

FanFest gives the Royals a chance to show their appreciation toward an enthusiastic crowd that generally lines up before the doors open. Does this unbridled excitement translate to more wins on the field? Not necessarily. But you'll have the belief—if even for a couple days in January or early February—that things are getting better.

88 The Maddening Run of Jose Guillen

Oh, what a tangled web we weave,
When first we practise to deceive!
—Sir Walter Scott

Former Royals outfielder Jose Guillen turned around that line from Scott's "Marmion." It was brutal honesty, which got Guillen into trouble during his years with the team from 2008–10. "When you tell the truth all the time, you have your heart right," he said. "When you lie to people, you're hiding something, and it doesn't feel good inside. The problem is that when you tell people the truth, they get offended and mad."

Guillen offended a lot of people. There was an outburst during the Royals' 12-game losing streak in May 2008 where Guillen referred to some of his teammates as "babies." Then on June 23, while the Royals were putting together one of baseball's best interleague records, Guillen went off again about how the team wasn't doing the "little things." And four days later, Guillen made some comments about not caring about the fans' opinions.

As one of the two true veterans on the club—Mark Grudzielanek being the other—Guillen felt it was his responsibility to be a vocal team leader. After a rough start to the 2008 season when he batted .165 through early May, most of his play backed up his words. In June alone, Guillen boasted a .345 batting average with a .611 slugging percentage after hitting nine doubles and seven home runs—one more than he had in the first two months. "Sure, he likes to say a lot, but he does so because he has a lot of passion and a lot of love for the game," Alex Gordon said. "He cares so much. It's good to have that kind of guy around here. He leads us in a lot of different ways."

This wasn't the first time Guillen had spoken his mind in a major league clubhouse. Not many quiet guys who can play the game like Guillen would find themselves on their ninth major league club in their 12th big league season. It's easy to scoff at Guillen's outbursts or say how he's wrong for speaking his mind. It's really easy to do so if you don't know Guillen's back story.

The trait of being outspoken came to Guillen honestly from his late father, Erbedo Guillen. Erbedo ruled his house of seven children (six boys, one girl) with something of an iron fist. "We knew if he caught us in a lie we were in trouble," Jose said. "I'd tell my brother that we'd need to get under the bed when Dad was coming because he was going to get us. When you grow up in that atmosphere, you don't want to lie."

Through a strict father, Jose learned not only the virtue of being truthful, but also of working hard and doing things the right way. It's those lessons that he has applied to his baseball career. Erbedo didn't want Jose to waste his time with baseball, a sport loved in the baseball-crazed Dominican Republic. He used to tell Jose that baseball was "for people who don't have anything better to do."

But ever since Jose started playing baseball at the age of nine with his friends in the street using sticks and whatever the boys could form into baseballs, his sole focus was on coming to the United States to make money playing the game. The only person who believed in him and pushed him to pursue baseball was his mother, Modesti. She made sure he had baseball shoes, a glove, and confidence that he could play. "If not for her, I have no idea what I would be doing now," he said. "I already didn't like school. I just wanted to play baseball. We didn't have a lot of money growing up, so I wanted to make it to the big leagues and take care of my family."

That dream came true when he signed his first professional contract for $2,000 with the Pittsburgh Pirates on August 19, 1992. He had celebrated his 16th birthday just three months earlier. When he signed with the Royals for three years and $36 million before the 2008 season, he was seen as the type of player Kansas City needed. During the previous decade or so, the Royals lost some swagger. The days of players with an edge—the George Bretts and Hal McRaes of the world—might as well have dated back to Ty Cobb.

Guillen provided the Royals a power-hitting outfielder with an attitude. He had other offers but signed with the Royals because of the money and the opportunity to play. At the same time, coming with a big contract to Kansas City, a team scarce of veterans, helped ensure that Guillen would take on the role of leader. "I don't really enjoy being a leader, but I feel like I have a responsibility," Guillen said. "I'm trying to help the young guys…I really believe in the players here. I believe in this team and that we're going to get better."

The Royals didn't improve much (at all) during Guillen's nearly three seasons in Kansas City. After finishing 75–87 in 2008, the club won 65 games in '09 and 67 in '10. But it was a way for the Royals to show their fans and the rest of Major League Baseball that they were willing to go after—and win the negotiations for—high-profile free agents. The Royals traded Guillen to the San Francisco Giants for a player to be named later—which turned out to Kevin Pucetas—in August 2010. In 340 games with the Royals, Guillen batted .256 with 327 hits, 45 home runs, 199 RBIs—and 240 strikeouts. And perhaps he was more duplicitous than he claimed. At the end of the 2010 season when he was left off the Giants' postseason roster, reports came out linking Guillen to HGH. He hasn't been in the majors since.

89 Pitching for the A's and Royals

As the Royals went through the 1968 Expansion Draft, they selected a familiar name to Kansas City baseball fans: Moe Drabowsky. He had been in the majors for 13 years before the Royals selected him 21st in the draft. During four of those seasons, 1962–65, Drabowsky was with the Kansas City A's.

Arguably, two of his worst seasons were with the A's, when he lost 13 games in both 1963 and '64. However, on April 8, 1969, Drabowsky got the first win in Royals history. "I'm very proud of winning the first game," said Drabowsky, who passed away from cancer in 2006.

He was a solid pitcher for nearly two decades, a career that included the 1966 World Series while pitching for the Baltimore Orioles. Drabowsky even set a World Series record for relief pitchers by striking out 11 Los Angeles Dodgers. But he became best known for his pranks. Some of Drabowsky's favorites included the hot foot, snakes in teammates' lockers (and clothes), and goldfish in the opposing team's water jug.

His favorite prank happened in 1966 at old Municipal Stadium while he was pitching with the Orioles. In his first trip to Kansas

City after pitching for the A's, Drabowsky made sure he had his list of important phone numbers handy. A's pitcher Jim Nash was throwing a beauty that game, a shutout with a few scattered hits. Drabowsky dialed the A's bullpen, disguised his voice, and shouted to coach Bobby Hofman: "Get [Lew] Krausse ready in a hurry!" And then he hung up. Krausse started feverishly warming up. Drabowsky and his Baltimore bullpen mates doubled over in laughter. Nash was cruising, so the sight of Krausse was bizarre, and they couldn't believe the gag worked.

After a few minutes, Drabowsky called back and confessed to his prank. "One writer said that I deserved one more victory on my record because Nash saw that bullpen activity, and he got so flustered that he lost his concentration," said Drabowsky, laughing. "That was not true. Nash beat us, but my fan mail definitely increased substantially after that story got out."

Then there were the contests he'd have with Kansas City roommate Dave Wickersham to see who could hold their breath underwater the longest. "Moe would fill the bathtub up with water and say, "Okay, let's see who can keep their head under water the longest, but you're not supposed to tap anybody until 45 seconds,'" Wickersham said. "So I went first. About 45 seconds passed, and he tapped me. I stayed under. He tapped again at 60 seconds. I stayed longer and stayed under there for 1 minute, 15 seconds!"

Wickersham, who still lives in Kansas City, was another name familiar to area fans when he was sold to the Royals before the 1969 season. He had pitched for the Kansas City A's during 1960–63. His best season was '64 when he won 19 games for the Detroit Tigers. "I so desperately wanted to make that Royals club in 1969," Wickersham said. "When I played for the A's, I didn't live here. But while I was with Detroit, I got married and moved to Kansas City. So when the Royals picked me, I'd already had this home built here and lived here in the offseason for four years. Nothing could've been better. My wife is from here, and her parents were living here at the time, so it was a neat thing."

Like Drabowsky, Wickersham pitched in the Royals' first game. He went five innings and didn't give up a run. "It was really great to be able to pitch that day and that season for the Royals," said Wickersham. "We had a lot of good people on that team with good chemistry. It was a great place to end my career."

Although they didn't make huge contributions, two other players, Aurelio Monteagudo and Ken Sanders, also played for both the A's and Royals.

Drabowsky led the American League relief pitchers in 1969 with 11 wins. "I really enjoyed [Kansas City], especially with the Royals," he said "That was a very secure time for me because it was an expansion club. I didn't think I'd wear out my welcome in less than a year."

90 The Duke

Several people have moved throughout the Royals organization. But you would be hard-pressed to find someone who has held as many positions as John "Duke" Wathan. He has been a player, coach, manager, and broadcaster and he's now in charge of special assignments for scouting and player development. With the exception of five years, he's been with the Royals since 1971. "I've got the greatest job in the world," Wathan said, "because I travel throughout our minor league system, get in uniform, and instruct and evaluate both the staff and the players. There aren't many people who are able to be in both scouting and player development. That's quite special for me."

Even though he travels to each of the Royals' minor league teams twice a year for four or five days each, he's able to spend much of his summer at his Kansas City-area home. "I really like the fact that I can be home more with my wife, Nancy," said Wathan, who spent 18 years in a big league uniform. "She put up with a lot, raising three kids while I was gone as a player. If anybody gives me any credit for raising three wonderful kids, I tell them it was her."

Wathan's career with the Royals started as the club's first-round selection in the free-agent draft of January 1971. Every year on his player evaluation, however, he was listed as "NP," which meant "No Prospect." Even though many felt he'd never make it to the big leagues, he kept working hard and doing whatever it took until he ended up playing 10 seasons in the major leagues from 1976 to 1985.

One of his crowning moments came in August 1982 against the Texas Rangers when he set the single-season record for stolen bases by a catcher. It's a record that stands today and could have Wathan's name next to it for years to come. "That record is special. I have that base from Texas as a barstool in my house. I still get people talking about [the record] when they meet me because you think of catchers being slow, and no way could a catcher steal 36 bases in a year," said Wathan, who perfected the walking lead. "I probably could have stolen more that year. I had 25 in June and fouled a ball off my foot and was in a cast for four weeks. I came back five weeks later and got 11 more. I might have been in the 40s or 50s. It's a lot tougher to steal a base now than it was back then. Pitchers then didn't use the move where they spin around to second, so it was a lot easier to steal third. That move never works, but it keeps runners close."

Whenever Wathan, whose dead-on impression of John Wayne led to his nickname, thinks about his career with the Royals, including the great players, the championship teams, and all of the jobs he's held, he can't help but laugh. "I've been very lucky," he

John Wathan, who managed the team after a 10-year career as a Royals player, looks on from the dugout in 1989.

said. "There's not much that I haven't done. Grounds crew would be next, I guess, if Trevor [Vance] would have me. I don't know what I'm going to do when I grow up and have to get a real job. Hopefully that'll never happen."

91 Eisey Overcomes Tourette's

Most people need second chances at some point in life. Jim Eisenreich made the most of his by returning to the major leagues with the Royals in 1987 at the age of 28 and spending a dozen years in the show. Before then, Eisenreich, who played parts of three seasons with the favorite team of his childhood, Minnesota, didn't know if he'd even get another opportunity.

While playing for the Twins, Eisenreich continued to struggle with the problem that had affected him since childhood, Tourette's syndrome. He had been out of professional baseball for more than two years, trying to get healthy from the neurological disorder marked by tics, involuntary sounds, or movements that a person makes over and over. He was told that it was psychological condition and was prescribed hypnosis and psychological sessions. Finally after many ineffective treatments, he was diagnosed as having Tourette's and received medication designed to help alleviate it.

Since 1996, aided by his baseball fame—which he says isn't really a platform—Eisenreich, who remains in the Kansas City area, has been helping educate and inspire kids and families facing Tourette's syndrome through the Jim Eisenreich Foundation. "I feel like every kid who comes up with similar conditions, whether Tourette-related or not, should have a chance," Eisenreich said.

"It's not an obligation, but I feel I should talk to kids and their families. As much as anything, parents need reassurance. It's not something for kids or parents to be ashamed of. I love to tell my story. Every time I tell it, I hope it helps the kids and their families. I know it helps me."

And what a story it is.

Eisenreich can't say exactly when the tics started, but it was sometime between the age of six and eight. He just knows that he was made fun of while growing up in St. Cloud, Minnesota. Eisenreich and his family didn't really know what he had. No one could explain the tics, the muscle jerks, and the constant eye blinking, which compounded the normal awkwardness and ridicule that childhood can bring. Eisenreich avoided most social settings like just going to movies. His relief came through sports, and being one of the best athletes in town certainly didn't hurt. "Sports helped me unbelievably," he said. "In reality that was my outlet to dealing with the physical and social problems with Tourette's. It was an escape. It took the focus away from what I was doing with my tics or whatever. I felt comfortable. On the social side, that's where I was accepted."

Two years after the Twins drafted him in the 16th round, Eisenreich reached the majors with Minnesota in 1982. In 34 games in '82, he batted .303. But fans were brutal, including those at Fenway Park, who yelled, "Shake! Shake! Shake!" He played in 14 more major league games during the next two seasons before being checked into a hospital to find out what was wrong. He went back to St. Cloud and started playing amateur baseball, golf, and even softball. "I was just trying to get my health back, even though I didn't know what that meant," Eisenreich said. "I also wanted another chance in baseball. I didn't know exactly what that meant, but I had to try."

It just so happened that an old teammate from St. Cloud State University, Bob Hegman, worked in the Royals front office.

Although Eisenreich says he's not certain that Hegman talked to then-general manager John Schuerholz, the Royals selected Eisenreich off waivers from the Twins for $1 in 1986 and signed him to a minor league contract. "When the Twins drafted me, it was a dream come true because I never imagined playing anywhere else," Eisenreich said. "With the Royals it was a second chance, but I wasn't thinking [about reaching the majors]. I was just trying to get in and take it day by day. I didn't have long-range goals."

After reaching the majors with the Royals during his first season, Eisenreich went on to play six years in Kansas City. In 1989 after batting .293 in a then-career-high 134 games, Eisenreich was selected as the Royals Player of the Year. He also hit his first home run, a three-run shot, for the Royals in Kansas City against the Twins. "My dad wasn't in the best of health, so he wasn't here, but he was back home in Minnesota watching," said Eisenreich, who doubled earlier in the game. "I won't ever forget that game."

Eisenreich spent the next four seasons with the Philadelphia Phillies, for whom he played in the 1993 World Series. (That was the one that Toronto Blue Jay and Kansas City resident Joe Carter won with a walk-off home run.) Then during a stint that lasted less than two years, Eisenreich won a World Series ring with the Florida Marlins in 1997. "I still have to look at the highlight videos to make sure we won," he said. "It's amazing to know where I came from—not just playing in big league baseball, but I got to play in the best games of the year and the last games. That's the highest notch you can go in baseball. The Hall of Fame is an individual honor, but a World Series championship is about the team."

That big league success is all because the Royals gave him another opportunity. "I've been blessed and lucky," Eisenreich said. "I never knew how long my second chance would last because even if you do make it, you don't know how long you can stay."

92 The Hammer

The 1994 season remains one of the most unforgettable seasons for the Royals over the past generation. The Royals got hot shortly after the All-Star break, winning 14 straight games—the second longest streak in club history—and flirted with first place in the newly formed American League Central.

That also marked *the year* of Bob "The Hammer" Hamelin. During his first full season with the Royals, Hamelin gave the club a true power threat. He hit a team-leading 24 homers, including a walk-off shot against the Chicago White Sox three games into the winning streak, and drove in 65 runs. He was selected as the AL Rookie of the Year, beating out Manny Ramirez. "That was a special season because the team was doing well, and I was doing well," Hamelin said. "We were going to get in the playoffs that year. I didn't play on many teams after that that were like our team in '94. When you win some games and gain confidence, you get an extra edge, which is what we had."

The 1994 season infamously ended with about 45 games remaining due to a strike that also wiped out the postseason. The Royals finished behind the Cleveland Indians and White Sox in the Central with a 64–51 record.

Hamelin struggled during his sophomore season of 1995, so much so that the Royals sent him down to Omaha in June when he had a .175 batting average and two home runs. "For the type of player I was, there's a fine line between being good and not very good at all," Hamelin said. "I don't know what happened for sure [in 1995]. You see it a lot of times. But I don't have any regrets. That's why this game is special."

During spring training in 1997, the Royals released Hamelin. He spent the next two seasons with the Detroit Tigers and Milwaukee Brewers before hanging up his spikes. When his career ended, Hamelin got away from baseball. He moved from Kansas City to North Carolina, where he started buying properties and fixing them up for resale. Then he started a manufacturing business, making storage buildings and sheds. Three years later he was ready to return to familiar territory. "The businesses were great experiences, but I wanted to get back in the game and do something that would let me stay near home with my boys [who were younger than six at the time]," Hamelin said.

He worked as a scout for the Washington Nationals and then the Boston Red Sox. "It takes awhile to learn the scouting side, and you can tell it's not an exact science because a lot of 'sure big leaguers' never make it," said Hamelin. "You have to make good decisions to get the right guy."

93 Two Veteran 1983 Additions: Gaylord Perry and Steve Renko

The Royals starting pitching staff was getting a little long in the tooth in 1983. Paul Splittorff was 36, Larry Gura was 35, and Vida Blue was 33. The Royals, however, added two more veteran pitchers.

Before the season the club signed Kansas City native and University of Kansas three-sport athlete Steve Renko, who was 38 when the season started and would be in his 15th major league season. And then on July 6, the Royals added a future Hall of Famer, the ageless 44-year-old Gaylord Perry, who was in his 22nd big league season and turned 45 during the season.

Both men also were instrumental in the infamous Pine Tar Game. When the melee started after George Brett's homer during the July 24 game at Yankee Stadium, Royals hitting coach Rocky Colavito told Perry to grab the bat. "I got the bat from the umpire, and then several other teammates had it," Perry said. "We didn't want the Yankees or the umpires to get a hold of it. Finally, our tallest guy, [6'5"] pitcher Steve Renko got it and ran with it. There was a group of security guards waiting for Steve as he went up the runway."

During his 22-year career, Perry developed a reputation as a pitcher with less than a bastion of ethics on the mound. "I can't say that I saw Gaylord do anything funny with Vaseline or a file or whatever, but regardless of the temperature, he had his jacket with him in the dugout folded in a special way," said Renko, laughing. "No one ever touched that jacket other than Gaylord."

Three days after the Pine Tar Game, Perry reached a milestone on July 27 that helped ensure his place in the Hall of Fame. He became the third pitcher that season—joining Nolan Ryan and Steve Carlton—to reach 3,500 career strikeouts. By the end of the '83 season, Perry's final big league year, he had 3,534 career strikeouts. "The fact that Kansas City gave me a chance to pitch meant an awful lot to me," he said. "I passed Walter Johnson [3,509] on the all-time list while I was with the Royals. I also pitched my last shutout with Kansas City." That shutout was Perry's last win in the big leagues. It was Saturday, September 3, less than two weeks before his 45th birthday. Perry held the Texas Rangers to six scattered hits during the first game of a doubleheader in Arlington.

Perry's Hall of Fame career, which included eight teams, detoured through Kansas City shortly after the Seattle Mariners placed him on waivers. He picked up four of his 314 career wins with the Royals. "We had some really good players and we had fun," Perry says of the Royals. "Guys have fun today, but maybe they don't show it as much as we did. We had some real cards with guys like George and Renko and Amos Otis. I had great times in Kansas City, and I love the people there."

Even though Perry was accused of doctoring baseballs with anything from saliva to Vaseline, he made hitters look silly. Perry, a five-time All-Star, was the first pitcher to win the Cy Young Award in both leagues. He also threw four straight shutouts in 1970. He was inducted into the Baseball Hall of Fame in 1991.

Then there was Renko, who played football, basketball, and baseball at Kansas. (He's the last three-sport letterwinner in the three main sports for the Jayhawks.) Although the Oakland Raiders drafted Renko, he chose baseball after the New York Mets selected him in the 24th round of the 1965 draft. In 1969 the Mets traded him to the Montreal Expos, where he spent the majority of his career.

He went on to a 15-year big league career, including spending his last season in 1983, playing for the Royals. "I looked forward to that season once I signed with the Royals," he said. "If there's anything tough in baseball, it's traveling, especially when you have a wife and kids. When I signed [with Kansas City,] we could stay at home, and I'd be around more for the family."

Renko had a 6–11 record with one save and 4.30 ERA in 17 starts (25 appearances) for the Royals. "It's like Gaylord said. We had a lot of fun that season," Renko said. "I didn't exactly have a ton of offers as a free agent before that season, but I'm glad the Royals offered me a contract. We had a good ballclub here in Kansas City. Plus it was special to pitch in front of my hometown."

94 The Nutty Buddy

"Be careful what you watch." Never has that phrase been more appropriate than when it applies to former Royals pitcher Mark Littell.

Sure, there's the image of Littell that longtime Royals fans can't shake. During the fifth and deciding game of the 1976 American League playoffs against the New York Yankees, Chris Chambliss ended the series with a home run against Littell.

In all due respect, Littell was a solid reliever for the Royals. Picked by Kansas City in the 12th round of the 1971 Amateur Draft, Littell had an 8–4 record with 16 saves and a 2.08 ERA in 104 innings for the Royals in '76. His numbers—8–4 with 12 saves and a 3.61 ERA in 104⅔ innings—were similar in '77. During the entire 1976 playoffs—Kansas City's first trip to the postseason—Littell had been solid.

And he had only given up one home run that season—until Chambliss. "Yankees fans, as they have been known to do, had thrown a bunch of trash on the field, and it forced a 10-minute delay before Littell faced Chambliss," said broadcaster Denny Matthews. "The first pitch after the delay—Boom!—and that was it. And the boom is for the suddenness of the home run, not its power. It barely got over Hal McRae's glove and the wall in right field."

That image—as painful as it was—is almost preferred to the one for which Littell, who was nicknamed "Airhead," has become famous in recent years. The far worse image is the video of Littell purposefully taking a baseball to the…well, you can guess where based on the name of the product.

It's called the Nutty Buddy.

While Littell was coaching he heard complaints about how his players wouldn't wear cups because they were uncomfortable. So Littell set out to change that. After making sketches and meeting with industrial designers—voila—the Nutty Buddy was born. To prove the Nutty Buddy's effectiveness, Littell was the guinea pig. Squatting atop a bench just a few feet from a pitching machine, wearing the Nutty Buddy, a helmet (backwards, which adds to the craziness of the video), and a smile, Littell takes a baseball to the cojones to prove the effectiveness of his Nutty Buddy.

The plan was marketing gold. Littell and the Nutty Buddy have been featured on Fox News' *Fox & Friends*, ABC's *World News Now*, CNN's *Anderson Cooper 360*, and ESPN's *Sports Science*. (If you enjoy a little sophomoric humor in your day, the original Nutty Buddy video and the *Sports Science* show are must-see videos.)

95 The Royals' Ties to the T-Bones

Chris Browne had a hectic schedule as a 15-year-old in 1985. He'd go to school at Rockhurst High School until about 2:45, be at work by 3:15, stay there until after midnight, go home, do his homework, and go to bed. Then he'd do it all over again the next day. "At times I'd do that for nine straight days," Browne said, "but I wouldn't trade it for anything."

Browne's enthusiasm is understandable. After all he had every boy's dream job in Kansas City during the 1980s, working as a clubbie for the Royals. At that time with the Royals, a kid would start by working in the visitor's clubhouse, eventually become a ball boy, and then move to the Royals clubhouse before ending up as a batboy.

That first job in professional baseball served Browne well. With the exception of going to school during the day, his schedule isn't much different these days. Since the T-Bones' inception in 2003, Browne has worked in various capacities for Kansas City's *other* professional baseball team. He's currently the club's vice president and general manager.

The memories of Browne's years with the Royals from 1985–91 have stuck with him. There were moments such as putting the ball on the batting tee for Cal Ripken Jr. in the tunnel behind the dugout or being told he could keep St. Louis Cardinals pitcher Joaquin Andujar's jacket after Andujar was ejected from Game 7 of the '85 World Series. (He still has it.) Or being offered (and taking) former Royals pitcher Bud Black's BMW to the Rockhurst prom.

Then there was his one-sided exchange with Baltimore's fiery manager, Earl Weaver. After a game part of Browne's duties included going into the visitor's dugout and packing all of the equipment. Late in a contest against the Orioles, Browne went to the steps separating the tunnel and the dugout, waiting for the game to end. He was standing right behind Weaver. "He was fidgety, nervous," Browne said. "And all of a sudden, he turns around and starts screaming at me, 'Get out of here, kid!' I'd seen all of the run-ins Earl Weaver had with the umpires and I'd just experienced one firsthand. He wasn't much bigger than me, but I was practically bawling."

The next day, Browne sheepishly went into Weaver's office and apologized. "You're all right, kid," Weaver said. "I'm just a little superstitious and don't like people behind me. Next time you want to come down, you sit next to me."

Out of all of the great players and managers Browne got to know, however, the one that stands out is George Brett, and that's why Browne gave his son the middle name Brett. The tales of Brett's generosity with the clubhouse guys are legendary. (He even mentioned equipment manager Al Zych in his Hall of Fame speech.) He'd also have a pool party and cookout each year at his house for the clubhouse guys. "After awhile, George took me under his wings," Browne said. "To this day he's a great friend and advisor. I've called him from time to time on a number of things. He's just awesome."

It's safe to say that Brett is the main reason Browne is in Kansas City and, ultimately, with the T-Bones. Shortly after college, Browne was working in the front office of the Jacksonville Suns, a then-minor league affiliate for the Detroit Tigers. In the mid-1990s, Don Kincaid had bought the Attack, Kansas City's indoor soccer team. Kincaid was with one of his neighbors, George Brett, talking to him about how the team was looking for front-office staff. Brett immediately started talking up Browne, who was hired by Kincaid and worked for the Attack in 1996. "I got some great experience in Jacksonville, but my goal was always to come back to Kansas City," Browne said. "Before Don hired me, though, he figured not all of the great stuff George said about me was true, so he called [Brett's wife] Leslie and asked her for the real story about me. Don and [Attack head coach/GM Zoran Savic] often reminded me of that."

When the T-Bones moved to town after the 2002 season, Browne was the second person they hired and he remains in contact with many of the former Royals. Throughout the years several former Royals have been coaches with the T-Bones, including pitcher Danny Jackson and outfielder Darryl Motley. Since 2012 Royals Hall of Fame second baseman Frank White has been the T-Bones first-base coach, while former bullpen catcher Bill Sobbe is the team's pitching coach.

In addition to former Royals on the T-Bones' coaching staff throughout the years, there have been other Royals sightings at CommunityAmerica Ballpark. Former Royals players—including

Motley, Ken Harvey, and Joey Gathright—have played for the T-Bones. And Willie Wilson, who's held his legends game at CommunityAmerica Ballpark, played one game for the T-Bones. He signed a one-day contract in 2009 and then retired, ending his professional playing career in Kansas City. "To still be talking to these guys is incredible to me," said Browne with awe in his voice. "And to be able to have the Royals as part of what we do with the T-Bones is special for me and for our fans."

96 Buck O'Neil

During the 1994 baseball strike, many fans used the PBS documentary *Baseball* to substitute for the September pennant races. On the night of "Inning 5: Shadow Ball," there was this captivating storyteller, offering anecdotes of Satchel Paige and Josh Gibson and other Negro League players that even the die-hardest of the die-hard, seam-head baseball fans hadn't heard. The storyteller was John "Buck" O'Neil.

Literally overnight the 82-year-old O'Neil became a national celebrity. "Buck had this mistaken assumption that we, who had made the series on baseball, were somehow responsible for his celebrity," filmmaker Ken Burns said during the memorial service for O'Neil at Municipal Auditorium in Kansas City on October 14, 2006. "I had always argued the opposite: that we had merely plugged in an amplifier, that it was in fact Buck who was responsible for our success. He wouldn't hear of it, and this became an ongoing thing between us."

The timing, though, couldn't have been stranger. O'Neil's rise in popularity occurred at a time when the Royals were in the midst of a steady decline on the field. The 1994 season, the Royals' first in the American League Central, saw the club make a serious push in the division for only the third time since winning the 1985 World Series. When the 1994 strike hit, the Royals were 13 games above .500. The club failed to finish above .500 again until 2003—and then not again until 2013.

The founder and longtime ambassador of the Negro Leagues Baseball Museum, former Kansas City Monarchs star Buck O'Neil stands next to his statue at the museum. (AP Images)

Meanwhile O'Neil's popularity skyrocketed. In spite of the Royals' struggles, O'Neil gave sports fans and the city a consistently positive baseball story. He had a rich history in Kansas City baseball. During his 12-year playing career—mainly for the Kansas City Monarchs, which included three trips to the East-West All-Star Game—he batted .288. O'Neil hit a career-high .358 in 1947 and won batting titles in 1940 and '46.

From 1948–55 O'Neil managed the Monarchs, leading the club to four league championships. He also managed the West squad in the All-Star Game four times, winning each contest. It stood to reason then that O'Neil could recognize talent when he saw it. The Chicago Cubs hired him in 1956 to do just that as a scout. They weren't disappointed. He signed the likes of Ernie Banks, Lou Brock, Joe Carter, and Lee Smith. Besides the great players O'Neil signed, he made a significant contribution to baseball during his 32-year career with the Cubs when in 1962 he became the first African American coach in the major leagues. In 1988, the same year O'Neil retired from the Cubs, then-Royals general manager John Schuerholz offered O'Neil a job as special assignment scout. He was associated with the club from that moment on. "The job with the Royals turned out to be even more rewarding than I expected," O'Neil wrote in his book, *I Was Right On Time.*

On October 6, 2006, O'Neil passed away. He was a month shy of 95. But O'Neil lives on both at the National Baseball Hall of Fame and at Kauffman Stadium. In 2008, two years after a special committee inexcusably passed over O'Neil for inclusion with other former Negro League players at the Baseball Hall of Fame—while he was still living—the Hall of Fame started the Buck O'Neil Lifetime Achievement Award. As part of that honor, a bronze statue of Buck greets visitors at the Hall of Fame.

In 2007 the Royals began the Buck O'Neil Legacy Seat program. For every home game, the Royals honor a nominee who "embodies an aspect of O'Neil's spirit" by allowing him or her to sit in the seat that Buck occupied behind home plate. That's certainly a big seat to fill.

97 Kauffman's Renovation: The $250 Million Face-Lift

It's hard to believe this old girl has reached 40. Sure enough, though, 2013 marked the 40th birthday for Kauffman Stadium. In many ways the stadium looks similar to how it did when it opened on April 10, 1973 as state-of-the-art Royals Stadium. A giant iconic crown scoreboard remains the centerpiece, though long gone are the days of the Lite-Brite type images of players' faces. (Actually, and somewhat sadly, those have been gone for several years—kind of like the old Atari games.) In its place is a 105 x 85-foot high-definition video screen that might be visible from Paola, Kansas. To put it in perspective, the size of the old screen was 40 x 60 feet. The old JumboTron was 30 x 40 feet.

The scoreboard remains flanked by the famous fountains where middle infielders Freddie Patek and Cookie Rojas took a dive when the club won its first division championship in 1976. In spite of the similarities, following a $250 million renovation that was completed before the 2009 season, the old girl looks a lot different—and not in a slapping some lipstick on a pig kind of way. It actually looks like a new stadium.

A year after the monstrosity of a CrownVision scoreboard was installed, the stadium was ready on April 10, 2009—a year ahead of schedule. Among the changes: the concourses are about double their previous size, there are now staircases at each end of the view level, and all of the concession stands received a face-lift. There are new entrance areas, a 5,000-square-foot team store on the main level behind home plate, and dugout concourse areas, which used to be the dark tunnel below the stadium. Now it's a brighter area with new concession stands exclusively for people sitting in the dugout box seats.

Some of the most dramatic changes happened beyond the outfield wall. When you look to the scoreboard, you're not eyeing a hill that leads up to I-70. As you sit in lower-level seats down the right-field line, the stadium feels more enclosed because of the outfield seats. When the stadium opened in 1973, there was a section of general admission seats down the right-field and left-field lines next to the bullpens. Now there are 400 Fountain Pavilion seats,

The Kauffman (Stadium) Center for Performing Arts

When the Royals officials were making their wish list for the Kauffman Stadium renovations, one item that ended up getting axed was a stage/pavilion area directly behind the scoreboard to hold concerts. Even though the idea was nixed, it wouldn't have been the first time concerts have been held at Kauffman Stadium. Besides postgame Christian Family Day concerts, the stadium played host to various concerts throughout the years. Here are some of the concerts held at then-Royals Stadium:

1973: Chicago
1973: Three Dog Night
1974: The Allman Brothers Band
1974: Crosby, Stills, Nash & Young with the Beach Boys
1976: Summer Jam—Fleetwood Mac, REO Speedwagon, Kansas
1976: Peter Frampton with Santana
1977: Summer Jam—Ted Nugent, REO Speedwagon, The Little River Band
1978: Summer Jam—Kansas, Eddie Money, The Steve Miller Band, Van Halen
1979: George Benson and B.B. King with Chic, Ashford & Simpson
1979: Summer Jam—REO Speedwagon, Santana, Little River Band

which surround—you guessed it—the fountains in left-center field. There's also a standing-room-only section below the fountains in right-center.

Behind those seats, there's a Hall of Fame building in left field and a sports bar on the right-field side, which features a rooftop area where people can hang out and watch a game. In between those two buildings is a walkway area that includes the statues of Frank White, George Brett, Dick Howser, and Ewing and Muriel Kauffman. There are more concession stands, a picnic area, and a retail store. A new and expanded kids area includes batting cages, pitching cages, a carousel, five holes of miniature golf, a base-running timer, and a bigger and nicer Little K with FieldTurf.

With the changes, Kauffman Stadium's seating capacity was actually reduced from 40,775 to 37,903. The renovation was well-received by most Royals fans, but there were some throughout the whole process that were calling for the club to start fresh and build a new stadium in downtown Kansas City. One big opponent of moving downtown, though, was former general manager Herk Robinson, who was the director of operations during the Royals' first year at Kauffman Stadium. "I know there had been sentiment to put the stadium downtown," he said. "It would've been wonderful if people could've guaranteed that downtown Kansas City would be like downtown Cleveland, or downtown Baltimore, and other similar places that are heaven on earth. I'll say respectfully that if you want to kill the Royals quickly, move the team downtown. When other stadiums went downtown, there was already an established downtown, and they became the crown jewel. But to put a stadium in downtown, hoping it becomes vibrant is a big risk."

Robinson also remembers the days when the stadium hosted rock concerts. (See sidebar.) He said he'd leave before the concert not knowing if the stadium would still be standing the next morning. Fortunately, Kauffman is still around—with just a nip and tuck here and there. "Kauffman Stadium is as good as any stadium that's ever been built," Robinson said, "which is reinforced when you see this much money put in to remodel it."

98 The 2013 Home Finale

It's every boy's dream to hit a walk-off home run. Justin Maxwell did that and then some for the Royals at the end of September 2013.

The Royals and Texas Rangers were among the four teams fighting for two wild-card spots. On Sunday, September 22, the Royals were playing host to the Rangers in the 2013 home finale. The Cleveland Indians, the wild-card leader, had won earlier in the day and held a four-game lead over the Royals with seven to play.

In the bottom of the 10th inning of the scoreless Rangers-Royals game, Maxwell batted with two outs and the bases loaded. He'd be facing former Royals closer Joakim Soria. With a full count, Maxwell, whom the Royals acquired in a trade with the Houston Astros on July 31, blasted Soria's pitch to the seats in left field with a 421-foot no-doubter. "I was just trying to hit the ball hard," Maxwell said. "I'd never faced Soria before, but I knew with the shadow [between home plate and the pitcher's mound] that the ball was going to jump on me."

Instead, Maxwell jumped on it in front of 27,899 at Kauffman Stadium. "I felt good," Soria said. "It was 3–2; I had to throw a strike. I can't give the umpire a chance to call a ball. I've got to throw a strike, hope he swings at it, and hits it at somebody. He hit it well."

Oddly, it was Maxwell's second walk-off grand slam in a home finale. He did the same thing for the Washington Nationals on September 30, 2009.

After James Shields threw eight scoreless innings, the Rangers threatened in the ninth. They had a runner on second with no outs against Greg Holland when Alex Rios, the runner at second, tried to test Alex Gordon's arm on a fly ball by Adrian Beltre. It was not a wise move as Gordon notched his 16th outfield assist of the season.

Although Maxwell's blast kept the Royals alive for another day, the club went 6–4 in its final 10 games and fell behind the hotter Cleveland Indians (10–0 in their last 10), Tampa Bay Rays, and Texas (each 8–2 in their last 10) for a wild-card berth.

However, the Royals' final record of the 2013 was 86–76, the team's best mark since it finished 92–70 in 1989. And the 2013 campaign gave the Royals optimism heading into the offseason. "This team came out every game and expected to win every game regardless of what happened the night before," Holland told *The Kansas City Star*. "You've got to grind it out that way. That's how you get in the playoffs. We came up short, but I think going into [2014], we're going to be pretty happy about where we're at."

99 SungWoo Brings Luck in '14

Adding to the craziness of the 2014 season and the idea of things happening for a reason, a man named SungWoo Lee traveled more than 6,500 miles (one way) to see the Royals in person for the first time. There's no way anyone could've anticipated what would transpire during the 10-day voyage.

SungWoo Lee's love of the Royals began 20 years ago. He was trying to improve his English by watching Major League Baseball games and he saw a broadcast of a Royals game from Kauffman Stadium. After Royals batter Jeff King launched a home run, the South Korean immediately fell in love with the "beautiful K" and he wanted to learn all he could about the Royals. He would get up at 3:00 AM to watch the Royals play a day game or he could wait until well after dinner to see a night game. He quickly became the Royals' biggest fan in Korea—heck, possibly the Royals' biggest fan outside of Kansas City.

After conversing with fellow Royals fans through Twitter (@KoreanFan_KC) for three years, the then-38-year-old SungWoo finally made plans to visit Kansas City in August of 2014. As his Royals friends in Kansas City caught wind, the entire city—fans, politicians, the media, former Royals, and the Royals organization—stepped up and allowed SungWoo to fulfill a fantasy experience for any Royals fan.

As part of SungWoo's trip, he...

- Toured the Negro Leagues Baseball Museum with the director of the museum, Bob Kendrick
- Ate lunch at Arthur Bryant's
- Was interviewed by local media
- Was featured in articles on Deadspin and *USA TODAY*
- Got an email from Mike Sweeney
- Received a tour of Kauffman Stadium by Jennifer Splittorff, the daughter of the late Royals Hall of Fame pitcher Paul Splittorff
- Received a personalized Royals jersey from the team
- Received red carpet treatment, including a personalized Chiefs jersey from the Chiefs
- Was featured on *SportsCenter*
- Received an autographed Frank White jersey from White

- Received a pin from George Brett
- Threw out a first pitch at Kauffman Stadium
- Danced around with the W that's put up near the Hall of Fame after each win.

And something happened along the way. The Royals became the hottest team in baseball. Since being down by eight games in the American League Central on July 21 with a 48–50 record, the Royals went 9–3 in the games leading up to SungWoo's visit. When he arrived on August 5, the Royals clobbered the Arizona Diamondbacks in Arizona 12–2. That was their second win in what became an eight-game winning streak. During SungWoo's visit—which also represented the first Royals games he saw at Kauffman Stadium—Kansas City played San Francisco, who the Royals would later meet in the World Series. The Royals finished SungWoo's trip with an 8–1 record and they were in first place in the division.

SungWoo's story became so big and sparked so much excitement for the Royals that a *30 for 30* short film about SungWoo was made for ESPN. The filming started for that in Seoul. It continued when the Royals brought SungWoo back for World Series.

100 Remembering Fred White

Author's Note: Although this book is, for the most part, a ranking of Royals moments and personalities from 1–100, No. 100 is more a case of saving the best for last. After all, Fred White was one of the best Royals. For 40 years, his name was synonymous with Kansas City baseball. His voice, along with Denny Matthews', was summer for many of us from 1973–98. And then after a bad breakup that put fans in an uproar, White re-joined the Royals as the director of broadcast services and Royals alumni. On May 15, 2013, White passed away from complications of melanoma. He was 76. On a personal note, White went from being one of my childhood heroes to a mentor to a friend. About seven years after he invited me to the radio booth for a game while I was in school, one of the first books I wrote was Play by Play*—with Matthews and White. Throughout the years, White was quick with an interview or just a story if I needed one. And most of the time, that ended with a chuckle. Perhaps more than anyone I've known, White loved to laugh. And when he did, his entire face would light up and, seemingly, his whole body laughed. The following is from one of those interviews. Fred White may not be the most important figure in Royals history, but he is the perfect person with whom to end a book on the Royals.*

You were around for all of the great Royals years, including the playoffs against the New York Yankees. As you think back to that rivalry and, especially, the postseason series, are there moments that stand out?

Fred White: The George Brett home run off Rich Gossage in 1980 defined his career and defined the Royals up until that time. The Yankees had beaten the Royals three straight years—1976, '77, and '78—so for George to hit that in the seventh inning of the deciding game, that was *the* moment that stood out to me. But then remembering the Royals in the postseason, there's Dane Iorg's little hit into right field, and Jim Sundberg's slide into home, of course, for the win in Game 6 against the St. Louis Cardinals was a huge moment. The Royals had a great history through the 1970s and '80s, and there were so many big moments that blur together. But George's home run off Gossage in 1980 was so loud that it's one you'll never forget.

How quiet did Yankee Stadium become after the ball went out?
FW: It was amazing. George will tell you to this day that he heard his own footsteps as he went around the bases. There was a big roar that just stopped at once. It was a monumental home run.

Speaking of the Yankees, you are a big fan of Stroud's, a famous chicken restaurant here in Kansas City. Wasn't that a must-stop for Yogi Berra whenever the Yankees came to town?
FW: There was a time, it seemed, when all of the American League teams would go to Stroud's. When Dick Howser came here to manage, he introduced the Yankees to it, and Yogi loved Stroud's. He just called it "that chicken place" because he never could remember the name of it. I'm not sure he could remember anyone's name. I loved being around Yogi because he had great stories, but he was a tremendous gentleman. Besides, there were great Yogi-isms, even though he didn't say everything attributed to him.

Here's one, though: the Yankees were in town, and Yogi brought his wife, Carmen, on the trip. He asked me, "When you come to the stadium, do you go through that [Country Club] Plaza place?" I said I did sometimes. He said, "Would you do me a favor? It's Carmen's birthday. Would you stop at Gucci and get her a scarf? And I'll pay you for it when you get to the park." I told him I would and asked him what kind of scarf he wanted. He thought for a moment and then said, "square."

Did you ever make an on-air gaffe?
FW: Oh, as long as there are live broadcasts, there will be slips regardless of the broadcaster. My biggest one happened on a Sunday afternoon when the Royals were in Chicago. This was several years ago before the Internet. I don't know where the ticker [a national service that sent out live updates to all baseball broadcasters] was located, but it was making a ton of mistakes. On the air I started talking about what a bad day the ticker was having, and

mentioning some of the mistakes it made. During the time I was talking about the ticker's problems, a pitcher named Terry Felton was in the game for Minnesota. The ticker then informed us of a pitching change in Minnesota. "Now pitching for the Twins, Terry Felton," is how it read. "Well," I said to about 130 radio stations and their listeners, "you'll never believe what the ticker is doing now. Now they're claiming that in Minnesota, Terry Felton has just relieved himself on the mound." Nope, that's not exactly what I meant to say.

Speaking of great calls, you had one while describing a player launching a high-arcing shot during an ACC basketball game. Didn't that line end up in the iconic baseball movie *Bull Durham*?
FW: I said that, "Anything that goes that high should have a stewardess on-board." At the time from what I understand, [writer/director Ron Shelton] was living in North Carolina and working on *Bull Durham*. I don't know if he was watching the game that night. It might've just been a coincidence, but I'd like to think the line in the movie might've come from that basketball broadcast.

With all due respect to Buddy Blattner and Ryan Lefebvre, you and Denny are the voices of summer to many of us.
FW: Matt, I'm simply a play-by-play guy from a small town in Illinois who has been pretty lucky and has had a lot of fun. I'm not sure what I would change about my life, why I would want to change it, or what I could ask for that's any better than this.

Acknowledgments

Although this isn't a history of the Kansas City Royals, per se, as one might imagine, putting a book like this together requires a lot of research, assistance, and support regardless of the author's knowledge—or lack thereof—of the topic. Thankfully, in my case, I grew up in the Kansas City area in the 1970s and '80s as a huge baseball fan and an even bigger Royals fan.

During my adult life, I've been blessed with the opportunity to write six Royals-related books with Denny Matthews, Dayton Moore, Fred White, and Frank White, in addition to books on the 2014 and 2015 World Series seasons. That's not counting the countless articles for the *Royals Insider* (formerly *Gameday*) magazine, Metro Sports, *The Kansas City Star*, and other outlets. That's not to mention the interviews with former Royals players for the currently-on-hiatus *Behind the Stats* radio show.

Because of my personal and professional ties to the Royals, a special thanks to Don Gulbrandsen and Tom Bast with Triumph Books, who gave me the go-ahead to write this. Thank you also to Noah Amstadter and my editor, Jeff Fedotin. Besides having the patience of Job on this project, Jeff happens to be a Kansas City native and lifelong Royals fan. I've worked with quite a few excellent editors over the years, but I don't think I've had one who's as knowledgeable and passionate about the book's subject as Jeff was with *100 Things Royals*. We had numerous discussions and email exchanges about the contents and the order. He had a huge (and wonderful) influence on this book. Besides those three gentlemen, there are multiple other people at Triumph who were responsible for this project. And I thank each of them.

To Royals general manager Dayton Moore for encouragement, stories, quotes, and, frankly, for bringing a winning culture back to Kansas City and making this update necessary. To members of the Royals front office and staff who provided research assistance or quick answers to goofy questions: Dina Blevins, Morrie Carlson, Toby Cook, Colby Curry, David Holtzman, Curt Nelson, and Mike Swanson.

To Jim Chappell, Matthew Hicks, Mark Stallard, Chris Browne, and Adam Ehlert—thank you all.

To Jeff Montgomery and Denny Matthews for writing the foreword and introduction, respectively. They both have been great ambassadors for the Royals, but they're even better people. We're lucky to have each of them in Kansas City.

To the former Royals who agreed to be interviewed for this book specifically, and/or provided help with the barbecue story: Buddy Biancalana, Jaime Bluma, Mike Boddicker, George Brett, Tom Burgmeier, Jim Eisenreich, Al Fitzmorris, Ed Hearn, David Howard, Joe Keough, John Mayberry, Brian McRae, Joe Randa, Steve Renko, Mike Sweeney, John Wathan, Dave Wickersham, Frank White, and Willie Wilson. I can't thank you enough for your time.

To the group of friends and family who serve as my core support and guidance, I owe a mountain of gratitude: Jim Wissel, Tom Lawrence, Chris Garrett, the Browns, Josh and Susan. As with past book projects, based on the amount of praying I did during the writing of this, particularly during the home stretch, without Christ this isn't possible. A final special thanks to my favorite in-laws, Todd and Pat Burwell, and my parents, Fred and Sharon. To Helen, Charlie, and Aaron, who make me thankful each day, and to my best friend, Libby, who would just as soon spend our date night at the K as she would some fancy restaurant on the Plaza.

Sources

The author would like to acknowledge the reporters and columnists who have covered the Kansas City Royals since the team's inception in 1969. As mentioned in the acknowledgments, many of the quotations found throughout the book were taken from personal interviews between these men and the author. Some were for this book while others were from interviews from previous books, articles, and radio shows. Most other quotes were taken from press conferences. Other quotes and information came from various sources. Those sources include:

Websites

baseball-reference.com
baseballhall.org
espn.com
foxsportskansascity.com
kauffman.org
kcroyalshistory.com
mlb.com
royals.com
tbonesbaseball.com

Periodicals

The Boston Globe
Chicago Tribune
The Kansas City Times
The Kansas City Star
The New York Times
Royals Gameday (Now *Royals Insider*)
The Seattle Times

Books

(Excluding books by the author)

Cameron, Steve. *Moments Memories Miracles*. Dallas: Taylor Publishing Company 1992.

Isaacson, Melissa. *Sweet Lou*. Chicago: Triumph Books 2009.

Morgan, Anne. *Prescription for Success*. Andrews and McMeel: Kansas City 1995.

About the Author

After growing up in the Kansas City area, Matt Fulks started his journalism career while attending Lipscomb University in Nashville, Tennessee, when his baseball career was cut short due to a lack of ability. He has been a regular contributor to various publications, including the *Royals Insider* magazine (formerly *Gameday*), the official publication of the Kansas City Royals. He is the author/co-author of more than 26 books (Amos Otis' number, by the way), including projects with Royals general manager Dayton Moore, and legends Denny Matthews, Frank White, and Fred White. Fulks, who's the director of Moore's C You In The Major Leagues Foundation, lives in the Kansas City area with his wife, Libby, their three kids, his mid-life crisis Jeep, and a Weimaraner named after Elvis. Sort of. More info is available at MattFulks.com (about Matt's books, not the dog).

Other Triumph Books titles by Matt Fulks

Nonfiction

Taking the Crown: The Kansas City Royals' Amazing 2015 Season, 2015
Out of the Blue: The Kansas City Royals' Historic 2014 Season, 2014
100 Things Chiefs Fans Should Know & Do Before They Die, 2014
100 Things Royals Fans Should Know & Do Before They Die, 2014
Coach John Wooden: 100 Years of Greatness, 2010
The Good, the Bad, & the Ugly: Pittsburgh Steelers, 2008

Collaborations

More Than a Season with Dayton Moore, 2015 (Updated in 2016)

Edited

Echoes of Kansas Basketball, 2006